Earl Bostic

Bostic in Harlem EP (Parlophone, 1957).

Earl Bostic
King of the Alto Sax

Derek Sculthorpe

McFarland & Company, Inc., Publishers
Jefferson, North Carolina

Also by Derek Sculthorpe
and from McFarland

Ruth Roman: A Career Portrait (2022)
Claire Trevor: The Life and Films of the Queen of Noir (2018)
Edmond O'Brien: Everyman of Film Noir (2018)
Brian Donlevy, the Good Bad Guy: A Bio-Filmography (2017)
Van Heflin: A Life in Film (2016)

Library of Congress Cataloging-in-Publication Data

Names: Sculthorpe, Derek, 1966– author
Title: Earl Bostic : King of the alto sax / Derek Sculthorpe.
Description: Jefferson, North Carolina : McFarland & Company, Inc., Publishers, 2026. | Includes bibliographical references and index.
Identifiers: LCCN 2025048478 | ISBN 9781476698830 paperback | ISBN 9781476658018 ebook ∞
Subjects: LCSH: Bostic, Earl, 1913–1965 | Saxophonists—United States—Biography | Jazz musicians—United States—Biography | Rhythm and blues musicians—United States—Biography | BISAC: BIOGRAPHY & AUTOBIOGRAPHY / Music | MUSIC / Genres & Styles / Soul & R 'n B | LCGFT: Biographies
Classification: LCC ML419.B676 S28 2025 | DDC 788.7/165092 [B]—dc23/eng/20251125
LC record available at https://lccn.loc.gov/2025048478

ISBN (print) 978-1-4766-9883-0
ISBN (ebook) 978-1-4766-5801-8

© 2026 Derek Sculthorpe. All rights reserved

No part of this book may be reproduced or transmitted in any form or by any means, electronic or mechanical, including photocopying or recording, or by any information storage and retrieval system, without permission in writing from the publisher.

Front cover image: publicity shot of Earl Bostic circa 1948 (author collection); *background* © Shutterstock.

McFarland & Company, Inc., Publishers
Box 611, Jefferson, North Carolina 28640
www.mcfarlandpub.com

In loving memory of my dad,
who introduced me to the world of jazz.

Acknowledgments

With grateful thanks to Vinny Barraza, archivist at Xavier University of Louisiana in New Orleans for all his help. Sincere thanks also to Thomas Haggstrom, assistant archivist at Creighton University Archives and Special Collections in Omaha, Nebraska. Additional acknowledgments to the National Jazz Archive at Loughton, Essex, the Library of Congress, the University of Chicago, the Smithsonian Institution, and the Oklahoma Historical Society. Also, to the Ohio History Connection, Utah Digital News, the University of Florida Digital Archive, and the New York Public Library. Sincere thanks to the University of Oregon, the University of Kentucky, the Minnesota Digital Newspaper Hub, the State Historical Society of Missouri, and Edwardsville Southern Illinois University. I am indebted to the Church of Jesus Christ of Latter-day Saints for access to genealogy archives. Thank you to my editor Charlie Perdue for his advice and enthusiasm. With thanks as ever to my family for their constant encouragement and support. Photographs are from my collection unless stated otherwise.

Table of Contents

Ackowledgments   vi
Introduction   1

1. T-Town Boy   5
2. Star Pupil   12
3. He Makes Snakes   16
4. Campus Idol   20
5. Days and Nights on the Riverboats   26
6. At the Harlem Ball o' Fire   34
7. Hildegarde   40
8. "Let Me Off Uptown"   43
9. Swinging with "Hot Lips" and "Hamp"   50
10. Going Solo   57
11. "Temptation"—A Different Direction   63
12. Breaking Down Barriers   71
13. A Few Million Miles on the Road   78
14. The Bostic Sound   85
15. "Flamingo" Takes Off   91
16. Accident   95
17. A University of the Saxophone   100
18. A Thousand Saturday Nights   109
19. The Nation's Favorite College Band   116
20. A Gentleman of Dignity   120

21.	Moving Spirit of the Alto Sax	128
22.	The King of King Records	136
23.	Farewell to the Fantastic '50s	142
24.	"Hello Sixty"	146
25.	A New Sound	151
26.	Interrupted Melody	159

Epilogue: The Song Is Not Ended	165
Appendix A: Collecting the Earl	171
Appendix B: Bostic as Composer	174
Appendix C: Discography	178
Appendix D: Radio, Film, and Television Credits	196
Appendix E: Partial Itineraries of Tours, 1945–1965	199
Appendix F: Sessions	213
Chapter Notes	219
Bibliography	230
Index	233

Introduction

"Today, Bostic stands as perhaps the most influential sax man in rock 'n' roll."[1]

Alto saxophonist Earl Bostic was a uniquely talented musician with a distinctive style that made his music instantly recognizable. His hard-driving rhythm and growling tone earned him the label of the first rock 'n' roller, before rock 'n' roll officially started. He was equally hailed as a progenitor of rhythm and blues. Nevertheless, although regarded as a true pioneer of popular music, he has always divided opinion, especially in jazz circles. He is seen as too jazzy for the rhythm and blues audience, and just too commercial for the cool jazz crowd. Bostic was always somewhere in between: never given credence by critics, he sold millions of records, his live shows were sellouts, and he kept the jazz instrumental alive in popular music during an era of vocalists. In many ways, he was a man ahead of his time.

I first became aware of Bostic at an early age, because my dad had some of his 10" records issued on the Vogue and Parlophone labels in England in the early 1950s. One of my earliest memories was of my dad recording Alan Dell's big band radio show from the old radiogram on a reel-to-reel tape recorder. Later, as a devotee of John Peel's radio show, I remember that Peel always championed Bostic at a time when no one else did. When I started buying records myself, I came across a reissue of *Dance Time* in a sale, after which I never looked back. He kept me going during student days along with my Blue Note sampler, when I shared a house with several others but, needless to say, I was the only one who liked jazz.

Bostic's sound immediately spoke to me. It always stood out from that of other saxophonists, perhaps because there was more of the blues in it, more warmth and vitality. It was so evocative that it immediately conjured up a scene in the mind's eye. There was an unbounded sense of optimism about it, allied to an element of nostalgia, but no pretentiousness, no striving to be art. There was too much joy in it for that. He was guaranteed to get any party started and everyone dancing. Above all, it sounded like he was enjoying himself, and that the music came from the heart. One relates to music on a deeply personal level, and clearly what is one man's bliss is the next man's nightmare. Music is an entirely emotional thing, and it is impossible to say in words why one responds to it, or why someone else does not. It is like trying to define art, or comedy. Who can say what makes Mozart great, or why the Marx Brothers are funny? If one needs to explain it, that defeats the purpose.

Sixty years have passed since Bostic's death. It seems curious that in all that time practically every other popular contemporary musician has been written about except him. Up until now the only notice the jazz literati have taken of Bostic has been insofar as his story overlaps with that of John Coltrane. The emphasis is always on the older man as a technician and that alone. There is no serious school of thought that deviates from this orthodoxy or suggests that he ought to be considered as an artist in his own right, and above all appreciated as a great entertainer. Surely, he belongs in the same line of descent as Louis Armstrong, Nat "King" Cole, Fats Waller, Little Richard, and Fats Domino, to mention just a few. Some independent-minded scholars have attempted to elevate his status with thoughtful analyses. The best of all was the eloquent article by the late Victor Schonfield, written many years ago but still resonating today. The world needs such free thinkers as Schonfield. He was, as *Jazz Journal* commented in his obituary, "a great advocate, catalyst, mentor and inspiration for many."[2] In recent years, there has been a fine dissertation about Bostic's music by musician and scholar Owen Callahan of Wesleyan University, titled *Up There in Orbit*, which is available to view online.[3] Eternal thanks must go to Marty Jourard for all his work starting the Earl Bostic website at earlbostic.com, and for keeping the flame alive.

First and foremost, Bostic was an entertainer. He did not live to impress jazz critics. He went over their heads and reached the people who danced to his music and bought his records. His approach was similar to that of other contemporary jazz mavericks who strayed from the ordained path, such as Louis Jordan, Lucky Millinder, Eddie "Cleanhead" Vinson, and others. They each followed their own star and could never be neatly pigeonholed. Their collective mission in the cosmos was to entertain royally, each in their own inimitable style—the key word with them all was personality. It made them highly popular with the paying public, but excluded them from any consideration as serious musicians. The jazz purists on the whole never forgave them for it, let alone for making a good living. Critics either studiously ignored them, berated them as mere honkers, belittled them, pushed them to the sidelines, or worse still damned them with faint praise. Jazz can sometimes be too self-regarding, whereas other genres are not written about nearly as often, or in such a precious way. Nor do they all take themselves quite so seriously. One wonders where all the great writers are on R&B, or Soul.

With this book it is my hope and intention to give Bostic at last the attention which he deserves, but has never hitherto been given. There are parallels between him and the great R&B singer Lavern Baker, who possessed a classy vocal style with never any straining for effect. Despite her status in the 1950s as one of the finest vocalists, and her abiding influence, she is not so well remembered today. Her star waxed and waned with changing tastes, and consequently there has been no decent biographical study of any substance about her until recently, let alone a proper biography. Many other of the popular but neglected entertainers have been given the honor of a biography in recent years, including Louis Jordan and Louis Prima. Surely if they are worthy of such an accolade, then so is Bostic.

My approach in assembling this biography is to broadly follow a chronological pattern, but with several chapters dealing with specific aspects of his personal story and musical development. In the appendices there is an extensive discography, along with details of songs he composed and his known credits on radio, film, and television. Since he toured a great deal over a twenty-year period from 1945, I also include an outline list of his tour itineraries. The reason for this is twofold. First is to give some idea of just how much time they spent on the road, and second, because I thought that it might be a useful point of reference to assist in fitting together his timeline. I hasten to add that the list is in no way complete, but it certainly helped to have this to refer to as I was trying to give structure to the whole. The bibliography covers the most useful sources, with plenty of avenues for further reading.

When I first embarked on this project I did so with a willing heart and a cup full of hope. And yet one cannot make bricks without straw. Unfortunately, there was little raw material to assist me at the beginning, no autobiographical memoir to draw on, no personal family archive that I could locate, no diaries or letters, and a decided paucity of photographs. Practically nothing was known about his early life or family background, and one account stated baldly that his parents were unknown. Only a few had ever written about him before and, aside from the rather soulless entries in encyclopedias, he appeared to be largely forgotten. My endeavors therefore centered on interviews, articles, sleeve notes of records, university archives, the reminiscences of friends and fellow musicians, the official records, state archives, specialist libraries, jazz repositories, and above all his musical legacy. From this I have tried to fashion a coherent narrative and give a rounded portrait that does justice to him. Anyone who has read any of my previous books will know that I tend to take the road less traveled. Only one of my biographical subjects has been written about before. The key word which perhaps links them is that they are, to all intents and purposes, forgotten. I hope with this that I can generate renewed interest in one of the most talented musicians of his generation and at last give him the appreciation he deserves.

1

T-Town Boy

"I was the best whistler in town."[1]
—Earl Bostic

Situated on the old boundary line between Oklahoma and Indian Territory, Tulsa, Oklahoma, was the place where the great nations of the Cherokee, Creek, and Osage overlapped. The elevation from the rolling prairie boasts a commanding view of the Arkansas valley. The city began life in 1836 when it was first settled by the Creek nation. They first established a small settlement around the Creek Council Oak Tree, just about where Cheyenne Avenue and 18th Street meet.

The discovery of oil in 1905 at what is now known as Glenpool, fifteen miles south of Tulsa, put the town well and truly on the map. Settlers flocked there, particularly from the East and the lower Midwest, and the population increased rapidly. Before long, it became known as the oil capital of the world. Although Tulsa chiefly owed its prosperity to the discovery of oil, it also had allied industries, including natural gas and some mineral deposits. The chief agricultural crops were grain and livestock. A large proportion of the incomers were Catholic and Jewish. There were many settlers from Texas and some African American families, among them, Earl Bostic's parents.

Earl's parents, Ike Bostic and Druzella (née Gipson or Gibson), were married at the Missionary Baptist chapel in Tulsa by license on August 10, 1912, by the Rev. C.L. Netherland.[2] At the time of the wedding, Ike was a resident in Tulsa town and Druzella was living in the suburb of Coweta in Waggoner County. Earl was their only child, and he was born April 25, 1913. Unlike some others in the jazz and entertainment field, he was born with the moniker that made him famous. He was christened Earl Eugene Bostic, but was always known to his family as Earl.[3]

Tall and of slender build, Ike Bostic was born in around 1886 in the border town of Van Buren, Crawford County, Arkansas, a port and trade center on the Arkansas River. It was the only sizeable town in the county,

Perspective map of Van Buren, Arkansas, County Seat of Crawford County, 1888, by Henry Wellge & Co. Earl's father Ike was born in Van Buren, where the Bostic family settled after the Civil War (Library of Congress).

which was mostly rural. Corn and cotton were the principal crops. On his draft card Ike gave his date of birth as November 29, 1889, although earlier records would indicate that the year was more likely 1886. He was the youngest child of Charlie and Maria Bostic, who first settled in Van Buren after the Civil War. Arkansas was a Confederate state at the start of the war. Van Buren itself was the site of a famous raid in 1862 when Union troops drove the Confederate forces south across the Arkansas River. The town was then occupied for two years, and a great many freed slaves settled in the area. It is possible that Charles served as a volunteer in the 32nd Colored Infantry during the war, because his age tallies with a soldier of that name in the muster rolls. At one time a baker by trade, he was later more regularly employed as a day laborer. He was born in Arkansas in around 1841, and it is feasible that both his parents may also have come from the state, although other sources suggest they had links to Missouri. In about 1862 he married Maria, who hailed from Texas, as did all her family. She often worked as a washerwoman in later years. The couple had eight children all told, but only four survived to adulthood. One of the daughters, Bessie, continued her education past the age of sixteen, which was quite unusual in those days. Ike attended school up to eighth grade, and by the age of thirteen he too began working as a day laborer like his father.[4] However, by the late 1900s when he was around twenty, he left Van Buren and found his way to Tulsa, just over 120 miles away to the northwest. Tulsa was then a boom town growing daily with plenty going on and lots of opportunities for work. There he became a cook in a hotel. By June 1910 he was lodging with many others in a large rooming house at 504 North Kenosha Avenue in the city.[5]

A probably apocryphal story was circulated in the press many years later that Earl had connections to a prominent family of Mexican landowners on his father's side. Although it sounds like a fabrication to generate publicity, it was stated that he inherited the title of Viscount on the death of one Viscount Eligio Arroyo.[6]

Earl's mother Druzella came from Texas. Her family had been resident in Coweta, Oklahoma, for at least two years prior to her marriage. The surname appears variously as Gipson or Gibson in the records. She was born in about 1890, or possibly as early as January 1888, one of ten children of farmer Charles Gibson and his wife Sarah, née Hart. Three of the children died in infancy. Charles was born in Missouri in about 1847, where his father was settled. His mother came from Kentucky. Charles married Sarah Hart at Freestone, Texas, on January 19, 1871. He was the freehold owner of his farm in McClennan County, where all the family worked. A resourceful individual, he also had his own blacksmith shop. In addition, he was a minister or preacher. There was a Charles Gibson living in Howard County, Texas, who volunteered in the 24th Colored Infantry in the 1860s. If this is him, it holds out the prospect that both Earl's grandfathers served in the Civil War. Charles's wife Sarah's family, the Harts, came from Tennessee.[7]

From at least June 1917, the Bostics were living at 20 North Detroit Street, in the predominately black district of Tulsa known as Greenwood.[8] Ike worked as a cook in the Elite café and Druzella was a dressmaker. As a boy, Earl was likely a pupil at the Dunbar Grade School, and he regularly attended the basement meetings at the Mount Zion church, which was the focus of spiritual life in the community at that time. He won prizes for Sunday school attendance.[9]

As the population of Tulsa ballooned in the early twentieth century, the crime rate also increased, and there were strong fears among the populace that the police were unable to keep order. Inevitably, tensions increased, and although African Americans made up just 3 or 4 percent of the population according to the 1910 census, there was a significant racial divide as in many other places in the United States during those years. Several of the officials charged with running the city were openly members of the Ku Klux Klan, including the mayor. As far as the black population was concerned, segregation was the norm; rail travel was segregated and voting rights were limited. Nonetheless, relations between the two communities were described as generally cordial, at least on the surface.

The Greenwood district where the vast majority of black residents settled thrived in the early years of the century. It was a bustling, self-contained community of businesses, shops, restaurants, theaters, cafés, and dance halls, with an active social life that revolved around the church and with its own high school that had a good reputation. As such, Greenwood became a beacon of positivity nationwide and was known as the black Wall Street. According to historians, a simmering resentment built up among the white population, fueled as much as anything by jealousy of their fellow citizens' success. The situation came to a head in 1921 when a minor incident involving a white girl and a colored boy in an elevator, which might easily have been brushed aside, was blown out of all proportion in the press and sparked a full-scale race riot. Beginning on the evening of May 31 and ending on the afternoon of June 1, homes in the Greenwood District were looted and destroyed by white rioters who ran amok, as people tried to defend themselves. Thirty-five square blocks were destroyed, with estimates of up to 300 dead and hundreds of homes and businesses lost.[10]

Earl was only eight at the time, but the riot and its aftermath must have affected his family, either directly or indirectly. They were still living on North Detroit Street, at the western edge of the area affected.

1. T-Town Boy

Whether or not they were rendered homeless like hundreds of others, the events of that single day were traumatic for everyone. There was a famous photo which showed the aftermath of the devastation with the whole area in ruins, and hardly anything on their street was still standing. Even the Dunbar Grade School that he probably attended was razed to the ground. The Bostics' experience may have mirrored that of the other residents. In any event, they would have been all too aware of what happened to respected elders in the community such as the Rev. C.L. Netherland, the local minister at the Mount Zion Baptist church who had married them. Before, he had a modern 10-room brick-built house and ran a prosperous barbershop business, but he lost practically everything in the riot. He was reduced to working from a folding chair on the sidewalk. In a book published in 1922 about the catastrophe, he blamed corrupt politics for letting the situation happen.[11] Mount Zion was the Bostic family church, and it had only just been rebuilt at a significant cost when it was burnt to the ground, along with twenty-one other churches in the district. For weeks and months after the devastation, families were forced to live in tent cities. Nevertheless, despite all they had been through and all they had lost, most of them stayed on and were determined to rebuild their lives. This they did, without any help from federal government, so much so that by 1925 there was a black business conference hosted in the city. It was a testament to the resilience of his people that must also have greatly inspired Earl.

Bird's-eye view of Tulsa, Oklahoma, where Earl was born and spent his formative years.

By the end of the decade, the family were living at 706 East Pine Street and Ike was a cook in a coal yard. This was in an area known as the Rosedale addition. Although his background was not middle class like, say, Duke Ellington's, the Bostics were not below the poverty line, although money was tight, as for most couples starting out. For example, a year after she married, Druzella obtained a sewing machine costing $33 on a mortgage scheme, a precursor to the hire purchase. A machine was essential to her paid work as well as that at home, so it was a necessary outlay, and one that would pay for itself in time.[12] Nevertheless, the family were better off in some ways than many on the same social level, and even others living on the same block, because both parents were in steady employment and they only had one child.

Only children are often viewed as insular, moody, and encountering difficulty making friends, but this did not seem to be so in Earl's case. If anything, it gave him certain material advantages. He had all his parents' attention and the family was clearly more comfortable than it would have been if there had been a lot more mouths to feed. If he had been one of many, he might easily have been lost in the crowd, and everyone would have had to make sacrifices. Besides, he had a supportive family, with plenty of relations on his maternal side. His aunts and uncles always took an active interest in him, and there were several cousins to play with, including Augustus and Juanita Reed, whose ages were similar age to his. As with many only children, he was close to his cousins, who in some ways took the place of siblings. Nor did being an only child hinder his development or social skills in any way. Essentially quiet, independent, and seemingly studious, Earl nonetheless had no difficulty making friends and appeared naturally sociable. His early involvement with the church, the Scouts, and school bands, allied to his later pronounced ability at public speaking, gave him confidence and made him an admirable person whom people looked up to. From a young age, he was someone others wanted to follow and get to know.

Earl's parents were both musical; Ike played guitar and his mother played the piano. One source stated that Ike was also a pianist. Despite his own musical talents, his father was dead set against all his son's musical ambitions. Earl was equally determined to pursue music regardless of anything. To begin with, he was an enthusiastic whistler and once avowed that he was the best whistler in town. Later, he became proficient on the harmonica. The first instrument he ever had was a secondhand ukulele, on which he taught himself some tunes. This made him popular around town and at school. His uncle Charles Gibson recalled how, when not at school, the young Earl helped in the restaurant where his father worked on North Lansing. Once he acquired the ukulele, he took to serenading the diners there while they waited. However, the minute his father got to hear about it, he was determined to put a stop to such nonsense. He took the ukulele and broke it in two, with the admonition to Earl that he would never amount to anything.[13] While it is understandable that his father wanted him to have a steady job with prospects, the vehemence of his determination seems hard to understand. Perhaps he had harbored musical ambitions himself at some stage, only to have to face the harsh realities of life. Far from being put off, Earl was if anything more determined than ever to pursue his musical dreams, and his mother was supportive.

2

Star Pupil

> *"When I started out to be a musician, the musicians around Tulsa were only making about $15 a week. My parents wanted something better for me. So I went to college, graduated and ever since I've been wooing my first love ... music."*[1]

Earl encountered two significant adult figures in his formative years who were crucial to his development as a musician. One was Leo Freymuth, his scout master, and the other was William Jett, his musical tutor at high school. With these two allies, and the clandestine help of his mother, Earl was launched on his path to musical success regardless of his father's opposition.

Since he was seen as a bright boy, teaching was considered the ideal profession for him, and early on his parents latched onto that as the best career choice for their son. It was highly respectable and would give him some standing in the community. Although he was intelligent and an excellent communicator, he did not have the vocation at heart. An alternative was the church, to which he seemed inclined at first, and at one point he had his sights set on following in the footsteps of his maternal grandfather and becoming a preacher. His studies in that direction were serious at one time, but he later abandoned them. Nonetheless, he did teach for several years, but it was always subordinate to his real calling, music.

Earl attended Booker T. Washington High School, which incidentally was established the same year he was born. Situated at the junction of Easton Street and Elgin Avenue in the Greenwood district, the original frame building was replaced by a three-story structure in 1920. The principal in that period was Ellis W. Woods, who was the main driving force behind the school's marked success. Woods served as principal for 35 years (1913–1948) and saw it grow from humble beginnings to become the first school accredited by the North Central Association. He surrounded himself with staff of caliber, and one of his key appointments was William M. Jett (c. 1901–1977), who also served part time at Carver High School.

Jett came from Virginia and graduated from the famous Hampton Institute. He later married the school's librarian. When Woods appointed Jett, the principal gave him the task of setting up a complete orchestra and first-class music department, which he did. Jett was also engaged as bandmaster of all the north Tulsa public schools.[2] He became a familiar and much-loved figure in town as he enthusiastically led the marching band, which took to the streets of the city every Friday evening to inspire the school football team, the Washington Hornets, on to greater things. They marched on a route from the school to Archer and Greenwood and down to the Hornet Stadium. A big event in alternate years was Turkey Day, when the Hornets played Muskogee Manual for the Thanksgiving Day Trophy and the people dressed in their Sunday best, as the band played on and everyone had a great time.

Earl played clarinet in the school band, and Jett soon noticed his outstanding progress, often remarking on him to his friend Ernie Fields, a fellow musician. Fields recalled that one time Earl took home the school's clarinet to practice further. His father heard him playing it and, just as he had with the ukulele, broke the instrument in two, adamant that he did not want his son to be a musician. Earl's mother cried and asked Ernie to call Mr. Jett and explain that she would pay for the instrument, but Jett said he would pay for it, and remarked: "She and everybody ... are going to be proud of that boy. The old man just doesn't know."[3] After that, Earl must have made sure he practiced well out of earshot of his father. It was probably around that time that he made his first arrangement of "St. Louis Blues" for the school band, which he did by humming the parts and writing them down. Other members of the band around the same time included Robert Lewis, who played bass, John Simmons, Hal Singer, and John Hope Franklin. Lewis later played with Ernie Fields, who ran the most illustrious dance band to come out of Tulsa, and of which Bostic was also a member. Singer, whose nickname was "Cornbread," lost his family home in the 1921 riot and was helped by the white employer of his father. Like Earl, he also became a saxophonist and the two enjoyed a friendly rivalry over the years. He lived to the age of 100. John Hope Franklin went on to study at Harvard and was one of the most respected historians of his generation.

Earl was an enthusiastic student and gave the impression of being interested in everything that was going on. Aside from music, he was also reputedly a major star of the track at high school for several seasons running. The school was rebuilt in the later 1950s, then again in 2003, and continues to thrive today.

Alongside his experience in the school orchestra, Earl first took up the saxophone when his scoutmaster Leo W. Freymuth organized a Boy Scout band, the Harmonious Nine. Freymuth immediately recognized his talent on the clarinet, but Earl began to show even greater interest in the alto saxophone. He set his heart on a particular instrument which he had seen in a shop window. Realizing that his parents could not afford to buy it for him, Freymuth presented him with his own alto, and Earl's joy was unbounded. He made rapid progress on the sax in no time at all.

Freymuth (1889–1972) led the choir of St. Monica's R.C. Church. He was employed as an accountant with the Mid-Counties Oil company, but in his spare time he took an active role in church life. The St. Monica church had been built just a short while earlier in 1926, and in the following year Freymuth organized the first Scout troop in Tulsa. He was especially prominent in his work among the black community in the north of the city and encouraged youngsters to take up music. After serving as a corporal in the First World War, he taught for several years in Tulsa County rural schools. He owned a large dairy farm situated to the northwest of Tulsa where he took the boys on days out, and from which he provided many local families with milk. He also distributed free lunches to the children at St. Monica's school when it was housed in buildings on East Haskell Street. He lived for the church, and long afterward he was known as the Patron Saint of St. Monica's. His devotion was recognized, and he was presented by Pope Pius XI with the Bene Merento Medal, an award for unusual and faithful service.[4] Highly capable and dedicated in his work, he was always modest and reticent in speaking of himself. He was essentially a pioneer in his work in the black community, which few if any other whites were doing then, and he made a substantial difference to many lives. An eyewitness described the early days at St. Monica's: "The building is simple, even rustic on the outside but inside it is lighted with dim candlelight giving it an air of mystery and depth."[5]

The Scouts met in the church and regularly in each other's houses to practice their various skills. Each was assigned a particular task; for instance, Earl was an expert in knot tying, and his friend Vernon Wickliff did first aid. Freymuth instilled a sense of belonging in the boys, who were a close-knit and happy bunch, and in many cases they stayed friends long afterward. They enjoyed lots of adventures together on days out, hiking, orienteering, and learning bushcraft. At age 14, Earl made a great impression as a public speaker. One who was there recalled; "Earl Bostic has been acclaimed the greatest talker in Troop No. 41. He carried away the laurels at our meeting and also on Labor Day at Mohawk Park."[6]

Freymuth organized Friday Night Socials and Mickey Mouse Dances, which were highly popular. Naturally, Earl came into his own as the star turn in the Harmonious Nine, which despite its name was sometimes a ten-piece orchestra. He was the first saxophone of three; the other two were Clarence Parker and Herrington Hamm. Wickliff played the banjo, and among the others, brothers Edwin and Edward Middleton played trombone, Oscar Washington was on bass, and James Bowen on piano.[7] They also took part in many fundraising events for the church, such as a minstrel show at the Holy Family parish hall, in which they acted and provided the music.[8] Spurgeon West was another saxophonist who played with them. He and Earl were reunited several years later in the Ernie Fields orchestra. Like Earl, West also went on to study for a semester at Xavier University. Oscar Washington became a composer who worked for several name bands before he switched to teaching. He too went to Creighton, and later taught at Bristow High School. In the 1950s, Bostic recorded one of Washington's compositions.[9]

Freymuth kept Bostic's picture on his desk for years afterward and appeared to consider him his star pupil. He recognized his talent immediately, and singled him out for praise. He once remarked, "I think some day he will be known as one of the best musicians in the southwest."[10] He maintained an interest in Earl's career thereafter and was instrumental in securing his scholarship to Creighton University, along with fourteen of his classmates. For many others he secured part-time jobs. At a farewell service for the boys in September 1930, as they were about to embark on university life, five of the No. 41 troop, including Bostic, were awarded Certificates of Service or Honorable Discharges from the Scouts.[11]

Freymuth was a well-liked and much-respected figure in Tulsa. A friend later said of him: "No one but the boys he helped can really know his true value in terms of his service to the Tulsa community. He was truly colorblind."[12] He saw it as his mission to steer his charges away from the crooked path in life. Indeed, Bostic credited his time with the Scouts as being crucial to keeping him on the straight and narrow and avoiding a life of crime and delinquency, which he felt he might easily have otherwise been tempted to pursue. In his case, music was his salvation, and the saxophone, first presented to him by Freymuth, was his path to glory.

3

He Makes Snakes

"There's a kid up there, man, he's fantastic. He makes snakes. This kid does everything on the sax."[1]

—Bill Davis

Earl soon gained a local reputation in and around Tulsa, and once recalled that one of his earliest gigs was unpaid. When he was around seventeen, he had his first experience of playing tenor sax with a Territory band led by Torrence Holder, who was the founder of the Twelve Dark Clouds of Joy. It was an exciting time for the teenage sensation and he proved his natural ability in the second incarnation of Holder's band.

Trumpeter T. Holder (c. 1898–1977), variously known as Torrence, Terence, or Tee Holder, was born in Texas. After some time with the Alphonse Trent outfit, in 1925 in Dallas, Texas, he formed his own band, which he christened the Twelve Dark Clouds of Joy or variations on the name. The actual number varied at any given time; there might be nine or even fewer. Based in Muskogee, Oklahoma, the band toured a circuit mostly between there and Texas, and appeared regularly at the Adolphus Hotel, Dallas. In the beginning, its material ranged from classical pieces such as the "Poet and Peasant Overture" to popular tunes of the day and jazz numbers. It was one of the outstanding Territory bands, but not well led, by all accounts.[2] There are several slightly differing versions of the history of the Clouds of Joy, and those involving T. Holder after he was ousted as leader in 1929 are fragmentary and often contradictory. The consensus is that Holder was a charismatic figure and a great trumpeter, but he was unreliable and a poor manager. He also amassed gambling debts, and in late 1928, matters came to a head when he left his band stranded in Oklahoma City, reputedly taking the band's funds with him. In his place, the quiet and reliable tuba player Andy Kirk was nominated leader. Thereafter they called themselves Andy Kirk and the Twelve Clouds of Joy and went from strength to strength. They made their first recordings in November

1929 and began to gain widespread attention. However, Bostic was never part of this group.

Undaunted after being ousted from his own creation, Holder immediately set about forming a new group. It was said of him that no one could get a band together as fast as he could. He joined forces with pianist and bandleader Jesse Stone from Kansas, and, along with one or two members from the original Clouds who had remained loyal to him, he gathered a formidable new ensemble of young talent whom he rehearsed relentlessly. It was this band that Bostic was recruited to, around 1930. Dates are notoriously unreliable but Buddy Tate said he recruited him in that year, and Leonard Feather further states that Bostic was with Holder between 1930 and 1932. Others place the date at 1928, but that would appear to be too early. Some of the confusion appears to arise from the fact that the band split in two but both parts, at least initially, used the same name.

Bostic was recruited into the band by saxophonist Buddy Tate (1913–2001). Although they were the same age, the jovial Tate had reputedly made his debut several years earlier at the age of thirteen with Roy McCloud's Night Owls when, so the story goes, his brother handed him a tenor sax one night. The ten-piece band was a family affair, and McCloud was his cousin. They had to improvise, and learned by listening to Louis Armstrong records and mimicking the sound. Tate was also with the St. Louis Merrymakers (at Wichita Falls, Kansas) and Gene Coy's band Troy Floyd, so he already had a wealth of experience despite his youth.

One night when Holder's band was playing a dance at Tulsa, it became apparent that the band needed a new saxophonist. The one it had (who was described as sounding like Frankie Trumbauer) had no interest in playing solos, and would rather spend time filing his nails between numbers. Buddy Tate heard from local musician Bill Lewis about a kid who could play like crazy. "He makes snakes," they said, meaning he could play fast. Tate recollected:

> So I went up and listened to him, sure enough. He was all over that horn, boy. He was triple tonguing and doing everything.... I walked up and introduced myself, says, "I like the way you sound." He says, "I know you, my name is Earl Bostic." [I asked him if] he was interested [in joining the band]. He said, "I never worked with a big band, I don't know if I could make it." I says, "You let us worry about that."

Tate asked him to come down and hear them play, to see what he thought about the idea, which he did. Tate continued:

> So when we got off I got all the guys over to meet him [Bostic] and he says, "The band really sounds fine, fellas, but you do need a saxophone player." So we told him about the money [he would make]. He says, "I'm ready." We carried him

right in the car. He wouldn't even go home, got a toothbrush, maybe a little overnight bag. So we carried him on down to Seminole.[3]

After that, he was introduced to Holder and they started to rehearse. At that first run-through, they thought they would test him to see if he could really play:

We picked King Oliver's "Louisiana Bobo." Something that had some teeth in it. We let Earl stomp it off. We usually played it fast but the tempo he started was something else. It was so fast one cat after another fell out. Only Earl and the drummer were left and finally the drummer had to quit. The funny thing was that we thought at first Earl couldn't read. But actually, he was a well-versed musician.[4]

Among the other personnel in the band at that time, besides Bostic and Tate on tenor sax, was Alvin "Fats" Wall or Wallace Mercers on alto. Jeff Carrington and Bill Dillard joined Holder on trumpet, with George Corley on trombone, Lloyd Glenn on piano, Leslie Nelson (guitar and banjo), Leslie Sheffield (tuba), and "Little" Joe Lewis on drums. Some of the other outstanding men in the Holder setup included trumpeter Hugh Jones and Claude "Fiddler" Williams. Clearly, Holder's later band has never had the attention that Andy Kirk's Clouds of Joy have enjoyed, but they were still a big attraction in their familiar spots of Oklahoma and Texas. As before, they played dances and were based in some venues for two or three months at a time. While on tour, Tate and Bostic roomed together, and Tate recalled young Earl's remarkable dedication and single-mindedness. All he was interested in when not on the bandstand was practicing his horn. He was so engrossed that Tate kept bringing food to him in the room to make sure he remembered to eat.[5]

It was Earl's first time away from home, and during the Depression era, times were harder than ever. His naturally self-contained nature helped him, and although he may have been assailed by feelings of loneliness or even homesickness on the road like everyone, his devotion to music was paramount and forever sustained him. Consequently, he seemed not to mind all the privations and perils of travel. At the beginning at least, that must have been part of the adventure, and playing alongside seasoned musicians was a delight to him. He soon got used to the peripatetic lifestyle, traveling all day in cramped cars and playing every night. Accommodation was variable, to say the least, but all wayfarers learned what places to avoid and useful tricks to keep the bedbugs at bay.

Bostic's involvement with Holder's band must have been sporadic, and especially so after September 1930 when he began his first year at Creighton University in Omaha, Nebraska. Although he rejoined the group at intervals afterward, his appearances must by necessity have been during vacations. For instance, he was not listed among the personnel who played in January 1932 in Texas and Little Rock, Arkansas, but he was with the band at the Lamord Ballroom in Longview, Texas, in September of the same year.[6] The second incarnation of the Holder band lasted until around 1932 or 1933, and folded because of the combined effects of the Depression and, it would appear, Holder's recurrent mismanagement. By the beginning of 1933, Bostic had left the Clouds and joined Bennie Moten, with his place in his former band being taken by Eddie Barefield.

Fired by his first practical experience, he began to realize exactly what he wanted to do in life. When he got the chance to go to university, he was able to begin to pursue his ambition to be a professional musician in earnest.

4

Campus Idol

> "[He is] perhaps the only famous musician in America who can credit a nun with being responsible for [his] achievements in the world of jazz."[1]
>
> —L. Masco Young

Bostic must have been one of the most highly educated of jazz men. He attended two universities, and possibly three. His academic studies ran happily alongside his musical apprenticeship in various ensembles for much of the early 1930s. University opened a lot of doors for him that might otherwise have been closed and helped enhance his natural confidence, giving him the tools to pursue his dream. It was also while he was a student that he met his future wife. The unusual combination of his formal and informal education gave him a unique outlook on the world, and surely contributed to his personal and professional musical development. Not only did he learn music theory, harmony, and how to play most instruments that he did not already know, but he also formed his own earliest dance orchestra, which served as the blueprint for his many subsequent and successful bands.

After graduation in 1930, Bostic went to Creighton University, a private, Jesuit-run establishment in Omaha, Nebraska. Founded in 1878, the university forged a good reputation for its strong business and sports faculties and among notable alumni are several baseball and basketball stars. It remains to this day a relatively small but prestigious school situated in the center of Omaha. His ex-Scoutmaster Leo Freymuth was instrumental in getting a scholarship for Earl, along with several others from St. Monica's, including his friends Oscar Washington and Vernon Wycliff. During his time there, Earl involved himself in various musical and extracurricular activities. He soon became an integral part of the band, and in October 1930 was appointed a technical sergeant with the R.O.T.C. (Reserve Officers' Training Corps).[2]

Earl's natural good sense of humor found an outlet and he took an

4. Campus Idol

Creighton University in Omaha, Nebraska, where Earl studied for his sophomore year between 1930 and 1931.

active role in several campus entertainments. In one such, he and Wycliff developed a skit based on the popular comic radio duo Amos 'n' Andy. The Bostic and Wycliff routine incorporated a tap dance, which went over well, and they also sang a few songs, with Vernon on the banjo.[3] According to some reports, Earl continued to play gigs around the city while he was there.

In 1930 the class numbered around 300, which was the highest it had been to date. Nevertheless, black students were in a distinct minority at the university at that time, which prompted commerce student and newspaper columnist Charles Wilson to set up a social club, the Creighton Colored Co-Operative Club. This had a membership of twelve, and although it is not known whether Bostic was among them, it seems likely. For some reason, The Chicago Defender took exception to the club, accusing it of "a tendency to Jim Crowism." However, Wilson made a strong rebuttal of its arguments and countered that the paper's editor had "jumped to conclusions."[4]

Whether it was partly that he never felt quite at home there, or because of the strictness of the Jesuit regime, or perhaps the often-inclement weather in Nebraska, Bostic decided not to stay. Likeliest of all, he sought greater scope for his musical ambitions, which he may have felt were not being satisfied at Creighton. At any rate, he only stayed for his freshman year before opting to study at New Orleans' Xavier University instead. His old Scoutmaster Leo Freymuth again secured his place there. The switch proved an inspired move for Earl and thereafter he blossomed. After all, the Crescent City was the heartland of the jazz music scene at an exciting time in its history, and he was right in the middle of it all.

At the time he moved to Xavier in September 1931, the university was on the way up, making a name for itself, and the intake of 77 students that year was the highest on record. As a measure of its success, the campus was undergoing expansion, and new central buildings were in the course of being erected at a cost of $400,000. This followed in the wake of a sports stadium built the year before. Unlike Creighton, Xavier was a fairly new university, only six years old. It traced its origins to the beneficence of Mother Katharine Drexel, founder of the Sisters of the Blessed Sacrament. She hailed from the wealthy, socially prominent family of a Philadelphian banker and financier, Thomas Drexel. Imbued with religious and charitable principles from the beginning, she traveled the world as a young woman, and a meeting with Pope Leo XIII in 1886 when she was 28 decided her mission in life. Thenceforward she dedicated herself to educating Native Americans and African Americans. On land once belonging to the Southern University, the Sisters established a high school in 1915, and in 1925, Xavier University of Louisiana was founded with the College of the Liberal Arts and Sciences. A couple of years later the College of Pharmacy was opened and the first degrees were offered. Medicine and the arts were two of the strongest areas of excellence and still are to this day. The

View of the interior of the chapel at Xavier University in New Orleans during a service. Earl first met his future wife Hildegarde White on the steps of the chapel when she was seventeen.

original source of income was a trust fund set up by the will of Drexel's father. Katherine Drexel withdrew from direct involvement after 1937, but remained connected to the university until her death in 1955 at the age of 96. She was the first American-born citizen to be made a saint.

Bostic spent three happy years at Xavier. Although he majored in English, he also studied harmony and music theory. In addition, he was already a good sight reader. He threw himself into the entertainment side of life there, as he had at Creighton. As soon as he arrived, he was organizing events and providing the music and arrangements for the Xavier Dance Orchestra as bandleader and saxophonist, which became his pride and joy. One of his first concerts during a weekly assembly happened to be broadcast on radio by Station WOW of Chicago, much to the surprise and excitement of the students. Among the numbers, Bostic introduced one of his own earliest compositions, "The Model" which soon seemed to get the joint jumping. As the *Xavier Herald* reported: "The rhythm of the music caused many feet to wish they were dancing. Even the Seniors lost some of their dignity."[5]

His talents became evident in all three orchestras, and as drum major, he made several noteworthy additions to the marching band, including a baritone saxophone, cymbals, and a tuba, which increased the band's impact. The members were arrayed in resplendent uniforms of white and gold. Despite his youth—he was still a teenager—he was assured and always inspired confidence. A witness wrote that he "has helped the band considerably by his knowledge of leadership."[6]

He made even more rapid progress with his dance band, which was essentially the earliest incarnation of his own orchestra. It was highly popular with both the high school students and those at the university, and under his leadership was soon ready for engagements on campus and off. The dance band was frequently in demand for all kinds of entertainments, such as Christmas parties, July 4 celebrations, and for the triumphant (or otherwise) homecoming of the college football team. It was said that the band, known as The Earls, rivaled both the basketball team and the football team in popularity. It featured in several radio broadcasts, including one aired over station WWL, Loyola of the South, on November 21, 1932. Among the songs the band played were "Dinah," "When Your Lover Has Gone," "Jig Time," and "Double Check Stomp," along with "The Model." The show was a big success, and as one observer wrote, "The most striking characteristic feature noted, was the display of harmony."[7] The selection of songs gives an insight into Bostic's preferences and influences at that early stage. Two were associated with Louis Armstrong, namely, "Dinah" and "When Your Lover Has Gone"; the latter was a popular song around 1931 and one that stayed in Bostic's repertoire for a long time thereafter. "Jig

Time" was a hit for vocal group The Three Keys, a lively number that showcased its inventive scat singing. "Double Check Stomp" was a Duke Ellington tune and a likely influence on Bostic's later stomp series. All of this begs the unanswered question of what "The Model" sounded like.

As if he were not busy enough, the genial Bostic was in addition a key member of the Glee Club, whose membership had doubled in a year. Their entertainments always went down well, and at one such, Bostic gave a clarinet solo, and again showed his propensity for humor when he acted as a clown with a friend, "Don" John Davis, in a skit entitled "A Bit of Nonsense."

His time at Xavier decided him on his career path, and he had by then abandoned his initial idea to pursue a life in the church. At least one of his old professors was disappointed that he took this decision and many years later even wrote to upbraid him about one of his songs, "Barfly Baby," which he found questionable. A teetotaler, Professor Lester Hines of Langston University had kept an eye on Bostic's career and felt that because he was by then a headline personality, he had a moral obligation to his following of impressionable youth not to make drinking seem too appealing. Suitably chastised, Bostic promised not to glorify the drinking spots in future and asked the forgiveness of his ex-instructor.[8]

Sister Mary Laetitia was the supervisor of the music department at Xavier when Bostic was there. Like many of her fellow nuns in the sisterhood, she was born in Philadelphia. Although at that time the faculty was geared to producing operas, Sister Laetitia was tolerant of whatever students wanted to do. Provided they worked hard and fulfilled all the necessary academic requirements of the course, she was supportive, and as a consequence, several others who pursued careers in jazz music got their first encouragement from her. One was Richard Payne, original bassist with the American Jazz Quintet. Payne was at Xavier just a short while after Bostic, and committed his memories of his time there to the compilation volume *Jazz in New Orleans* (2001).[9] Another was the jazz vocalist Germaine Bazzle, who was taught by Sister Laetitia while in the fourth grade at the Xavier High School and credited Sister Laetitia with inspiring one of her signature improvisations.

Sister Laetitia introduced Bostic to practically all the instruments in the orchestra which he did not already know, including the piano and violin. She also gave him instruction in baton-twirling technique for the marching band. He was a willing student and eager to try everything. Although already proficient on the tenor and alto saxophone as well as the clarinet, his natural love of music meant that he reached a standard well above average on the guitar, piano, and trumpet.

While he was at Xavier, Earl first met Hildegarde White, then seventeen. As she recalled, she was introduced to him by a mutual friend one evening on the chapel steps after the novena service. At the time she was a high school senior and he was about 19, the idol of the campus, in her words. He had the air of someone who was going places. "Earl took me home that night," she remembered, "but I wasn't any real competition to the older co-eds who had their eye on the attractive out-of-towner."[10] Although neither knew it at the time, it was the start of a long and unusual courtship that played out over the course of the next ten years.

Bostic was a mainstay of the music department at Xavier, and his dedication, work ethic, and natural organizational skills made him indispensable—so much so that the faculty asked him to stay on an extra year as Director of Music, which he did. He not only continued to conduct the symphony orchestra along with the activities of his dance band, but also taught at the school. He continued to play gigs around the city and soon gained a reputation as one of the hottest young players around. He laid down the gauntlet to all local and visiting stars alike, and a later commentator recollected: "When the big bands were playing in New Orleans all the sax stars had to pass by Earl in the after-hour jam sessions. If they got too warm on the sax, Earl would finish them out on the clarinet."[11]

According to most accounts, he graduated in 1934 with a bachelor of arts degree in English. Thereafter he taught in various schools, both in New Orleans and in San Antonio, Texas, where he was based for a time, possibly as long as a year. Among his pupils during his teaching days was one Joe Newman, a talented boy who, while he played trumpet in the Daniel Public School band, came under the tutelage of Bostic. Newman recalled: "Earl Bostic had become bandmaster at my school and he started the first band there. I was a tiny little guy, about eight, and he stood me on a chair to solo on a tune called 'Washington and Lee Swing,' a march."[12] Little Joe went on to study at Xavier high school himself under Sister Laetitia, and was invited to play with the university band. He had a great career in jazz as the lead trumpeter for Count Basie and had his own highly successful band.[13] Bostic sometimes encouraged his musician friends to go to college, and Buddy Tate, for instance, said that Earl had tried to persuade him to study harmony, and in retrospect Tate wished he had taken his advice.

Bostic's time at university decided him in his career as a professional musician. Moreover, it gave him a degree of confidence he might not otherwise have had, and combined with his growing experience as a sideman in various bands, touring during the summers, he had the best possible start to a successful life in music. His long-term ambition was to make his way to the big time and eventually to reach New York. Although he was a long way from where he wanted to be, everyone who encountered him was impressed by his quiet determination, and none ever doubted that he would get there one day.

5

Days and Nights on the Riverboats

"There was a saying in New Orleans when some musician would get a job on a riverboat with Fate Marable they'd say 'Well, you're going to the conservatory.' That's because Fate was such a fine musician and the men who worked with him had to be really good."[1]

—Zutty Singleton

Before he attended university, Bostic had already had experience playing in bands and touring, and continued to do so at night and between semesters in gigs all around New Orleans. After completing his formal education, which set him in good stead, he continued his informal education and served a long apprenticeship, including valuable work on riverboats for the legendary Fate Marable. He worked hard and crisscrossed the country as a sideman for several bandleaders until he finally reached his goal, New York, the mecca of the jazz music scene, after four years.

Among Bostic's influences at that stage, some of the early ones appear to have been clarinetists who later moved on to the saxophone, a route he had followed himself. Captain John Handy was reputedly influential for him, as he was for fellow saxophonist Tab Smith. Handy came from Mississippi but was long associated with the New Orleans scene. He started on clarinet and switched to the sax in 1928, but he did not record until late in life. His hard-driving sound on the alto had elements of swing and was also influential on R&B. Handy remembered that Bostic came to see him whenever and wherever he played in the city. Bostic himself cited as his greatest early influence Sidney Bechet (1897–1959), who in turn thought highly of him. Although mostly associated with the clarinet, Bechet played soprano sax. Inspired by him, Bostic achieved a yet higher register on the alto than Bechet had on soprano. Artistically, the two might have had much in common, but they were entirely different personalities. Bechet was described as abrasive, and was known as being especially difficult with younger artists. Bostic, with his round, open face practically radiating bonhomie, said that he always enjoyed helping youngsters. Several others with whom he crossed paths over the years, all senior to him in years, such as Lester Young, "Professor" Buster Smith, and Benny Carter, were considered influential on him in some way—for instance, in the use of a tenor sax reed on an alto mouthpiece. Bostic's early solos were most frequently compared to those of Carter in terms of his flowing lines. However, Bostic has also been credited as being influential on Carter in turn. Alto player Willie Smith (1910–1967) was a near-contemporary of Bostic and yet he too was often credited as a direct influence on Bostic's approach. Smith worked for Jimmie Lunceford and Harry James, among others. Along with Johnny Hodges and Carter, Smith was considered one of the great alto-saxophonists before the advent of Charlie Parker. Duke Ellington was someone else Bostic listed among those he most admired, and who informed his career at different stages, especially with his choice of material both at the beginning and much later, as with the song "Flamingo," which he made his own. Hodges must have been a formative influence too, albeit less directly so on his actual playing style.

Despite all the strands of his various inspirations, from the beginning Bostic appeared to be his own man and to a remarkable degree already had his own style, which was evident from his earliest appearances on record. This seemed to come from his sheer singlemindedness, and the years of constant practice on his own in which he sought and achieved complete mastery of his chosen instrument. Ever since he started playing, he took it seriously and practiced assiduously. He approached music like a job; he would start at 8:00 a.m., practice until 12, and after an hour off for lunch he would continue until 5 p.m. This he did every day, when possible, apart from Sunday. Such devotion reaped its own rewards and helped to make him one of the most distinctive players who was not especially beholden to anyone.

Bostic left the T. Holder band sometime around the end of 1932, and by at least February 1933 he was playing with Benny Moten on a tour in the South that included dates in Memphis, Tennessee, Lexington, Kentucky, and at the Champion Theater, Alabama.[2] Moten, out of Kansas City, Missouri, was a leading light of swing in those years. Among the personnel of this outstanding group was trumpeter Oran "Hot Lips" Page, vocalist Jimmy Rushing, and none other than the great pianist William Count Basie. Bostic had replaced Eddie Barefield in the Moten setup, and Barefield took over his place with T. Holder. Despite the great success of the Blue Devils and Moten's other bands in the 1920s, they were struggling at this period in the early 1930s, as indeed were many others, mostly on account of the Depression. Throughout the whole time, Bostic needed a steady income and taught in a grammar school in the winter months. According to several reports, he spent over a year in San Antonio after his graduation. The Moten band came to a premature and tragic end in 1935 when Moten died suddenly as the result of a botched tonsillectomy. Thereafter, Count Basie took over. Bostic would appear to have moved on by then.

Around 1933 or 1934 Bostic played with trumpeter Ernie Fields, his old comrade from Tulsa days. Often, he would alternate with another buddy, Luther Spurgeon West on sax. The Fields ensemble was one of the best known Territory bands gaining in reputation at that time. Although he never became a big star, Fields had a solid career and toured both at home and abroad during the war entertaining the troops. His sound moved more toward R & B as it progressed, and he had perhaps his biggest success much later in 1959 with a version of the Glenn Miller hit "In the Mood," which got as high as no. 4 on the *Billboard* chart.

From about 1934 in New Orleans, Bostic joined up with the pianist Joe Robichaux (1900–1965). Robichaux had first formed his own ensemble in 1931 and later recorded some stomping up-tempo numbers for Vocalion Quintet. Those sides were issued in 1933–1934, just before Bostic joined. According to "Father" Al Lewis, Bostic lived with Robichaux on Magnolia Street and Louisiana Avenue in New Orleans.[3] When Bostic was with him, Robichaux was looking to expand, and his orchestra at its peak boasted fourteen or fifteen pieces. Unfortunately, they were

Earl played with Fate Marable on board the *Washington*, which ran between New Orleans and St. Louis, Missouri, during 1935–1936.

not allowed to play live in New York because of a dispute with the Musician's Union. It was then that Bostic first wrote expressly for Robichaux his arrangement of "Let Me Off Uptown," which, although he never recorded it himself, was later a famous hit for Gene Krupa. The Robichaux sound often drew comparisons to that of Fletcher Henderson. Robichaux's band toured Florida, and went on to Cuba around 1935, but Bostic had seemingly left by then. According to several accounts, he went to work with Sam Morgan.[4] Although Robichaux questioned whether Bostic was ever a member of Sam Morgan's band, Harold Holmes said that he was. Holmes maintained that he saw Bostic in Mobile, Alabama, and later played opposite him in Brooklyn Park, New York, on Davis Avenue.[5] Morgan's was one of the most popular Territory bands, which mostly toured the Gulf Coast circuit (Galveston, Texas, to Pensacola, Florida). Sam Morgan died suddenly in 1936 at the age of 48, after which his orchestra broke up. Whether Bostic played with Morgan or not, it is possible that he played with Papa Celestin, who was there at the same time. Bostic was reputed to have spent a year in St. Louis, Missouri, possibly between 1934 and 1935, and may also have briefly been in Minneapolis–St. Paul.[6] As accounts differ and memories were sometimes hazy, there is some uncertainty on the exact sequence of events.

Between 1935 and 1936, Bostic joined Fate Marable's Mississippi riverboat combo. At the same time, he played in night clubs all over the city. Since he was a teenager, Marable had played the piano and calliope on boats sailing on the Streckfus Line, which ran between New Orleans and St. Paul, Minnesota. He started as far back as 1907, when as a callow youth he was first employed by Joseph Streckfus senior to play the calliope. Few could handle the curiously cumbersome-looking steam-driven organ mounted on the deck, and none as well as Marable. Visitors flocked from miles around to see and hear him in action. The evocative, curiously plaintive sound of the calliope was somewhere between that of a fairground organ and a ship's whistle and could be heard from a long way off.

When Bostic played with them, the band was jointly led by Marable and trumpeter Charlie Creath. Bostic was just out of his teens at the time and they were well-seasoned men in their forties. According to many, including the renowned writer Leonard Feather, Bostic learned a lot of his jazz aboard the riverboats. It was there that Feather first encountered him when he was taken on board and shown around by Fate himself, as the band played. It was the Englishman Feather's introduction to the United States, the land he would eventually make his home. He described the orchestra as fairly conventional, but recollected: "Now and then a jazz solo would slip through. Impressed by a very young, unknown saxophonist, I asked Marable his name. It was Earl Bostic."[7]

Marable instilled a high level of professionalism in his musicians. He expected them to be able to sight read, and those who failed to do so were given short shrift. Known as a disciplinarian, he stood no nonsense and instilled a businesslike attitude in his bandsmen. Gambling, drinking, and poor timekeeping were a distinct no-no. This regimen suited Bostic, who came to expect the same commitment in turn from his own band members throughout the various incarnations of his orchestra. However, many thought Marable too strict, and they did not last long. Rehearsals were on Tuesday and Friday mornings, and if anyone happened to miss a rehearsal, they were fined more than if they missed the actual performance. Captain John Handy for one disliked working for Marable on account of what he considered excessive and needless rehearsing. Those who could not read music at first sight either found a way to do it or were shown the door. The material they played was decided by the Streckfus line, and it was largely a case of keeping them, and the dancers, happy. The repertoire took in light classical pieces and popular dance tunes. In the early days at least, musicians had to play about fourteen long numbers all through, with encores. These numbers changed every two weeks. It was no sinecure working the riverboats, but it made genuine musicians of those who succeeded and who could say that they had graduated from the Marable floating conservatory. The salaries paid were good; the average was about $45 a week with a good-behavior bonus of $5 payable at the season's end. Fate had a happy knack of finding young talent and famously gave Louis Armstrong his first big break. Armstrong readily acknowledged all he owed to the great bandleader. A roll call of names who served some of their apprenticeship with Marable reads like a *Who's Who* of jazz, including George "Pops" Foster, "Baby" Dodds, and Henry "Red" Allen.[8] Creath, the band's co-leader, was with Marable between 1935 and 1938. Although Creath began as a trumpeter playing in traveling circuses, he suffered several bouts of ill health over the years and after one illness switched to playing the saxophone and accordion. He ran his own band at one time and had made some collectable recordings in the 1920s for Okeh Records. Despite his influence, Marable made hardly any recordings, and those which do survive give only fragmentary evidence of the obvious excitement the actual bands must have engendered at the time. Among his highlights with his Society Syncopators was a version of the classic "Frankie and Johnny."

Bostic played on board the *Washington*, which ran between New Orleans and St. Louis. The boat had been built in 1881 and refitted in 1921. The musicians lived on the boat for the duration of the tour, stopping at numerous ports along the way, such as Baton Rouge and Natchez, where they would play for local excursions. They shared cabins containing berths of two or four, some of which could be extremely uncomfortable

5. Days and Nights on the Riverboats

The legendary Fate Marable pictured on the cover of *The Jazz Record*. Marable led an orchestra on board the riverboats for the Streckfus line along the Mississippi for many years, an effort that was often called a floating conservatory of jazz.

with the immense heat in summer. The clientele they played for was largely white, but sometimes day excursions were run especially for colored audiences. Between October and April, the boats were moored to the shore and dances took place on board.[9] During the summer season, the band played for day trippers as they boarded after 9 a.m., with a break around 11 a.m., and then a staggered sitting to enable bandsmen to take their lunches in succession. The band then convened at 3 p.m., playing until 4:45 p.m. The moonlight excursions band struck up at 7 p.m. for forty-five minutes, and from 8 p.m. until just before midnight they played for dancing. Such long sessions of playing required a decided stamina, and Bostic clearly made the grade in that department.

The *Washington* was last used in 1937, and despite its long, sterling service it was dismantled the following year. Times and tastes changed. The excursion boats fell out of favor. People sought their entertainment in different ways, and the heyday of the riverboats was visibly passing by the time Marable became ill in 1941. When they heard the news of his illness, many of the musicians who had worked for him over the years rallied around and a benefit was organized by Nat Storey. Bostic was among those who took part; some of the others included "Red" Allen, Zutty Singleton, "Mouse" Randolph, Kaiser Marshall, and Vernon King. When Marable died of pneumonia in January 1947, it was truly the end of a colorful and defining era in jazz that lived long in the folk memory and forever in the imagination.[10]

Bostic next turned up in Columbus, Ohio, where he joined the Clarence Olden Orchestra. He was definitely there by November 1935, and while living in Columbus, he stayed at 846 Spring Street with William Louis and his wife, whom he had known from Tulsa.[11] Olden (1904–1981) came from Paducah, Kentucky, and there was a clear link with Fate Marable, not just because he was also from Paducah, but because Olden had first been inspired to become a musician by a visit from Fate himself.[12] The Olden band toured locally in Marion, Ohio, and later went to Buffalo, New York.

Also in Ohio, Bostic toured with the saxophonist and successful bandleader Marion Sears, who was based in Cleveland. At one time the band included his more famous younger brother Al Sears, who was also a sax man, and with whom Bostic would later work as a sideman in New York. The basement club was situated at Cedar Gardens on East 97th and 9706 Cedar Avenue in Cleveland, Ohio. Previously a Chinese restaurant, it was owned by Joseph Hecht, and opened as a nightclub in 1934. Although located in a predominantly black neighborhood, the club was popular with white customers who provided most of the business. Hecht, who was white, brought in the restauranter Ulysses "Sweets" Dearing as his manager and had an all-black staff. In its heyday, it was described as Cleveland's version of Harlem's Cotton Club, with a full floor show, dancers, and singers. *The Pittsburgh Courier* called it "the most famous night spot between New York and Chicago."[13] Marion Sears led the featured band there, which began as a seven-piece. Bostic passed through this band around 1936 or 1937, although he does not seem to appear on a contemporary photograph.[14] He may also have first worked alongside pianist and arranger Al Freeman around that time.

Shortly after his stint with Sears, Bostic worked as a sideman in a band led by the teenage trumpeter Freddie Webster, which also included pianist Tadd Dameron. This band may have been the fourteen-piece orchestra that toured locally. Webster and Dameron were lifelong friends and natives of Cleveland. Webster was a great and highly influential talent from whom Miles Davis took his cue. Webster died tragically early at the age of only 30. Dameron was also a composer and is credited as the most influential arranger in the age of bebop.

In about 1937, Bostic traveled further north and spent a brief time with the obscure Clyde Turpin in Buffalo, and it is known that he later played in Rochester. Thereafter the trail becomes hazy, and he most likely followed up with further experience with other small-time bands in the vicinity. All the while, he was getting closer to his goal—New York. In the new year of 1938 he finally made it.

6

At the Harlem Ball o' Fire

"Bostic is an earnest young fellow who should go far."[1]
—Harry Miller

Once he reached New York, Bostic soon found congenial work as musician and arranger with some of the biggest names in jazz at that time, including Don Redman. He formed his own band, which became the mainstay of the world-famous Smalls' Paradise club in Harlem, where they played for a record four years. In addition, he composed several songs and made some of his earliest recordings with Lionel Hampton, which displayed his development in what was the heyday of the swing era.

Bostic reached New York in January 1938, and one of his first engagements was as a sideman in the Edgar Hayes band. Pianist Hayes led an interesting swing band from the early 1930s onward, and at the time Bostic joined, drummer Kenny Clarke was also playing with them. One of their biggest hits was a version of "In the Mood." The orchestra recorded in that period, and some of their recordings were gathered on the limited-edition LP *Edgar Hayes & His Orchestra 1937–1938* (Swingfan, c. 1978), which gives a good insight into their oeuvre. However, Bostic is not named among the personnel and it would appear he had moved on by then, because he was only with them for about two months. He left Hayes in March after the band set off for a tour of Europe.

By April 1938, Bostic joined the Don Redman orchestra, then somewhere near the height of Redman's popularity. Redman began under Fletcher Henderson as arranger, and by 1931 had his own band, which was renowned for its driving rhythm and outstanding soloists. Yet his greatest contribution to jazz was probably as one of the most sophisticated of arrangers who helped instigate swing. By the time Bostic joined the lineup, Redman was leading a large seventeen-piece orchestra and featured in regular radio broadcasts. The tour began on April 1 when they played at the grand reopening of the Austin, Texas, Cotton Club. On the 17th of the month, they were at the Rhythm Club in Detroit.[2] Bostic's friend from riverboat days, "Shorty" Baker, was Redman's trumpeter. The orchestra appeared at the Apollo, New York, in May, and were at Springfield, Ohio, in June. They had an extended engagement at the Surfside Club, Long Island, over the summer, playing dinner dances and midnight suppers. Redman disbanded his orchestra in 1940 to concentrate on arranging. Several compilations of material from around 1938 have been issued over the years which give a good idea of how the orchestra sounded at the time, for instance, *The Little Giant of Jazz 1938–1940* (RCA, 1972). This includes their inventive, playfully swinging takes on "Auld Lang Syne" and "Margie."

Bostic's ambition had always been to get his own band together, and the chance came along sooner than expected when he was invited to play after hours at Edwin Smalls' Paradise on Seventh Avenue in Harlem. Smalls' predated the far more famous Cotton Club, and outlived that establishment. There were a great many clubs in New York, but even among those, Smalls' Paradise stood out. It was the only one under colored ownership and which had a wide appeal across racial boundaries. The opulent Cotton Club differed in that only those with money or who were already famous were allowed in. Smalls' was established in 1925 by the nattily dressed philanthropist Edwin Alexander Smalls, a real character in the Harlem firmament. During its glory years, all kinds of people frequented the club; movie stars, writers, artists, athletes, businessmen, and "socialites of all races."[3] There was no telling who might turn up. Many famous names passed through, including George Raft, Ethel Waters, Joe Louis, and Tallulah Bankhead. On a typical night the last show at the Cotton Club ended around 2, and closed about 3:30, so clubbers for whom the night never ended eventually made their way to Smalls', where the floor show went on until 6:00 a.m. As Sonny Greer remembered:

> "It was the complete show with 25 or 30 people, including the singing waiters and their twirling trays. Show people from all over New York, white and colored, went there Sunday mornings. It's hard to imagine now, musicians coming out from the breakfast dance at eight or nine in the morning with their tuxedos on, and showgirls with evening dresses on."[4]

That was in the glory days of the Roaring Twenties, but even throughout the Depression era and after, the club held its own. Glenn Miller, Tommy Dorsey, and Gene Krupa dropped in after hours and jammed with other musicians who happened by. Although the venue lost some of its cachet over the years, it nonetheless kept going, and by the time Bostic and his ensemble were the mainstays there, it was a thriving concern and still leading the way in some regards.

Bostic first played at the club around 1938, and from August 1939 onward his became the resident house band until at least 1943, but he was invited back in 1944, and he may even have rejoined at intervals after that. His music formed the soundtrack to the times. When he first started, he only had five arrangements in his repertoire, which the band had rehearsed for five days straight. Recognizing it as his first big chance, Bostic was determined to create a good impression. To make it look as though he was in demand and had a lot more scores at his disposal, he got hold of a sheaf of printed stock arrangements from song publishers. He showed himself to be a man of many parts and did everything in the band; in addition to the alto sax, he played piano, trumpet, guitar, tenor sax, and clarinet. He was the chief arranger, and even showcased his vocal skills when required. Often, they were billed as Earl Bostic and His Earls of Rhythm. At Smalls' he worked mostly with a seven-piece orchestra. He usually favored two saxes to back up his own, plus two trumpets, piano, and drums. Although not a big band, it packed a lot of punch, led by Bostic's driving sound. Despite the band's size, it had power to get across. One witness admired its youthful energy, and asserted: "For a seven-man combination, this outfit produces enough jive to cause this Harlem nightery to jump." A lively night was guaranteed, and the dance floor was always full when the Earls were playing. Even so, they had more than just hot numbers in their repertory, and could change the tone at will. As the same witness remarked, "[the] outfit can also show its mettle with the more dignified pieces."[5]

Bostic always insisted on rehearsing a lot, having never forgotten his early training on the riverboats. He was dedicated, and expected his band to be the same. Jimmy Brown was one of the key sax players in that period. Some of the other personnel who gigged with the band then included trumpeter Ed "Moon" Mullins and the double-bassist Norman Keenan. It was a feature of Bostic's orchestras that the musicians each had more than one string to their bow, and most of his men could play two or even three instruments, so that if need be six or seven men could play eleven or twelve instruments between them, which gave them a remarkable versatility. They often featured guest vocalists, including Miss Rhapsody (real name Viola Wells), who was with them around 1940. A largely forgotten talent, she was once described by Jimmie Lunceford as "the best singer since Bessie Smith."[6] Later, blues singer Olive Brown also sang with the band. At times Bostic included his own compositions directly inspired by the club, such as "Smalls' Special" and "Harlem Serenade."

In March 1940, Bostic had lodgings on the same street as the Smalls' club, at 2441 Seventh Avenue. By October that year, when he registered for the draft, he was living at 230 West 138th Street, Manhattan.[7] By then, employment was becoming more regular for him, but was not guaranteed. In 1939 he had worked for half the year, and in 1940 he was working on average for around 36 hours a week. As far as is known, Bostic did not serve in the war, perhaps on account of his eyesight, as even his earliest photos show him wearing glasses. With the coming of the war in December 1941, Bostic played a lot of USO shows and traveled to army camps across the country. His lively sets struck a chord with servicemen, and the verdict was that "The doughboys take to them in a big way."[8] He took part in radio broadcasts and had plenty of gigs, including several at the Apollo. One of those, in December 1941, was with a band that featured renowned pianist Lester Fauntleroy, "Skippy" Williams on tenor sax, and no less than three trombonists, among them the great Wilbur de Paris. Earl's music not only hit the spot among those who frequented the clubs but satisfied the critics too. Jimmy Hines of *The New York Age* admired the "dance-compelling melodies emanating from Earl Bostic" at one bash

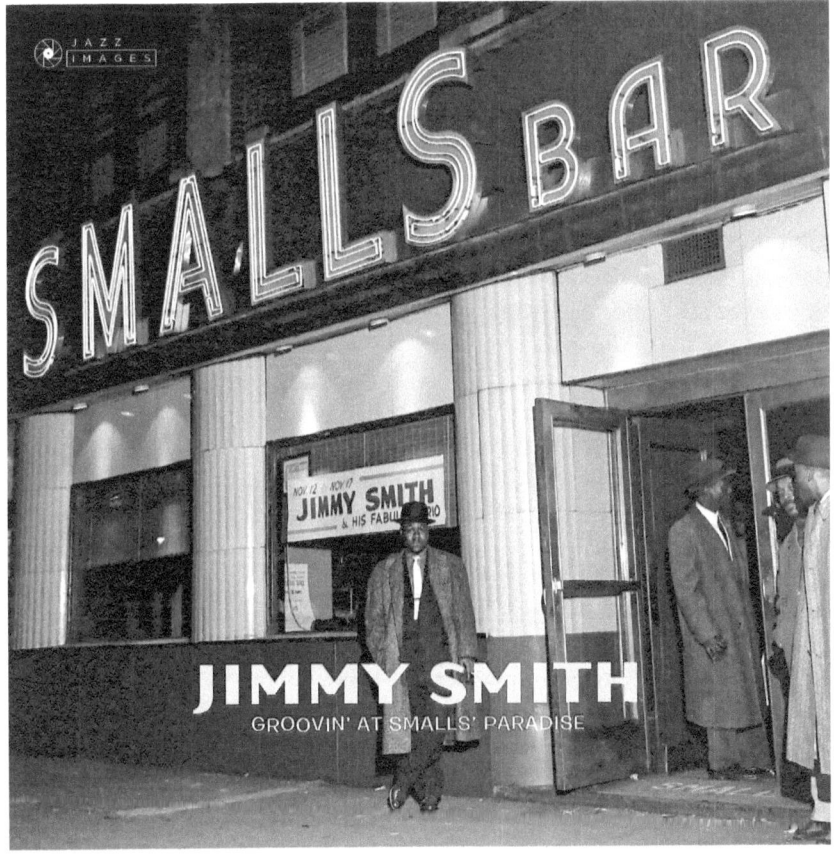

A view of Smalls' nightclub in Harlem, taken from the cover of a Jimmy Smith live recording. Earl led the resident house band at Smalls' from 1938 to 1943, and last played there in 1944.

celebrating the Harlem Dukes closing party at Smalls'.[9] In this early period of his career he played in what Hugues Panassié called a "bright, voluble style."[10]

By 1942, the Earls of Rhythm had become a veritable institution at Smalls', which was affectionately known as the Harlem Ball o' Fire. Earl showed his virtuosity, and one observer described him as "better than average" on the electric guitar and clarinet. The same writer noted that "[He] holds his own well in [the] personality side which in the long run pays dividends."[11] His stint was a record at Smalls'. Although a lot of male attention may have been focused on the shapely dancers, the music was widely appreciated. Critic Herbert Nichols praised Bostic and the Earls of Rhythm, writing that they had "a fine book full of swingy and imaginative arrangements and what's more the band has an extraordinary intonation backed up by a solid rhythm section."[12] Bostic was reputedly a good dancer, and according to at least one source may even have been a professional.

There was no knowing who might turn up at Smalls' and not just among the guests. A certain troubled teenager by the name of Malcolm Little even worked there as a waiter between 1942 and 1943. Little became famous many years later as Malcolm X. By his own recollections, he loved the atmosphere there and felt entirely at home. The circumstances that led to his being fired from his job sent his life in a totally different direction than might otherwise have been. Whether or not he ever paid much attention to the music during his stay there, he must nonetheless have heard the Bostic band in full flow.

Bostic's long stint at Smalls' led him to finding regular spots at most of the leading nightclubs in the city. He had plenty of other engagements, such as the Mimo Club, Harlem, in a similar combo to that which he showcased at Smalls. The vast majority of clubs in those days had a white clientele, but he managed to please all, regardless of race. He even managed to impress the notoriously hard-to-satisfy white folks who frequented such upmarket venues as the Copacabana, the Stork Club, the Zanzibar, Tony Pastor's, Club 78, Ruby Foo's, and many more. For instance, in August 1941, one reviewer raved that Earl and His Earls of Rhythm "caused [a] sensation at [the] Omega Showboat last Friday night."[13] He was invited to all plum spots in other clubs, and was a regular attraction at the iconic Apollo Theater, on 125th Street. Nights were busy there, with some ace performers on the bill, such as the talented young organist Hazel Scott. Even so, Bostic also took the eye, and at one show, critic Alfred Duckett noted "Orchids to debonair Earl Bostic for the sax solo on 'Body and Soul.'"[14] He was busy in this period and played for several others. Between 1942 and 1943, he featured as a sideman for Al Sears with his big band during his residency at the spacious Renaissance Casino at Seventh Avenue and 138th

Street in Harlem. His remuneration for his nightly work there was probably less than $8 or so, but he was nonetheless grateful for anything that supplemented his income at what was sometimes a precarious time.[15]

The show at Smalls' Paradise was regularly reorganized across the seasons. Bostic was a major player in the fast-paced revue "Swinging in Victory" in 1943, to mark the eighteenth anniversary of the club's opening. Indeed, the Earls of Rhythm were still as popular five years after their debut. From August 8 to the end of October 1944 a new revue opened, probably his last, in the Orchid Room, called "Tipping on Down." This featured several entertainers on the bill, including soprano Dell St. John, tap dancers Ray & Ray, and baritone Phil Gomez. They were augmented by the glamorous chorus line of Eight Orchidettes, but the Earls who provided the music for dancing were the biggest draw in themselves and still reeling in the customers.

Despite all his apparent success, however, not everyone appreciated his music, even while his career was taking off. There were times his experimentations did not go down well. For instance, on Easter Sunday 1943 at a gig at the City Auditorium, Buffalo, Bostic was fired from a band and, according to one account, "virtually laughed out of the place," although it was unclear why. It gave him no little satisfaction when he made a sensational return to the same place as a headliner six years later, at which time they could not get enough of him, and the manager of the venue remarked that he could have sold it out twice over.[16]

7

Hildegarde

"If I ever find that I can support a wife, I am going to let you know."[1]
—Earl's promise to Hildegarde White, circa 1938

Although Earl usually had plenty of female company, what suited his personality seemed to be to settle down with a wife and family. As an up-and-coming musician, arranger, bandleader, and well-dressed man-about town in the fashionable Harlem and uptown night spots, he was hardly short of admirers. However, he remembered his promise to Hildegarde White, the girl he met at Xavier when he was nineteen. Nor did she forget, and despite the way their romance played out on a tortured path over a decade, she never doubted that one day her dream of matrimony would come true.

Bostic stayed in regular touch with his folks back in Tulsa and kept them updated with all his news. From at least 1935 his parents lived in at 1809 West Easton Place, in an all-white neighborhood, where his mother was employed as a maid for oil company employee Lloyd Owen and his wife and son. It was a hard life for Druzella, who got little time off. Indeed, she was still working sixty hours a week. Meanwhile, Ike was a cook in a hotel.[2] Father and son had long since been reconciled about Earl's choice of career. According to one story, by the time Earl was becoming known, Ike presented him with a ukulele, with the words, "Son, I was wrong."[3] His father lived to see just the beginning of Earl's fame and at least the turning point when Gene Krupa took up his song "Let Me Off Uptown." Ike Bostic died suddenly on October 16, 1941, just a few weeks short of about fifty-three. The suddenness would indicate that he too had heart problems. Coincidentally, Earl was fated to die at a similar age.[4] It was a melancholy trip back home for Earl to make all the arrangements and attend the funeral.

On an upbeat note, Earl decided that things were going well enough in New York to enable him to get married to his long-time sweetheart Hildegarde White. Theirs had been a long, drawn-out courtship that often looked as though it would never end happily. Throughout it all, she never doubted that one day they would be wed. It was not unlike the romance of many another struggling musician, such as that of Glenn Miller and his wife Helen, with long gaps in between, then seeing each other out of the blue and picking up where they had left off.

Hildegarde Theresa White was seventeen when she and Earl first met. She had lived all her life in New Orleans, where her family had been settled for several generations. Slightly less than two years younger than Earl, she was born June 21, 1915, the daughter of Fred White, a porter, and Blanche (née Conrad). She had one younger brother, Fred, two years her junior. The family home was then at 1833 Burdette Street.[5]

After Earl left Xavier and began his travels, he and Hildegarde did not see much of each other for several years, although they kept in touch. They only got together again after he went to New York and began working for Don Redman. It happened that he returned to New Orleans for a dance around that time, and she made certain she was there to see him. She invited him to dinner, and while he was in town they got to know each other all over again. He told her of all his plans for the future, and promised her, "If I ever find that I can support a wife, I am going to let you know."[6] She never forgot those words, and throughout the years that followed always believed that one day it would happen, despite her friends' belief that she was crazy to cling to a dream. They again did not meet for a long time after that, as he was busy in the midst of his career. In the meantime, she moved to Chicago, where she lived for about three years, and also dated other men, but always maintained that she was not serious about any of them.

To begin with, she and Earl regularly exchanged letters, but as time went on, the letters slowed to a trickle and then stopped altogether. She had not heard from him in about two years when a mutual friend of theirs happened to mention she was taking a trip to New York. The friend gave Earl Hildegarde's new address and he wrote to her. She recollected: "I remember well the thrill of seeing that familiar handwriting after so long a time but I don't think, despite my long-held faith, that I was prepared for what it said."[7] Earl told her all about how his "Let Me Off Uptown" had just been recorded by Gene Krupa, and that he felt that he was now in a position to support a wife. He invited her to New York for a visit to see if she still felt the same way. Although she never answered his letter, she had already decided to go. She said that she wanted to meet up with other friends there and hoped to see the Joe Louis fight. Now the moment was at hand of seeing him again, she was not sure how she felt, and it was not without trepidation that she set off on her journey, assuring her flatmate that she would definitely be coming back.

When Hildegarde and her friend arrived in New York, they went straight from Grand Central Station to Smalls' Paradise in Harlem where Bostic was playing. They sat at one of the tables at the back of the club. She recalled: "As I sat watching Earl on the bandstand, all the memories I had accumulated over ten years seemed to crowd themselves into my consciousness. I was almost afraid to speak to him." So much so that she got her friend to send a note round to him. She continued:

> "I watched as he opened it during a lull in the music. Without a word he turned and walked off the bandstand toward us. Then he was standing before me. Neither of us said anything for a long moment then he said: You're not going back." It's funny how at the most important moments of our lives, words elude us. I had waited so long for Earl to ask me to marry him and now in a simple phrase the dream had come true.[8]

Without thinking she blurted out that she had to go back because she had a return ticket. Needless to say, the ticket was never used, and afterward they often laughed about it. They kept the ticket as a reminder and put it in a frame in their house. They married not long after her visit, on November 30, 1942, in Baltimore, Maryland.[9]

8

"Let Me Off Uptown"

"He could do anything on sax, and he could write like crazy."[1]
—Buddy Tate

From the time he reached New York, Bostic was busy not only as a sideman and arranger for name bands, but as a composer in his own right. He developed his own special signature style as an arranger that meant he was constantly in demand, and he worked for a wide array of leading players, from Cab Calloway to Paul Whiteman. With the latter he gained valuable experience in how to arrange for a radio orchestra. In that period, Bostic was an integral part of what became known as the Harlem Renaissance.

Arrangers seldom had much of the credit for their work, but they each had their trademark style and were clearly crucial in developing a particular sound for each musician. Unseen and largely unknown, they might be called the invisible facilitators for all manner of bands. Records seldom mentioned arrangers in their lists of personnel despite their importance, and in many cases they remained unacknowledged. For years they not only were uncredited, but received a far lower pay scale for their work than composers, and were often perceived as second-class citizens in the industry. The impetus for change came from Hollywood in the 1930s with the advent of sound in the movies. Arrangers pushed for recognition, and this led to the founding of the American Society of Music Arrangers (ASMA) in January 1938. Later, some notable arrangers achieved a large measure of fame, such as Billy May and Nelson Riddle—the latter particularly in his association with Frank Sinatra.

Bostic worked as an arranger for Paul Whiteman on his *Chesterfield Radio Hour* show, which ran in 1938 and 1939 on CBS. Whiteman was then one of the most famous personalities in mainstream jazz and popular music. He first came to prominence as orchestra leader with the introduction of Gershwin's ambitious "Rhapsody in Blue" in the 1920s, in which the composer sought to marry the worlds of jazz and classical music.

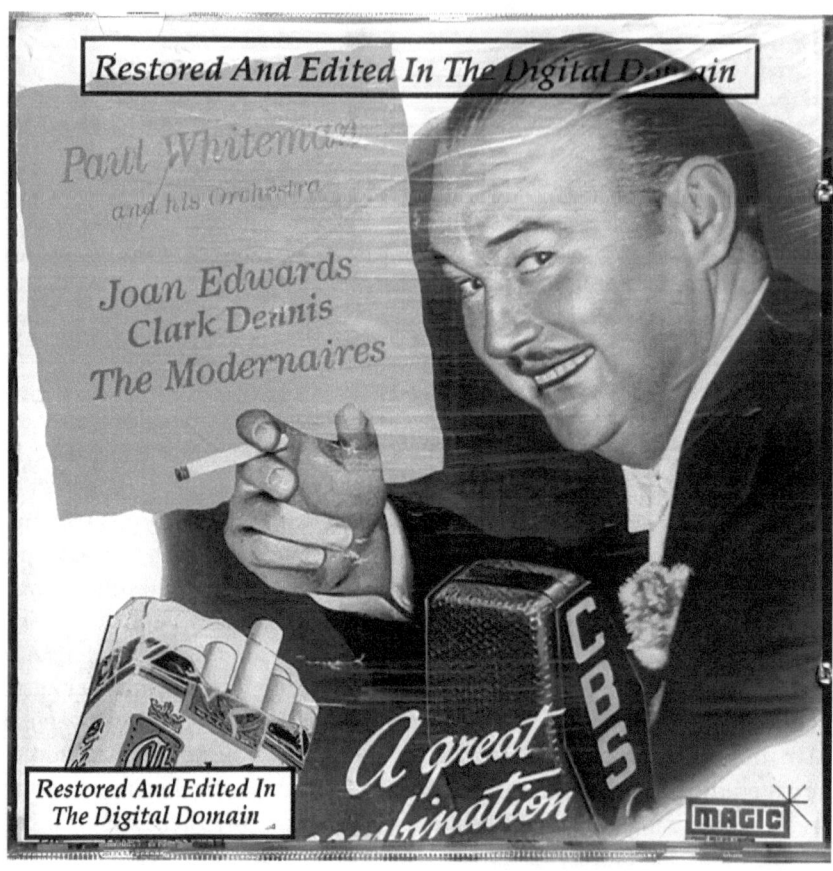

Bostic worked as arranger for many big-name bandleaders, including Paul Whiteman on his weekly *Chesterfield Radio Hour* show, broadcast by CBS in 1938–1939.

Whiteman thereafter became known as the "King of Jazz" and developed a polished sound that greatly appealed to audiences in the 1930s. Although he led an all-white band, Whiteman was sympathetic to black musicians and keen to hire them, but his manager persuaded him that it would not be good for his career. Nonetheless, he must have done so on a small scale, because he gave Bostic a chance and was clearly impressed with him. Among the personnel in the Whiteman orchestra at that time was Jack Teagarden, for whom Earl also arranged. The *Chesterfield* shows aired on Wednesday evenings at eight. Whiteman would feature guest vocalists and a close harmony group, The Modernaires, who were especially popular. Arranging for radio was an art that had specific requirements. Time was of the essence, and there were cues to take note of so that the all-important sponsor's message could be heard at regular intervals. Working to a tight deadline limited the scope for experiment but concentrated the mind. Most of the numbers came in at under two and a half minutes, but that was ample time for those with imagination. Among the songs that Bostic may have arranged is "I Kiss Your Hand, Madame," a number he recorded many years later. The playful 1939 recording similarly has the saxophone at the fore. It has changes in tempo and some inventive passages, and finishes on a familiar high note. After Whiteman left the show in November 1939, it was given over to Glenn Miller. Although some of the broadcasts from the Whiteman era have been released over the years, there is no mention of the arrangers. Two sets from the summer of 1938 were issued on CD several years ago as *Paul Whiteman & His Chesterfield Orchestra*, and another from 1939 as *The CBS Shows* (see Discography).

Also in 1939, Bostic worked as arranger for the great Cab Calloway. A born showman, Calloway was famed for his musical inventiveness and elegant sartorial style. Like many of the great bandleaders he was a stickler for discipline, especially where timekeeping was concerned, and his musicians were always well paid. One of Bostic's most notable arrangements for the band was the appealing "Trylon Swing," which featured four saxes (two altos and two tenors). The tenors on the recording were Leon "Chu" Berry and Walter "Foots" Thomas, the latter of whom later joined Bostic in his own band.

That same year, Bostic made his tantalizing recording debut. This occurred when he was briefly associated with Lionel Hampton for the first time. The session, dated October 12, was for the Victor label. Along with Hampton, the stellar line-up included no less than the legendary guitarist Charlie Christian, "Red" Allen, trombone virtuoso J.C. Higginbotham, drummer Sid Catlett, double bassist Artie Bernstein, and pianist Clyde Hart. The songs included "Haven't Named it Yet" and "I'm on My Way from You." Earl's style of playing was already clearly established, and he showed great spirit on such tracks as "The Heebie Jeebies Are Rockin' the Town."

Among others Bostic arranged for was Ina Ray Hutton, known as the blonde bombshell of rhythm. She was famous as the first female bandleader with her all-girl band The Melodears during the 1930s. In 1939, she disbanded her group in favor of a male ensemble, who were billed as Ina Ray Hutton & Her Orchestra. At the same time, she reverted to being a brunette. One of her popular numbers was "The Five O'Clock Whistle" (1940). She filmed some short choreographed musical interludes in the early 1940s, and it is noticeable that some of her groups included three saxes. The sax was to the fore in "Knock Me a Kiss." Various disputes kept her away from recording for a number of years in the 1940s. She reformed the band around December 1945, with several releases following in February 1946, including "Make Me Know It" issued on Regal Zonophone. Contemporary reports suggest that it may have been around this time that Bostic arranged for Hutton; however, by December 1946 she disbanded once again.

Bostic had been composing since his teens, and eventually several of his songs gained the attention of some well-established names. Among his earliest and most famous hits were "The Major and the Minor" and "Let Me Off Uptown." The first of those, "The Major and the Minor" (1941), was a big hit for guitarist and bandleader Alvino Rey, who recorded it for the Bluebird label. On its release, a delighted *Down Beat* review called it "the best sounding wax Rey has ever made," and "the first one he has that

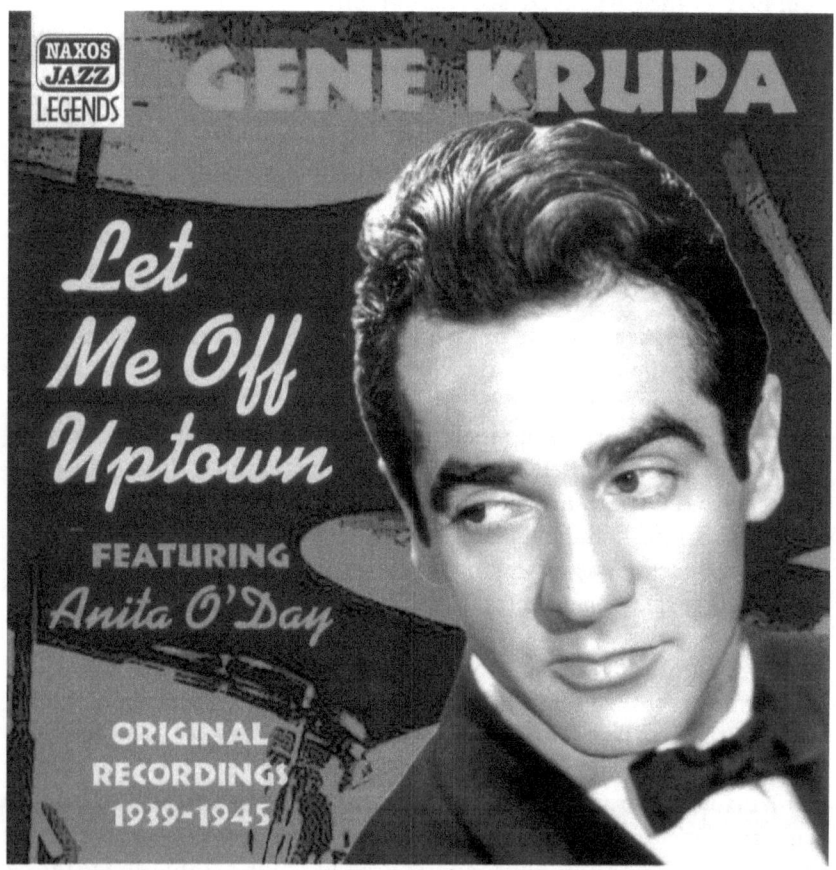

Bostic's composition "Let Me Off Uptown" was a big hit for Gene Krupa and his featured singer Anita O'Day in 1941. Krupa's was one of the many releases that feature the song.

swings."² *The Baton* immediately hailed the tune as a "superior instrumental."³ Bostic later released his own version on record in 1944. According to one source, the wartime romantic comedy *The Major and the Minor* (1943) was said to have contained some of Bostic's music, but none of that listed can be attributed to him and it would seem to be unrelated.

"Let Me Off Uptown," which he had written in the late 1930s, was probably his most successful number. It was a song that several other people recorded but he never did. Almost immediately it was taken up by Gene Krupa, and, with lyrics added by Redd Evans, was sung to great effect by Anita O'Day accompanied by outstanding trumpeter Roy Eldridge on a recording made in June 1941. The combination of O'Day's swinging, conversational vocal style coupled with the sophisticated harmonies of Eldridge caused a sensation. Over one and a half million copies were sold and it became one of the biggest hits of Krupa's career. With the "Uptown" in question being Harlem, it was almost a paean to black culture, and the playful, interracial nature of the song was in some ways a large part of its importance and appeal. Interestingly, critics have noted that O'Day's distinctive voice had "the timbre of an alto saxophone."⁴ A musical short featuring the band playing the number was also released in 1942. The song became associated with O'Day, the "Jezebel of Jazz" forever afterward. It probably did more to get Bostic's name known in the early 1940s than any other. Many in their turn were attracted to it, and it was recorded by Lucky Millinder, Larry Clinton's Bluebird Orchestra, The Delta Rhythm Boys, Tony Pastor, and many years later Dakota Staton. Benny Goodman often did a version of it in live performance on tour in Europe when Anita O'Day was his guest singer, although it appeared that he never actually recorded it. Frank DiFabio and His Trio recorded an instrumental version in 1961. Some of Bostic's other compositions from that early 1940s period were directly inspired by his time at Smalls' Paradise, for instance, "Smalls' Special," "Paradise Shuffle," and "Harlem Serenade."

Charlie Barnet also recorded "Let Me Off Uptown" in 1941.⁵ One author wrote that Bostic was a featured soloist for Barnet in the early 1940s.⁶ Perhaps more well known for his multiple marriages, Barnet was an accomplished saxophonist who could play the whole range from baritone to soprano when required. A pioneer of integration, he had made his debut at the Apollo in Harlem as far back as 1933, being one of the first white bands to do so. From the early 1940s, he brought many colored musicians into his orchestra, despite the stiff opposition to this among some promoters. It was not because of any burning desire on his part to be a civil rights pioneer, but purely because he only ever sought to hire the best men for the job. A firm admirer of Duke Ellington, he based his playing style on that of Johnny Hodges. Familiar swing tunes he was remembered for included "Skyliner," "Cherokee," and "Pompton Turnpike," all of which were popular on the AEF (Allied Expeditionary Forces) Radio during the war, especially on an afternoon show called *Duffle Bag* broadcast daily around 4 p.m. Earl later included several of these and other Barnet numbers in his repertoire to great effect.

During the turbulent war years there was a more regular turnover of personnel in bands as men were drafted, or found steadier and more lucrative work in airplane factories or defense plants. So it was in the various combos that Bostic led at Smalls' and elsewhere. John Johnakins was offered a job in his band when one of the other sax players left or was fired. Johnakins was engaged as a baritone and alto saxophonist, but he also played the clarinet. He later recalled Bostic's attention to detail in regards to arrangements:

> "Earl had some arrangements where ... to get a heavier ensemble, it was more profitable to switch to a baritone and get a heavier chord according to the way you voice it. Bostic was a good arranger so he could voice it so that I could play the alto when three saxophones were playing, then, during the introductions or interludes where you want to be heavy, then he had me switch to baritone.... He played so marvelous; he was fabulous."[7]

Before, during, and after his stints with "Hot Lips" Page and Lionel Hampton, Bostic contributed arrangements for trumpeter Louis Prima, including "The Blizzard" (1944). The larger-than-life Prima hailed from New Orleans, and his Dixieland-style swing sound became increasingly popular. His first big hit was "Angelina," and in the postwar period he became yet more of a showman. Gene Allen, who played baritone saxophone for Prima, recalled some of the arrangements that Bostic wrote for the band:

> Earl was a fine gentleman who encouraged me a lot, and I got to know him well. He wrote some of the flag-wavers like "Chinatown, My Chinatown" that we used to open stage shows. It was taken at a break-neck tempo, with some interesting saxophone parts, which allowed Louis to do his high-note trumpet work over the opening choruses with the band storming away. Another one of his charts was an old waltz called "I Love You Truly," which was played in double-time and was very "notey" for the saxes—one of those arpeggiated up-and-down things that gave the section a real workout. It was like practicing while working.[8]

Bostic also co-wrote with Prima "Brooklyn Boogie," a song that famously featured members of the Brooklyn Dodgers. After Prima, Bostic worked for Leon Gros, Artie Shaw, Jack Teagarden, and several others. Many years later Bostic recorded Shaw's "Special Delivery Stomp." Teagarden's head arranger was Phil Moore, and this was one of the few instances of a colored

8. "Let Me Off Uptown"   49

arranger working for a white band. Promoters and agents were dead set against any such mixing at that time in history, principally because of the reaction when touring in the South. John Chilton said that Bostic arranged for Teagarden around 1939. Among the songs he may have worked on was "Rippling Waters" by Willie "The Lion" Smith. Smith expert Johnny Simmen specifically praised the arranger. He remarked, "I don't know who wrote the arrangement, but the writer did a very good job indeed, having the Lion's right-hand figures played by four clarinets against effective brass-scoring. Much of the Lion's playing is kept intact by this device."[9] Some sources indicate that Bostic worked for Teagarden on a freelance or ad hoc basis over a period of years, and one maintained that it was for as many as seven years.

9

Swinging with "Hot Lips" and "Hamp"

"It's hot swing at its hottest and wildest—but it has form and cohesion. And it has several of the finest instrumentalists in the business."[1]
—Lionel Hampton orchestra review in *Billboard*, 1943

Bostic joined "Hot Lips" Page in 1942 and stayed for six months, then left to take up an offer from Lionel Hampton. He was employed as a man of many parts with the Hampton orchestra and stayed with him for around a year. With both outfits and in other combos he recorded several sides during that time. Before the end of the war, he decided to try again with his own band and went solo.

Oran Thadeus "Hot Lips" Page was born in Dallas, Texas, and was first taught clarinet and saxophone by his mother. From the age of twelve he started playing the trumpet and began to specialize. From then on, he gained wide experience touring with the likes of blues singer Ma Rainey and later with Walter Page's Blue Devils. He formed his own band in the mid-1930s when he relocated to New York, enticed by the invitation of Joe Glaser, the manager of Louis Armstrong. Page had a stint at Smalls' Paradise in 1937, the year before Bostic, but found the going difficult and went touring instead. A genuine innovator with a warm, charismatic personality, Page could play in a range of styles and was in many ways a pioneer of R&B in a similar way to Bostic. The two got along well and admired one another. They played alongside each other several times both before and after Earl joined his band. There were at least two recorded sessions in 1944. Page's orchestra had a decidedly playful spirit, heard at its best on such numbers as "Double Trouble Blues" and "They Raided the Joint." His pleasing blues style on vocal and standout ability on trumpet played off against great backing by some of the outstanding sax men of the age. The tenors alone consisted of Ben Webster, Don Byas, and Ike Quebec.

9. Swinging with "Hot Lips" and "Hamp" 51

Bostic was joined on alto by Floyd "Horsecollar" Williams, who was later replaced by "Butch" Hammond. Earl was present during what "Hot Lips" experts believe was the finest incarnation of the orchestra in the early 1940s. At that time, they were the featured band at the Famous Door club on 52nd Street, where Bostic amazed everyone with his skill, and the other musicians marveled at the way he took his solos in one breath. He was perhaps heard to best effect on disc on "Good for Stompin'" and "You Need Coachin'." When he recorded with them later, he was striking on several tracks, especially so on "Kansas City Jive," with its almost big band style arrangement. He displayed his mastery in his solos on "Texas and Pacific" and "Birmingham Boogie." The latter two appear on the recent compilation *The Earl Bostic Collection* (Acrobat, 2015). A perennial favorite of the band was "The Sheik of Araby," which Earl returned to many years later.

Earl spent some time playing with "Hot Lips" Page in 1943 and again in 1944.

In many ways, Page has been curiously overlooked, and his early death at the age of forty-six meant he was sometimes a forgotten figure. Nonetheless, recent years have put him back on the map and there was a timely book about him published not long ago. Luckily, his recordings have been reissued regularly over the years on both vinyl and CD. Bostic's time with the band is well represented on several records. All the tracks appear on two of *The Chronological Hot Lips Page* series, namely, *1940-44* (Classics, 809, 1995), and *1944-46* (Classics, 950, 1997), both issued in France. Of special note is the companion release *Hot Lips Page 1937-49: The Alternative Takes* (Neatwork, 2003), which features different versions of six songs.

Earl kept experimenting with different combinations, and in between stints with Page, he got together a new group with which he opened at Ernie's in Greenwich Village. The lineup featured Leroy Fletcher on tenor sax, Roger Jones on trumpet, Herbie Goodwin, piano, and Chester Stewart, drums.[2] Of those players, Jones stayed with Bostic the longest in the orchestra that he was then working toward assembling, and became an integral part of it.

In June 1943, Bostic left "Hot Lips" Page to join Lionel Hampton, and swapped places with Rudy Rutherford, who replaced him in the Page band. In addition to playing alto, Bostic was attracted to the offer from Hampton, who engaged him for his all-around ability. Not only was he appointed the musical director for the band, he was called on to play acoustic and electric guitar, trumpet, and clarinet. Hampton did all he could to entice Bostic and even gave him time off for arranging.[3]

The young alto sax man was an up-and-coming talent, and had offers from a host of big-name bandleaders. What put him off seemed to be the long tours away from New York, which at least at that stage of his career just did not suit him. He wanted to augment his experience in a first-rate orchestra he admired and perhaps chose "The King of Swing" because he felt the offer was a good one that would raise his profile further, give him even greater experience, and gave him some scope to do other things. He proved a great addition to the band. Just after he joined, Hampton remarked, "I consider myself lucky to have Bostic. That boy can do about everything. He digs a mean sax, doubles on clarinet, trumpet, and guitar. Hot arranger too. Tulsa, Oklahoma, kid."[4]

Hampton was born in Louisiana, but his mother took him to Chicago as a boy. She enrolled him in a Catholic school although she was not herself of that denomination. In a curious echo of Bostic's story, Hampton too was taught the basics of music by a nun at the school who was a disciplinarian. He began as a drummer in a Chicago newspaper band sponsored by *The Defender*. After touring California with various bands, he came upon

9. Swinging with "Hot Lips" and "Hamp"

the vibraharp almost by chance. While playing with Les Hite, the bandleader was absent in Los Angeles, and Armstrong led for a while. Hampton began fooling with a vibraphone that had been left in the studio, and Armstrong was so taken with what he heard that they recorded "Memories of You" (1930), which is considered the first appearance of the vibes on a jazz record. Up until then, the instrument, which had been invented in 1916, was considered a novelty, and was mostly associated with vaudeville. Thereafter, Hampton took up the vibes full time, and spent four years with Benny Goodman (1936–1940). From 1940 he started out on his own, but at first found the going difficult. By 1942 to 1943 he had established himself, and from then on for the next fifty years he had one of the most popular and successful orchestras in jazz history. Moreover, he established the vibes as a versatile and important instrument in the music. Its importance

In 1943, Bostic accepted an offer from Lionel Hampton to join his popular orchestra and stayed for almost a year.

was reflected in the rise of several exceptional practitioners, notably Milt Jackson and the Modern Jazz Quartet.

During the war years, the Hampton orchestra was considered somewhere arguably close to its best. By the end of 1943 they topped the annual *Pittsburgh Courier* poll. Singer Joe Williams spent about six months with the band around the same time as Bostic and said they were really rocking then. He recalled that "it was a real swinging pleasure" to hear and play with them.[5] Hampton always had a strong saxophone section. Bostic led the way on alto, with Arnett Cobb on tenor and Charles Fowlkes on baritone. Earl got to know Cobb well and he became a good friend who later joined Bostic's band. At other times, the great Dexter Gordon also played on alto. Hamp's trumpet section was no less impressive, consisting of the three Joes, Joe Morris, Joe Wilder, and Bostic's old pupil Joe Newman, along with Lamar Wright, Jr. Fred Beckett and Booty Ward were on trombone, with Milt Buckner on piano. With the sensational 19-year-old Dinah Washington making a name for herself as the resident singer, there was seemingly little else it could want.

When asked how he managed to attract some of the best young players around while others missed out, Hampton replied, "I guess it's because I keep a 'free' band. I give every man the opportunity of free expression of his musical self. All of my men take solos. They told me, from time to time, that they enjoy working with me because they can PLAY in my band. I refuse to strap my men in a musical straight-jacket."[6] A striking feature of Hamp's approach was that he gave each soloist their chance, and numbers routinely went on and on until they had all had their full turn in the spotlight. He was a terrific encourager of young talent and gave a flying start to a host of amazing musicians.

Bostic worked well within the Hampton setup, within which he was one of the most popular musicians. It was notable that the vibes featured prominently as an integral part of Earl's sound in most of his later bands, and especially so in the big hits of his early 1950s heyday. He was interested in all instruments, and reputedly also became proficient on the vibraharp himself, perhaps even more so while playing with Hampton. Bostic's surprising skill on the trumpet has also been commented upon. Among several highlights during his time with "The King of Swing," he was especially impressive on the famous signature tune "Flying Home No. 2," and on "Hamp's Boogie Woogie." The orchestra also recorded a great version of Earl's "The Major and the Minor" for V-Disc, for the armed forces serving overseas. Among the numbers he arranged for Hampton was Redd Evans's catchy dance favorite "Arkansas."[7]

Hampton organized some ambitious presentations in which he sought to showcase the true versatility of his orchestra and specifically his

9. Swinging with "Hot Lips" and "Hamp"

unique interpretation of modern music. One of the most noteworthy was a Palm Sunday concert on April 2, 1944, held at the Symphony Hall in Boston. Divided into two halves, the program included Hampton's "Bach Is in the Groove" augmented by seven violinists from the Boston Symphony Orchestra. Bostic was prominent among the soloists on the opening number "Lady Be Good" alongside Arnett Cobb, and Bostic alone began the second half with "The Major and the Minor" and was again to the fore on "Lisa."[8]

In July 1944, Bostic left the Hampton band after thirteen months, and went back to Smalls' Paradise. He was replaced in the former orchestra by George Dorsey. Hampton often lamented the way he lost at regular intervals some of his key talents, such as Bostic, Illinois Jacquet, and Dinah Washington, and was unable to replace them with any musicians of equal caliber or dedication. In some ways, it was not surprising, because although the band was among the most popular and lucrative over a long period, Hampton notoriously did not pay well. His wife Gladys arranged the financial side of things in such a way that many an unsuspecting musician ended up with a lot less than they expected or deserved. The great Charles Mingus, for instance, his bass player, once wrote a song for him, "Mingus Fingers," despite the sage advice of his friend that Hampton never paid songwriters. Sure enough, Mingus eventually had to take Hampton to court in order to try to get paid for his song.

Hampton's later years were blighted by bouts of ill health and some bad luck, including a stroke on stage in 1991 and the crippling effects of chronic arthritis. A devastating fire at his apartment when he was in his eighties destroyed much of his lifetime accumulation of music, awards, and memorabilia, although luckily, he survived to reach the grand old age of ninety-four. Known for his philanthropy, he was instrumental in providing funds for public housing projects in Harlem and elsewhere. As much as anything, he was remembered for his natural exuberance combined with discipline and his great knowledge of music. He saw jazz as a brotherhood and had no time for divisions or cliques. Thus, he was able to straddle eras and different genres with ease and was all-encompassing in his approach. His legacy was also in the way he enriched the music for upcoming generations in the many personnel who played in his remarkable orchestra, not least such exceptional talents as Art Farmer and Quincy Jones.[9]

In September of that year, 1944, Bostic recorded in New York with the Buck Ram All Stars for Savoy. It is worth noting that among the personnel on the four tracks of that session, Don Byas was on tenor sax, with the great Red Norvo on vibes, Remo Palmieri on guitar, "Slam" Stewart on bass, and Cozy Cole on drums. These recordings were not heard until many years later. Two of the four tracks, "Twilight in Tehran" and "Morning Mist," appeared on the compilation LP *The Changing Face of Harlem—The Savoy Sessions* in 1976. The other two, "Swing Street" and "Ram Session," were released on the double LP *Jam Session at Savoy*. All four tracks of the recording session were finally released together on the Cozy Cole CD *Cozy Cole 1944* issued in 1995. Bostic's distinctive throaty but melodic sax was heard to especially good effect on "Ram Session." The easy style of his colleague Don Byas on tenor began the appealing "Morning Mist" and Bostic did the honors to end the piece, finishing on his by now familiar sustained high note.

As well as his return to Smalls' in 1944, Bostic also played several times with "Hot Lips" Page again, and recorded some excellent sides for various record labels including Apollo, Commodore, and Hub.

Sometime around late 1944 or early 1945, Bostic first heard about a hot new talent on the saxophone who was fast making a name for himself in bebop circles. Twenty-four-year-old Charlie Parker from Kansas City, Kansas, nicknamed "Yardbird" or "Bird," was headlining at the Heat Wave club on 52nd Street. As he did with all new kids on the block, Bostic often went down to see Parker wherever he happened to be playing, and the two played together in a near-legendary session. Bostic was taken with him, and was perhaps already thinking about scouting him for his own band, which he was in the process of forming. Hal Singer recalled the meeting between the two when Bostic sat in. Singer recollected: "Then for the jam session, 'Bird' called 'Cherokee.' The two horns were Bird and Bostic. Both of them were great and had a great feeling towards each other. There was great admiration for each other's drive and technique."[10] According to those who witnessed it, there was no telling which one of them had "won" the competition, because it seemed like it was not so much a contest as an exciting meeting of minds and contrasting styles, each outstanding in their own way. It was one of the earliest meetings they had, but by no means the last, and how jazz fans would love to have heard them if they could only have been caught on record for posterity.

10

Going Solo

"He [Bostic] knows this instrument inside out, back to front and upside down."[1]
—James Moody

The end of the war saw Bostic advance his ambitions, and he struck out with his own band again. His music had great energy at that time, and although he did not find his distinctive sound immediately, he was constantly working toward it, and made several successful recording sessions for various labels. During the next couple of years, he gained huge experience playing in clubs and theaters, and was constantly honing his sound until he finally hit on the right combination that would eventually catapult him into the popular imagination.

It was a time of transition, and Bostic, like everyone else, was adjusting his approach to suit the changing tastes of restless audiences, but more pertinently to develop his own ideas. Even a year before the war came to an end, he had already resolved to re-form his own band. Ever since he left Lionel Hampton in July 1944 he was effectively on his own, although he did play and record with others on occasion thereafter, notably "Hot Lips" Page. In October, he was back in his familiar stomping ground at Smalls', as *The Record Changer* described, "playing a show that will astonish all visitors."[2]

By the start of 1945, he was already seemingly well established in his own right, and in January and February, he was playing the round of the clubs of New York with the talented young soprano Ruth Weston as his chief vocalist.[3] In March he was part of the orchestra of choice for singer Lena Horne in her headline show at the Capitol Theater. As well as her regular accompanist and arranger Horace Henderson, Bostic played clarinet alongside Edmond Hall, with Benny Morton on trombone a standout among the other personnel.[4] Bostic was also present on several of Horne's V-Disc recordings, made for the armed forces, for which she specifically requested him.

In May, just as the war in Europe was coming to an end, Bostic opened at the famous Kelly's Stables on West 52nd Street in Manhattan. There followed several other club dates in the vicinity. By the summer he was already a fixture at Murrain's, previously known as Mimo's, on 132nd Street and Seventh Ave, playing three shows daily. Manager Art Paris was "loud in the praises" of his new signing.[5] Bill "Bojangles" Robinson was the star in residence there, along with the curvaceous and sprightly Smith Sisters dance trio. Although the club was just as popular as ever, it was a sign of the volatile times when it closed later that year.

July saw Bostic playing for cornetist Rex Stewart on a standout session for Savoy. Stewart (1907–1967) started out studying the piano and violin as a boy, but before long specialized on the cornet. After dropping out of school to join the Ragtime Clowns, he went on to have wide experience

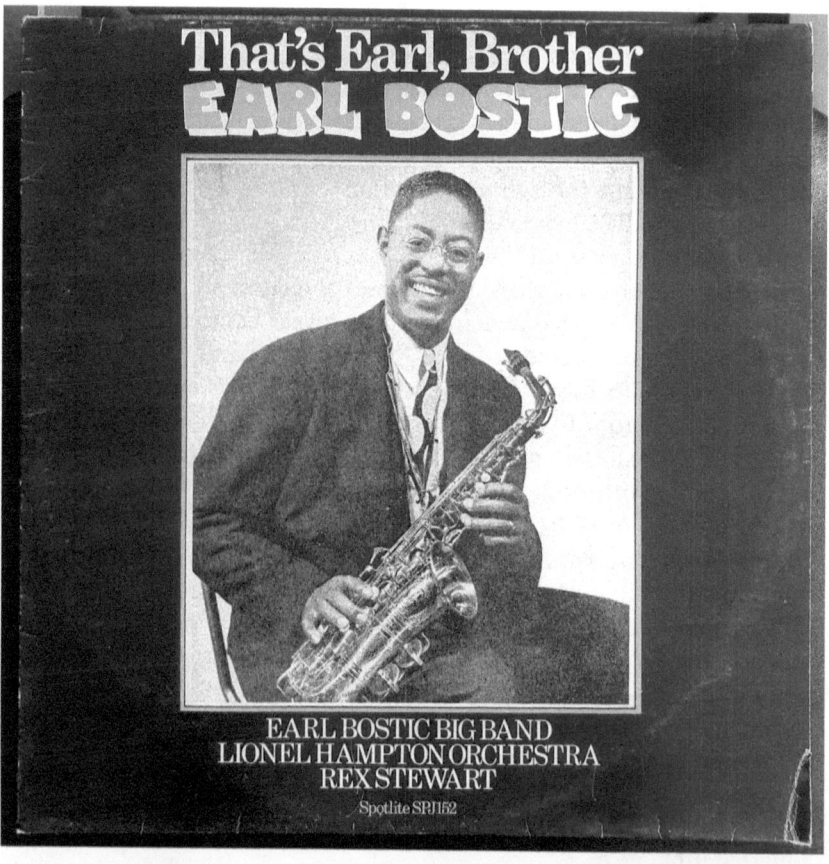

The LP *That's Earl, Brother* (1985) collected many of Bostic's early recordings, including some from his excellent session with Rex Stewart in 1945.

10. Going Solo

in numerous bands before in 1934 joining Duke Ellington's orchestra, with whom he spent eleven years. In 1945 he left to run a series of his own great little swing bands. Earl appeared on the four tracks recorded that day, and sounded assured on "The Shady Side of the Street," an intriguing exercise loosely based on "The Sunny Side of the Street." Fluent and controlled, it was considered by many as one of his strongest statements to date on record. This track pops up most frequently on compilations of this period. All four numbers can be heard on *The Chronological Rex Stewart 1934–46* (Classics, 1997). The tenor saxman who played alongside him on the session was Cecil Scott.

In September, just a couple of weeks after VJ Day, Bostic was firmly ensconced at the Onyx Club, which, like Kelly's, was on the famous West 52nd Street, nicknamed the street of jazz. The Onyx began life as a speakeasy during Prohibition, at which time it was run by a notorious bootlegger. By the mid–1940s the club had become a thriving venue for jazz, and played host to most of the greats, including Art Tatum. Bostic's tenure at the club began on September 15 and finished on November 2. Ben Webster was there around the same time.

Bostic's reputation was growing steadily, and in between his longer residencies in New York he also featured as guest artist at several other clubs, including out-of-town venues such as The Paddock in East Hartford, Connecticut. In November he was invited there to join Gage Amber's New American Jazz outfit for the second time, having proved so popular on an earlier visit. Hartford had not seen such an unusual talent and the gig sent jazz fans into raptures. The local music correspondent raved about his dexterity, exclaiming: "Boy oh boy! That man Earl ... can do Louis Armstrong stuff on sax. Which sends lovers of jazz. Those hands move so fast. Those lips are so tricky when they blow! Oh man you just don't know whether or not Earl's goin' [to] go off in a thunder cloud suddenly."[6]

From late November until the beginning of December, Bostic played the Elks' Rendezvous at 133rd and Lenox Ave. The club, famous for its girls dancing on the tables, was associated with Louis Jordan, then charting his own course in what became known as rhythm and blues. It was while Bostic was based there that Delta bluesman "Cousin" Joe first encountered him. Joe, originally known as Pleasant Joseph, spent much of his early life working on a plantation in his native Louisiana. He began touring in the 1940s, and first became famous when he took part in recordings for Sidney Bechet, after which he settled in New York. He enjoyed a long career and benefited from a revival of interest in the blues which led to successful European tours late in life. Joe later claimed that he alone was responsible for getting Bostic his breakthrough into the big time. According to the way he told it, Bostic would have remained an unknown playing in the basement at the Rendezvous if it had not been for him. This seems something of an exaggeration considering that he had already had fifteen years varied experience including a four-year record run at Smalls' Paradise, not to mention that he was a successful composer in his own right and the arranger of choice for some of the biggest names in jazz. Joe was greatly impressed by the young player, and recalled, "He played so much horn he was making nine thousand notes a second." Joe said that he was working on a gospel album for which he approached Bostic to write the beginnings and endings of the tunes, and arranged for him to be paid $100 extra for the session. One of Bostic's distinctive arrangements for Joe was "Beggin' Woman," which he recorded with the Sam Price Trio. Joe was often billed as Brother Joshua on those sides that had a more obvious gospel influence, such as "When Your Mother's Gone," on which he was backed by the Bostic band.[7] Six tracks from the various sessions Bostic made with "Cousin" Joe appeared on the LP *Cousin Joe from New Orleans in His Prime* (Munich Records, 1984) from Holland.

Earl was still much in demand as an arranger, not just for jazz and blues musicians but in other genres. For example, he arranged for the influential gospel group The Golden Gate Quartet. Among their recordings in that period was the old favorite "Bones, Bones, Bones" (Ezekiel in the Valley) and the uplifting "No Restricted Signs (in Heaven)." "I Will Be Home Again" from that time was one of their more secular numbers, given a sympathetic Bostic arrangement backed by piano and guitar. This song was famously covered by Elvis Presley, who in his turn was greatly influenced by the Quartet.

Earl's first session under his own aegis took place in New York in November or December 1945 for Majestic. This was with his sextet, which had Roger Jones much to the fore as trumpeter and vocalist. Jones showed how well he could handle blues numbers, on "Hurricane Blues" from that session, and later displayed equal ability with ballads. Often compared in his style to Al Hibbler, Jones stayed with the Bostic band for around five years off and on. Other songs in that session included old favorites such as Gershwin's "The Man I Love," on which Bostic showed a deft touch, and he gave a masterfully swinging interpretation of his own composition "The Major and the Minor." The closer "All On" was an up-tempo Hampton collaboration. *Down Beat* commented that it had "some of the speedy forensics in which Earl delights and which is in direct contradiction to his reed ability."[8]

In January 1946, Bostic signed for Gotham Records, co-founded by Sam Goody and Ivin Ballen. Bostic's next recording date took place in February, shortly after he opened at the Village Corners on Seventh Ave. South. On these sides, his alto dominated on the fast-paced "Liza," and

10. Going Solo

"Jumpin' Jack" was a light-hearted introduction to Bostic as vocalist. His easygoing humor was never far from the surface and found its expression over the years in several fun songs, which were in the same mold as "Cleanhead" Vinson and others. Bostic was also heard in the call-and-response "That's the Groovy Thing" along with the rest of the band. The jump blues tune was recorded in two parts and became one of his biggest national hits for Gotham. "Baby You Don't Know It All" was a showcase for the blues style of "Cousin" Joe in his guise as Brother Joshua. As good as it was, the song seemed undistinguishable in many ways from other typical blues numbers of the time. Indeed, few of the tracks presented anything to set them apart from similar bands, and the most obvious influence was that of Louis Jordan. Of them all, "Tippin' In" stood out for its combined melodic and rhythmic quality, which became the Bostic hallmark. It had the feel of one of his much later treatments and seemed to presage his future direction. Tony Scott had a distinctive clarinet passage on that song. Renowned for his cool style on clarinet, Scott was an interesting figure in jazz circles. He studied at Juilliard and during the war had his own army band. His abiding love of folk music of the world and meditation meant that he was associated with what became known as New Age music.

Bostic recruited some inspiring new members to his orchestra during the period when he was getting them together. One such was Percival "Sonny" Payne, who was his drummer from 1945 until 1947. The enterprising Payne was just nineteen when he joined and had previously studied with drummer Vic Berton. Bostic had played alongside Payne in the "Hot Lips" Page band. He was a great swinging drummer who went on to make a significant contribution to the success of the Count Basie orchestra, with whom he spent over a decade from 1954 onward, and was Frank Sinatra's personal drummer on all his Basie numbers. He later led his own band and toured with Illinois Jacquet. Payne was a popular figure, and when he died aged just fifty-two of pneumonia, Harry James paid all his hospital bills and funeral expenses.

Other regulars in Earl's orchestra included saxophonist Walter "Foots" Thomas (1907–1981), along with Roger Jones and bassist Vernon King. As well as his work on trumpet, Jones often took the vocal on ballads, including "My Special Dream" and "Barfly Baby." A fellow Oklahoman (a native of Muskogee), early on in his career he had played with "Jelly Roll" Morton but was mostly associated with Cab Calloway, for whom he was also an arranger. He played with Bostic from around 1947. King, a devotee of swing, stayed with Bostic for several years and was still playing with him in his 1950s heyday. Other players included tenor sax man Ted Barnett in 1947, who had once been with "Lucky" Millinder.

After his first Gotham session, Bostic returned to his regular club dates and by spring was back at Murrain's. They also made a hit at the Glen Island Casino at New Rochelle. A real highlight for him in that period was his appearance in two concerts in the prestigious Cavalcade of Jazz series in April 1946. Both were organized by Bob Streeter. The first took place at the Town Hall, New York. The teatime session saw bands led by cornetist Muggsy Spanier, trumpeter Wild Bill Davidson, and others blow up a storm. Over a thousand devotees of the music packed the hall, among them the correspondent of *Down Beat*, who was especially taken with Bostic's contribution. He wrote, "The *Beat's* legman noted with amazement a series of wild choruses in E flat by alto saxist Earl Bostic with a new polytonal idea of having the rhythm section in B flat."[9] Bostic's second appearance was even more notable, at the Academy of Music. This was the first time that jazz had ever featured at the Academy and Bostic was part of a stellar line-up alongside some of his familiar cohorts, not to mention his early hero, Sidney Bechet. The others were "Red" Allen, J.C. Higginbotham, Benny Moten, and Hank Duncan, most of whom he had played with before. All featured collectively and in solo spots. It was a joyous evening that this time had a theme, and presented a potted history of jazz as interpreted by twenty leading musicians. Hence, there were examples of Dixie, boogie-woogie, and barrelhouse, which rubbed shoulders with the sophisticated sound of Gershwin. After two and a half hours, "Red" Allen, Bechet, Bostic, and others "climaxed the event with their own rousing interpretation of 'Obobereeba.'"[10]

Between 1944 and 1946 Bostic was establishing himself as a bandleader, and gained a growing reputation as one of the hottest young players around. The *Esquire* yearbook for 1946 noted that he was one of the most improved players of the year. It was an exciting time as swing was passing its zenith and bop was the latest thing. He found steady work and was successful up to a point, but had not come across the magic ingredient that would set him apart from the rest. Never scared to take a risk, in the following two years he made great strides toward finding his signature style that would take him to the top of his profession.

11

"Temptation"—
A Different Direction

> *"Featuring plenty of warm alto by Bostic, 'Temptation' has a neat bounce and a catchy beat, making it highly danceable without racing."*[1]

Bostic's career was already on an upward curve when he won the *Pittsburgh Courier* poll as the top alto saxophonist of 1947 and was voted the runner-up in the same category in the *Esquire* poll, which earned him the epithet of "Crown Prince of the Alto Sax." In addition, his orchestra was hailed as the All-American Band of Tomorrow. He was a big draw in the clubs of New York, Washington, D.C., and elsewhere, and recorded several times in the year. The recording ban of 1948 meant that he did not return to the studio until 1949. In the interim, he had taken a big risk and changed musical direction completely. His new sound was presaged in a surprising version of "Temptation" which led to him being signed up by King Records of Cincinnati, with whom he would remain for the next seventeen years.

From December 1946 until the new year, the Bostic Sextet played at the prestigious Club Bengasi in Washington, D.C. That led to an invite from the swank Club Baron, Harlem (February 7 to March 21), which was described as a theater-cabaret type venue, where he accompanied singers Gwen Tynes and Evelyn Freeman. From late March he was offered an open-ended engagement at the Horseshoe, New York.

That same month, Bostic was among the all-star lineup at the *Pittsburgh Courier* Poll Winners Concert held at Carnegie Hall. Among the plethora of famous names were Ella Fitzgerald and Dizzy Gillespie. Bostic came just ahead of the great Johnny Hodges in the alto sax poll, and his orchestra was voted second in the band category. The concert was unsurprisingly sold out well in advance and a superb night was enjoyed by all. Bostic played with a small combo on that occasion, consisting of Charlie

Harris on double bass and Fox Warren on drums. Harris once featured as one of three bassists in the Lionel Hampton band, and went on to spend thirteen years with Nat "King" Cole during his glory days. Critic George F. Brown singled out Bostic's version of "The Man I Love" for special praise. He observed: "Bostic plays beautiful horn and the crowd thought so too."[2]

Duels between the musicians were a regular part of the itinerary in concert, which attracted a lot of publicity and big crowds. These were sometimes billed almost along the lines of prizefights and even likened jocularly to gunslingers' contests. Several promoters particularly favored duels for maximum interest and enthusiasm—for instance, Arthur Monteiro, who arranged the matchups between seven duos in a big Stomp Off held at the Rollaway Ballroom at the Manhattan Center in April 1947. Advertised as the Musician's Mobilization to Save *New Masses*, a Marxist periodical, the event featured some great names including clarinetists Sidney Bechet against Buster Bailey, and trombonists J.C. Higginbotham versus Miff Mole. In Earl's case he was drawn against Don Stovall. Stovall, from St. Louis, Missouri, was often compared in his playing style to Bostic, and like him he had started out on the riverboats with Fate Marable. Although Stovall briefly had his own ensemble, he never recorded as leader. He worked mostly for others, especially "Red" Allen, but after leaving Allen in 1950 he retired from music altogether and afterward worked for a telephone company. Although the concert was a big hit with jazz fans, the funds raised failed to help save *New Masses*, which went under the following year.[3]

Earl's reputation for superfast playing and astonishing high notes went before him. By then a hot proposition, he was soon enticed back for a longer stay at the Bengasi in Washington, D.C., beginning on May 17. While there he regularly brought down the house with his exciting solos. He made an impression at Watt's Zanzibar Club in Philadelphia. This was more surprising because it had a reputation as the ultracool bebop spot in the city. He once gave his own succinct definition of the new jazz form: "Bop is music played with the accent on the harmonic structure rather than the melodic structure of the tune."[4] Despite the so-called war between bop and swing, his own view was that one day soon the two would converge and forge a new kind of music. While in Philly, his band set an attendance record at the Elate Ballroom on Broad Street. The previous records had stood for over a year and had been set by two other hot properties of the saxophone, Louis Jordan and Illinois Jacquet. Bostic had the venue bursting at the seams with a crowd of over 2,500.[5]

He created more waves when he started what turned out to be a long residency at the 845 Club in the Bronx in June.[6] The *Courier* award gave him much kudos and meant that he was still a center of attention. In

11. "Temptation"—A Different Direction

August it was announced that his run had been extended by another seven weeks at the 845. The great time the band had at the club gave rise to a popular number that soon became a regular request in their set list, the urgent jump blues tune "845 Stomp." Around this time, "Away" was often billed as his theme tune, and the close harmony group Gotham's Four Notes later recorded an appealing vocal version of the song.

Earl was also busy in the recording studio that year, and had several releases on the Gotham label, including "Cuttin' Out," "I'm the Guy Who Loves You," "My Special Dream," and "Here Goes."[7] These and others featured his fairly settled lineup, consisting of Roger Jones, Vernon King, Shep Shepherd, George Parker, and Ted Barnett. Shep Shepherd (1917–2018) was a multi-instrumentalist who had previously worked for Artie Shaw, and he went on to be associated with Bill Doggett, with whom he wrote his big hit "Honky Tonk." From childhood on he was fascinated with marching bands. The story goes that as a boy he used to drum on the tables so much his mother bought him a toy drum to save wear on the furniture. Among highlights of the sessions was the humorous "Cuttin' Out" with Barnett's tenor to the fore, and the infectious "Hot Sauce Boss," a real floor-filler which was essentially a rock 'n' roller, inspired by the famous hot sauce which was a big favorite condiment of the band members, who adored Louisiana cuisine. The song made a decided impact in Harlem, Chicago, and Los Angeles. Jones displayed his vocal versatility on the ballad "My Special Dream." After a degree of controversy, Bostic was at pains to explain that "Joy Dust" was not a paean to a certain drug, but referred to gold. Of all the songs recorded, "Temptation" was the one that made the greatest impact at the time. A standout track recorded late in 1947 was the sublime "Serenade to Beauty," which provided a welcome change of pace and a neat contrast with his more energetic work. Although often overlooked in his repertoire, this warm and soulful treatment of his own composition showed his marked ability to handle a variety of moods, and proved beyond doubt that he was a romantic at heart.

Earl also made his big-screen debut when he appeared in the Stepin Fetchit short *I Ain't Gonna Open That Door* (Astor Pictures, 1947). In essence it was the answer song to the big novelty hit "Open the Door, Richard" and consisted of lazy Richard (Fetchit) and his determination not to get out of bed to answer the door. Bostic and his orchestra provided the musical accompaniment and were seen briefly on screen. The 10-minute film was directed by William Forest Crouch, who helmed a handful of similar musical shorts. Bostic was playing in Boston at the time and was working to a tight schedule. Hence, during the period of filming he took almost daily flights to and from the studios in New York and gigged at night.

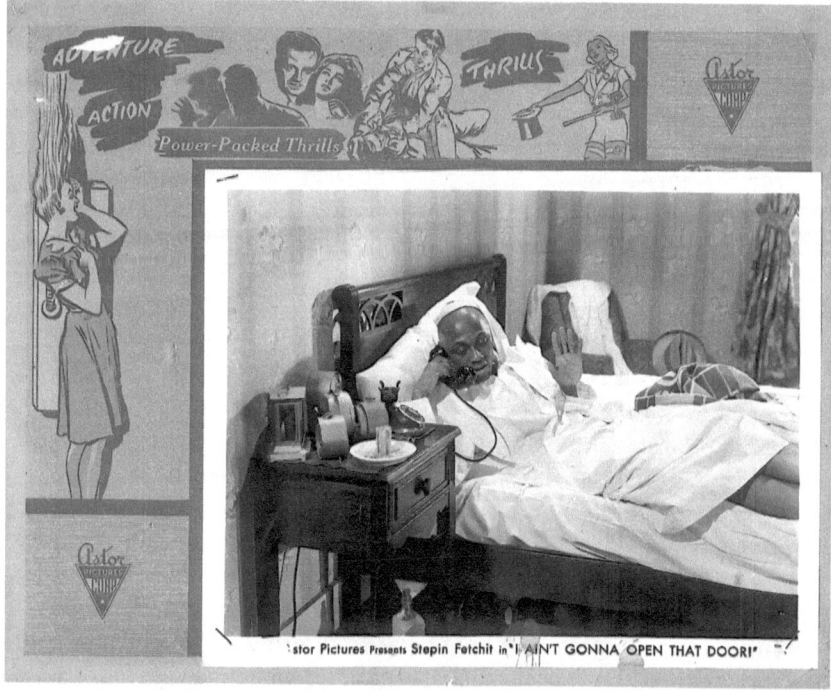

The Bostic orchestra's sole big-screen appearance was in the musical short *I Ain't Gonna Open That Door* (Astor Pictures, 1947), starring Stepin Fetchit.

From September 19 the band played a two-week residency at the Club Bali on 14th Street in Washington, D.C.[8] Then it was back to the 845, before rounding out the year at the Apollo with a seasonal revue.[9] Earl was also heard on various radio networks. He was given a permanent Saturday night spot on the *Hospitality Club* for the Mutual Broadcasting Service, introduced by Willie Bryant, the emcee, host, and creator of the show. This was a coast-to-coast broadcast that boosted his profile no end. The opportunity arose directly from his being signed up to Universal Attractions in November 1947 by Ben Bart, who had founded the agency based in New York only a couple of years before. Bart enticed some of the big names in the jazz and R&B field to join the roster, including Dinah Washington and later James Brown. Earl came under the wings of agent Dick Boone, who became his manager and played a crucial role in his burgeoning career. He organized many of his big tour packages in the 1950s. The popular Boone spent many years with the agency, and was especially associated with guiding the fortunes of Washington and Cootie Williams as well as Earl.[10]

When Ivin Ballen acquired Gotham Records from Sam Goody in January 1948, much of his impetus to do so was that he wanted to sign

Bostic.[11] The label spent the impressive sum of $10,000 to build him up with advertising and write-ups. The timely *Courier* award, allied to the runner-up spot in the *Esquire* poll, greatly advanced his cause in terms of publicity and prestige. He was widely hailed as one of the top three alto sax men in the country. The year 1948 was significant in recording history as the second time a recording ban came into being. This was instigated by the American Federation of Musicians (AFM), as was the previous ban, which had lasted from 1942 to 1944. These actions were prompted by James Petrillo, the AFM president, who believed that musicians who made their living largely from live performance were losing out financially compared to those who mostly made records. Nonetheless, it did not unduly affect Bostic because he had a steady flow of releases and re-releases thanks to his new record contract and the material he had recorded during 1947.

The hit song of the year for him was "Temptation." Written by Nacio Herb Brown and Arthur Freed, it was introduced by Bing Crosby in the 1933 movie *Going Hollywood*. After that, there were countless versions, from acts as diverse as "Screaming" Jay Hawkins and the Everly Brothers, and practically every jazz outfit worth their salt recorded it. Bostic's lively version made an immediate impact in the nascent R&B charts, and in May 1948 it reached number 10 on the Harlem Hit Parade. It topped sales in record shops for five straight weeks, and featured high in many other regional and specialist charts. Moreover, it soon became a jukebox favorite. There was something different about this interpretation which made it stand out at the time. In June it was chosen to feature as the music played at baseball games between innings and at other intervals at both the Polo Grounds, home of the New York Giants, and Yankee Stadium. Hitherto, the music featured mostly consisted of marches, semiclassical tunes, or folk songs. Bostic's "Temptation" was not only something radically new and exciting, but it was also significant as being the first time any colored band had been heard.[12]

In March, he was back on familiar ground at the Bengasi in Washington, D.C., blowing up a storm. Around the same time, his "Earl's Rumboogie" was voted the best "hot" record of the month by fan magazine *Radio Best* in March 1948.[13] On April 3, he appeared with his sextet at another annual *Pittsburgh Courier* Poll Winners concert. Although he was second to Johnny Hodges on that occasion, it was a close-run thing, and there was no shame losing out to Hodges in any event. Once that gig finished, he embarked on a lengthy tour, the first of many. This began in the spring and continued well into the following year, with hardly a break in between. It started in Washington, D.C., and mostly consisted of one-nighters across the Midwest, the Eastern states, and parts of the South. This pattern was punctuated by some longer dates, such as a split week at the Club Sudan and the Carnival Club in Detroit, and a fortnight at the Hi Hat in Atlantic City in midsummer. There were several return dates, for instance, to Emerson's Rainbow Room in Philadelphia, where for his second 10-day visit it was standing room only every evening. Nightclub audiences were notoriously fickle and it was practically unheard of that a band would generate as much enthusiasm, if not more, over a year later at the same place, let alone repeat the feat subsequently.[14]

By then, Bostic was enjoying driving his latest acquisition, the stylish 1948 Studebaker Commander, to add to his growing automobile collection. It was reported that he had three shiny new Studebakers delivered to his hotel when the tour reached his home state of Oklahoma. These consisted of a sedan, a convertible, and a station wagon. The latter usually stored all the instruments. He observed at the time: "Getting cars is a real problem now but with the resumption of normal production, I feel sure that all the other bandleaders will follow our plan and equip their organizations with similar setups. In the light of traveling difficulties often encountered, particularly in the South, such a setup is not only practical but cheaper as well." It was also his intention to invest in a brand new "fleet" annually.[15]

He returned to New York City in July, when he played a sellout concert at the Renaissance Casino, about six years after his previous appearance there with Al Sears. As a contemporary report observed: "A milling mob of 1,287 admirers and dance lovers crowded into the casino to listen and jump to the exciting music stylings of the new idol of the swing set."[16] In August the orchestra was back at the Apollo as part of a curious vaudeville type show built around magician Dr Neff's Madhouse of Mystery. Bostic with his small combo played at intervals during the evening's entertainment. His unit comprised two reeds, three rhythm, and one brass, and among his songs the "845 Stomp" went over well. His singing on "Cuttin' Out" was also praised. In between his sets, patrons were wowed by a slick magic act, but for many the music was the highlight of the evening's entertainment. There was always an element of the showman in his performances, and he had clearly not forgotten his days with the high school band. As the critic of *Variety* observed, "Bostic returns for the closer, giving out with a frenzied tune and injecting a personal element into it by marching up and down the aisles, simultaneously blaring away on the sax."[17]

In October, Bostic broke new ground with some of his first college dates at the universities of Michigan and Illinois, among others. He had a much-needed two-week break around Thanksgiving when he was finally able to make it home to his new house in Addisleigh Park, Long Island, that he had purchased some months before.

During the whole period while he was on tour, he was constantly experimenting with his sound, and going on the road as he did, he soon found out what clicked with audiences and what did not. Against this background, he began to hone his sound, abandon some elements he previously thought essential in his music, and develop it in an entirely different direction. The recordings he had made thus far were successful up to a point, but on the recent Gotham sides there was a tendency to sound not dissimilar from other groups who followed too closely the Louis Jordan blueprint. This was particularly the case with some of the up-tempo rhythm and blues numbers. After he changed tack, Bostic tended to move away from using vocalists and concentrated on instrumentals. He took a great risk and made a radical change in his whole approach. Victor Schonfield in his masterful analysis of Bostic highlighted this as the turning point in his story. As Schonfield wrote perceptively: "The solution he finally chose towards the end of the year 1948 was as drastic as it was successful, and demonstrates artistic courage and intelligence of a high order. He simply turned his back on his previous work and set about constructing a new style, keeping only his original power and fire." Schonfield went on to outline the way in which Bostic altered his tone, but lost none of his attack in the process. His tonal range increased dramatically, and he developed greater focus on essentials, combined with a decided ease of playing. Schonfield observed that despite the new approach Bostic never lost "an overall feeling of ease and space" in his music.[18] Henceforward, there would always be the strong melody, the driving rhythm, allied to a sense of drama and movement, with an airy feeling of space. He gave the overriding impression that it was played easily, without any strain. Of course, it had taken a long time for him to reach this point and his music was still not the finished article, but from here on in he had found his unique sound as assuredly as when Glenn Miller found his. It was an ease borne of experience, because by now Bostic was such a maestro of his instrument that he was able to relax and had a clear idea of what he was trying to achieve.

Whatever changes he implemented in his interpretation of the blues, he was keen to reassure his long-term fans that he was not abandoning his stomp credentials. He once remarked, "Don't worry, I'll still stomp awhile. We still love to ride 'em, you know."[19] A real breakthrough was his appearance at the Savoy Theater on Lennox Avenue. To be accepted by the discerning clientele of the Savoy, known as the fountainhead of jazz, was the ultimate recognition that an artist had truly arrived.

Bostic's change of musical direction practically coincided with a change of record label. Alerted by the buzz caused by "Temptation," Syd Nathan, owner of King Records of Cincinnati, bought out Bostic's contract. He was able to do so because he operated a licensing agreement with Gotham. Nathan also bought out most of Bostic's masters as part of the deal, and they were reissued over the following months. Founded in 1943 as an outlet for hillbilly music, King soon branched out and developed as the home of early rhythm and blues stars, including Ivory Joe Hunter, along with bluesmen such as Champion Jack Dupree, and idiosyncratic jazz artists, among them Eddie "Lockjaw" Davis. Bostic was a key signing and stayed with the label for the next seventeen years, his entire remaining career, recording over 400 sides in that time. It was fitting that he earned the nickname of the King of King Records.

After his respite at home during Thanksgiving in 1948, Earl rounded out the year in Indianapolis, finally getting some more time off for Christmas before the whole thing was due to start all over again in January. The new year of 1949 would bring an end to the recording ban and see him back in the studio for his first King session, and beginning to put into practice his exciting new ideas which would soon bear fruit.

12

Breaking Down Barriers

"If music be the food of love, play on."
—Shakespeare, *Twelfth Night*[1]

Bostic did much for the advancement of civil rights throughout his life and yet in many ways considered music the ultimate healer in society. He was an eloquent speaker and offered his services on many occasions for the cause when it was not the fashionable thing to do. It is possible he might have become a more active political figure later in life. At the same time, it was not just his words but his deeds that mattered, and the way in which his music worked its magic with audiences, appealing strongly to all, regardless of race. His ultimate faith was in music, which he saw as a unifying force for good in the world. He always believed that it alone had the power to reorder fractured lives and heal all divisions. Many years later he was justly honored for his contribution to civil rights.

In August or September 1948, Earl purchased a beautiful house in the exclusive Addisleigh Park suburb in St. Albans, Queens, New York. There was some debate about the amount he paid, with one report stating that the sum was $21,000, and another putting it closer to $40,000.[2] The house was situated at 178-16 Murdock Avenue. Built in 1926 in the Colonial Revival style, the property measured some 2,500 square feet.[3] It had ten rooms and was set on a large plot of land on an attractive tree-lined avenue. Due to his extended touring schedule around that time, he was unable to move in for a couple of months, until he finally managed to have some time off at Thanksgiving. He spent about $6,000 on furnishings, and according to one story was intending to do some of the interior decoration work himself and arrange everything "just as he likes."[4]

The neighborhood to which he and Hildegarde moved had first been developed in the 1900s, but in those days, it was a whites-only enclave which operated restrictive covenants that prevented colored families from settling there. Although these covenants were strictly speaking still in force until after World War II, affluent black families had already been settling there since the 1920s. In view of its beauty and proximity to the city, some of the biggest names in jazz and sports were drawn to St. Albans, and specifically Addisleigh Park. These included the musicians Fats Waller, Mercer Ellington, Cannonball Adderley, Lena Horne, Count Basie, and Wild Bill Davis, and athletes like baseball player Jackie Robinson and boxer Joe Louis. Ella Fitzgerald moved in just a few months after Bostic, also on Murdock Avenue, at 179-07. Illinois Jacquet, another resident, expressed the view of many when he called it "a neighborhood to be proud of, a monument to black achievement." One of the other locals who lived there during childhood recalled the vibrant and inclusive sense of community: "Basie had the largest swimming pool around here and his backyard was the size of a city block. He and his wife Catherine would let all of us kids use it and there were always barbecues and parties."[5] According to one story, Wynonie Harris used to give wild parties which Bostic, Arthur Prysock, and other musicians attended. Earl also had a "rumpus room" in the house where he used to practice. The neighborhood remained mixed—for instance, one of his next-door neighbors was black and the other white. At one time Hildegarde's younger cousin Ardenne Moore, who worked in a dress shop, lived with them. Meanwhile, Earl's mother Druzella, now nearing retirement age, was still in service working sixty hours a week as a maid to the president of a paper company and his wife, a couple in their sixties, at East 26th Street in Tulsa. Druzella had family and friends nearby, including her sister Aslean Reed, who worked as a masseuse and was an active member of the Vernon AME church.[6]

Hildegarde was in her element in the classy new environment, and thoroughly at home. In an interview she said that she "maintains the kind of home I like" for Earl. He was always generous, and for their tenth anniversary he gifted her a downpayment on an apartment house elsewhere in Long Island, one of his earliest property investments.[7] Hildegarde became a doyennne of the social scene in the Addisleigh Park suburb and beyond. She was a queen bee among the jazz wives, who formed their own social group and called themselves the Rinky Dinks. Among her friends were Catherine Basie and Barbara Jacquet. While their menfolk were busy away on seemingly endless cross-country tours or in the recording studio making money, their wives were equally busy back home thinking up ways to spend it. Sometimes described as statuesque, Hildegarde was a stylish lady who loved to keep up with the latest fashions. She was not alone among the wives and sweethearts who, just like the rest of American womanhood in the postwar period, simply had to have a fur coat to know that they had truly arrived. The Rinky Dinks often took vacations and traveled abroad together. For instance, they spent three months on a sightseeing tour across Europe in the early 1950s. However, they were not just frivolous social butterflies. They raised money for all kinds of charities and organized events for good causes. Hildegarde was especially associated with children's charities and other projects to aid children, not just in New York but in Louisiana, Texas, and Alabama. These projects included daycare centers. The Savoy Ballroom in Harlem was the frequent site of their functions, and later, under the influence of their dynamic president Ruth Bowen, their formal dances took place at such upmarket venues as the Hotel American and the Waldorf Astoria. In many ways, they mirrored what socially prominent women were doing across the country. Some of them, particularly Hildegarde, clearly enjoyed committee life and being at the heart of organizing everything. Her zeal sometimes put her at odds with others in the community, and there was a much-publicized falling out with Maria Cole, wife of Nat. When Maria was elected president of the Hilltoppers Club in New York, Hildegarde promptly resigned and later formed a branch of the Rinky Dinks on the West Coast.

Bostic was acutely aware that as a highly successful musician living in a select suburb of Long Island, he was able to do a lot of good for the advancement of his people. He took a close interest in all that was going on at the time. In 1948 he proposed an idea to strike a blow for civil rights. It was his suggestion that black and white artists should come together for a series of nationally broadcast radio shows. With a cast list that included some of the biggest names such as Duke Ellington, plus some of the leading white artists, the notion soon gained widespread support. At a meeting in Houston, Bostic spoke with great clarity and conviction about his vision for the enterprise: "There will be no inflammatory harangues by the speakers," he declared. "On the contrary, they will calmly attempt to enlist the moral aid of good thinking citizens that a condition that threatens our national unity and welfare must be altered for our national good." He understood just how important music was as a force for good, and especially the way it broke down barriers. "I think that such an impressive array of talent will insure a huge audience. The rest must be easy. I have that much faith in the sound judgement of the American people. They will do the job."[8]

Bostic was chief among those who supported new ventures to further the study of music for all races. One such enterprise was the MacArthur Conservatory of Music in Indianapolis, set up by Ruth MacArthur. This pioneering establishment employed an interracial staff of twelve teachers and consisted of 200 scholars made up of college students and private pupils. All levels and ages were encouraged, ranging from six to sixty years. The conservatory was accredited by the state of Indiana, and approved by the Veteran's Administration under the GI Bill of Rights. Integrated courses of two and three years were offered in band-orchestra directing, which enabled students to arrange for, direct, and play in any field of music, from classical to popular. Bostic, Louis Armstrong, and Eddie Condon among other professionals were impressed by the scope and ambition of the new school, which had twenty rooms in a three-story building. The outstanding feature was that the curriculum covered the compositions of modern composers such as Duke Ellington alongside the classical greats, Beethoven, Bach, and others. The first students graduated in June 1949. At that point, there were ten undergrads playing in dance bands, and three leading their own bands. The conservatory had several years of marked success, and during its existence there were many music clubs and venues which sprang up locally in Indiana as the music scene thrived. Ironically, desegregation led to a decline in enrollment in the later 1950s, and the school closed altogether in 1963.[9]

Earl maintained that change would come in time through the ballot box, and while encouraging people to vote, he realized all too well the importance of engaging the electorate: "The problem is to interest the people in the issues so they will vote," he once observed. "The political standard of the colored people in this country is being improved because they are being educated to vote on questions that influence them."[10] He did important behind-the-scenes work on influential committees to advance projects aimed at desegregation, such as the Musicians' Committee for Integration. An appeal to rectify bias in the International Musicians' Union drew his support and that of some of his friends, including Nat "King" Cole. Their backing was crucial to advance the cause because in some Musicians' Locals, black musicians were effectively being denied the right to work, and a petition to the union president did not even receive a reply, nor did two followup letters. It was only the support of respected public figures that brought the issues into the open and forced grievances to be addressed.[11]

While on tour he tried his best to support local black businesses, many of which were concerns thriving against the odds. At Columbia, Missouri, two local entrepreneurs, tired of constant segregation, set up the first black-owned movie theater in town, which opened as the Frances in 1948. They had to face opposition; for example, they were not allowed to show first-run movies. Nevertheless, like many, they showed great adaptability and resourcefulness, and the venue had multiple uses. On one side was a convenience store, and on the other a cinema that doubled as a nightclub after hours. The building was situated at 109 N. 5th Street, Columbia, in the First Ward. Bostic played a date there at Eastertime 1949, which was a special event for him because it was one of the few times he did not play the alto sax but instead showed his prowess on the piano.[12]

In the years after the war, Bostic believed that attitudes were changing, even south of the Mason–Dixon line. He cited his gig at the Youth

Center in Greensboro, North Carolina, in 1948, which had gone down so well with local teenagers that the band repeated the engagement the following year to even greater acclaim. To Bostic, music of quality was the key. As he observed, "People want entertainment that's good. I think you'll find that more and more merit is being used as the basis for the entertainment selected."[13] He was at the forefront of driving change in that time during which his band made several pioneering tours of the South. Those tours were facilitated by equally pioneering promoters, one of whom was Ralph Weinberg, who organized tours down south for Bostic in 1949. Some shows, such as that at Macon, Georgia, in September, were billed as a Battle of Music, in that instance between Bostic and his old school buddy Hal "Cornbread" Singer. Weinberg (1895–1953) hailed from Maryland and began as a wrestling promoter. He had sound instincts for showmanship and brought some of the biggest names in entertainment to the South, including Frank Sinatra when he was with the Tommy Dorsey Band. Weinberg established a network of theaters and dance halls and booked concert dates as far west as Texas and as far south as Birmingham that were safe for black bands. His policy was to rope off a section where white patrons could come and enjoy the music, but the dance floor and bandstands were strictly reserved for black performers and audiences. The striking feature of the concerts was the surprisingly relaxed atmosphere that prevailed, and there was seldom if ever any friction.

It was also thanks to influential disc jockeys such as Hunter Hancock that things were beginning to change. Hancock, a Texan-born white DJ, was one of the first to regularly play music by black artists, of whom Bostic was one of the most popular. His half-hour *Harlematinee* daytime show was first broadcast on KFVD in Los Angeles in 1947 and proved so popular that it was soon extended to three and a half hours. He had a large following among the colored population and was one of the few white DJs who was honored with awards.[14]

Among many firsts attributed to Bostic, he broke the color bar at many venues, including the upmarket Atlantic Beach Casino in Morehead, North Carolina, in 1950, and Loew's Victoria in Baltimore.[15] His innate positivity, good nature, and optimism imbued all he did, and his music was a great force for good which he hoped would bring about real change. He was all too well aware of the cruel irony that both white and colored were dancing to the music with the same enthusiasm on either side of the rope that divided them. He was impressed by Johnny Ray for his stance at that time. Ray was at the height of his popularity in that era and, like Bostic, was one of those who paved the way for rock 'n' roll. In 1952, Ray refused to play a Jim Crow dance in Mobile, Alabama, until the rope preventing black audience members from watching was taken down.

It was nonetheless a difficult and potentially dangerous prospect touring in some parts of the South. There was one alarming incident for Earl and his orchestra when a crudely constructed bomb was placed under the stage where the band was playing at an Independence Day dance at the Grand Terrace Café in Birmingham, Alabama. Luckily, when it exploded the band were taking their break so the bandstand was vacant, but part of the stage was blown away. It was dismissed at the time as a prank with a toy firecracker, so as not to alarm everyone, but it was a reminder of just how precarious the situation was in some parts.[16]

Bostic continued to be a pioneer into the 1950s and beyond. His band were not only the first colored artists to play the Celtic Room in Nashville, Tennessee, but the venue was hitherto strictly white only. This occurred in March 1955, and again took the form of a "battle of music" in which resident jazzman Papa John Gordy met Bostic the challenger to see who came out on top. Gordy declared that no self-respecting jazz band in the South would have a saxophone in their lineup, whereas Bostic maintained the saxophone was essential. Gordy publicly bet $5000 in Confederate money, no less, that his Dixielanders could outplay Bostic's orchestra any day of the week. The mere mention of Confederate money was enough to get anyone's dander up and Bostic took up the challenge with gusto.[17] His band members were in a determined mood and came out clear winners. The night was a great success and the venue was packed. It was so successful that a second night and third night were added, both of which, everyone agreed, went to Bostic. There was still an appetite for more, but they had plenty of other engagements to fulfill on their tour.

There were significant and hard-won victories on the road to establishing civil rights. One of the key pieces of legislation was the desegregation act of 1954. However, all advances were checked by events in the South that came to a head in the mid–1950s. A turning point was the lynching, in Mississippi in 1955, of teenager Emmett Till, which was a landmark case. The brutal murder of the fourteen-year-old Till shocked the nation and had wide repercussions. A seemingly trivial incident in a grocery store, about what was or was not said to the wife of the store owner, was the spark which set the tinderbox alight. Not only were Till's alleged killers acquitted, but they subsequently sold their story to the press. For Bostic and many others, this case crossed a line in the sand. As an immediate reaction to events, he canceled all his outstanding booking dates in Mississippi. He commented, "I just don't care to play in that state since the Emmett Till case." There were lots of problems in several other Southern states, but he declined to make any further comment at that stage about his dates in Alabama until he heard the outcomes of the Autherine Lucy and bus boycott cases. Once the position became clear there, he decided not to play in that state, too.[18] The situation was deteriorating, but several of his friends and peers continued to play in the South, among them Nat "King" Cole, who was attacked and knocked to the ground by four men during a white-only show in Birmingham, Alabama, in April 1956. Bostic remarked: "For me, I don't expect to run into the trouble Nat had in the South because I don't accept bookings in Alabama or Mississippi. Naturally, if you appear down South at all, you'll appear before segregated audiences. That's just the way of the South."[19] He was disappointed that at a stroke all the good work he had done during his tours in the previous ten years had seemed to be canceled out, but such was not the case. He lived to see that in fact he had played his part in the change that eventually came about.

Bostic had supreme faith in music as the key to a better world, not just to dissolve walls between people but in all situations. For instance, he advocated music as a deterrent to delinquency. To that end, he submitted a plan of action to the National Council on Adolescent Study. He suggested a fund be set up to provide musical training to problem children. Based on his own personal experience, he was a firm believer in the power of music to transcend many of the difficulties faced by adolescents. In practical terms he delineated how the concentration involved in learning an instrument was the catalyst to instilling discipline and a love of music. He reasoned that once learned, it could provide not only an income, but a source of continual interest and an outlet for the creative urge.[20] He was an optimist by nature, and even a visit to the United Nations conference at Lake Success in September 1948 left him full of hope about the prospects for world peace—so much so that he was inspired to write a new composition to celebrate, which he called the "United Nations Stomp."[21]

All of Bostic's impulses were for the common good and he tried to do all he could to promote and advance change. Music had given him everything and he believed that it could help change the world. Only time would prove him right, and it could well be argued that he and all the musicians of the 1950s did far more at a stroke to heal divisions between peoples than all the well-intentioned politicians in history.

13

A Few Million Miles on the Road

"It was pretty rough traveling up and down the highway in the early '50s. Your life was always in danger."[1]
—Stanley Turrentine

By November 1949, Bostic and his band had reputedly clocked up their first million miles on the road. This was in a little under four years of touring. In the following ten years they covered a few million more crisscrossing the country, and ventured into Canada. Although they broke a lot of new ground, with several tours south of the Mason–Dixon line, life for a touring band in the postwar era was hard, and arguably took its toll on Bostic's health. As the recording ban was lifted, he returned to the studio and began to put his new musical ideas into operation on some excellent sides which saw his star rise further.

At the beginning of 1949, Bostic headlined a short tour of the South with two rising young singing stars, Roy Brown and Velma "Chubby" Newsome. Brown was an ex-prize-fighter from Louisiana who made a name for himself with his hit song "Good Rockin' Tonight," subsequently covered by a legion of big names. He was highly influential on the likes of Jackie Wilson and Little Richard. Like Brown and Bostic, "Chubby" Newsome was riding high in the *Billboard* charts and hailed as the singing sensation of 1949. Together they played sell-out dates at the Palace Theater, Birmingham, Alabama, and Memphis, Tennessee. The turnout for the show at the Palace was described as outstanding, and Bostic and his band clocked up a four-day gross at the theater that was just short of the all-time record for the venue.[2]

The year started for Bostic in the studio with the recording of his first session for King records in Cincinnati after the year-long recording ban had been lifted. The lineup at that point consisted of regulars Roger Jones on trumpet and vocals, Shep Shepherd on drums, and Vernon King on bass. The band had two newcomers, tenor saxophonist Lowell "Count" Hastings and pianist Jaki Byard. Hastings had been around a while and his earliest recordings dated from 1939. He worked for Tiny Bradshaw and others before joining Earl, and later went on to work for a great many more big names including Louis Jordan. The talented Byard was only nineteen at the time of his debut, a multi-instrumentalist with a deep knowledge of jazz piano and European classical music. Byard's playing was notable on "Swing Low Sweet Boogie." Among the other songs recorded, several had a similar feel to previous jokey R&B numbers, for example, "Watch Where You Walk Boy," on which Bostic and Roger Jones were both heard to comic effect. Several tracks showed his tremendous energy, such as "Blip Boogie" and the frenetic "Earl's Imagination." "Earl Blows a Fuse" featured some virtuoso playing, and herein he displayed a more focused vitality which neatly summarized how far he had progressed and pointed to future directions.

His next recording session took place in New York in May. All three songs were prime examples of the popular novelty R&B vocal style with Bostic doing the honors. It was all harmless fun and on "Earl's Blues" he lamented in comic cartoon style the catalog of troubles caused by his woman. Of more interest was the session in August, which produced "Choppin' It Down" that had signs of his trademark playing on a smooth rock 'n' roll number, and more especially "Filibuster," on which he gave a robust workout of his special technique by now finely honed.

His records were doing good business and gaining much attention from all quarters. "Where or When" was voted the best release of April 1949 by the Music Criticism Assembly of the University of Pennsylvania. All members of the group were music majors. They declared that Bostic gave "an unusually sympathetic interpretation, not only of the mood and meter of the work, but also an almost flawless execution of an exacting instrument."[3]

His musical ambitions were always great and at this stage in his development he had lots of ideas for future projects, although only some of them came off. In August 1949 it was announced that he was planning to get together a sixteen-piece symphony orchestra, employing twelve saxes, with piano, guitar, bass fiddle and drums. For this he had reportedly sounded out several top-flight saxophonists who expressed an interest.[4] Whether he ever managed to assemble such an orchestra is unknown, but if so, it was never recorded. Around the same time, it was reported that he also had plans to enter the world of Broadway musicals. He worked for about nine months on the score for *Rockin' in Rhythm*, which was described as a musical comedy. According to one story, four potential producers expressed an interest in the venture. The *New England Bulletin* commented, "While not calling for too elaborate a cast or sets, the opus is loaded with ear catching tunes, eye-catching scenery, and a substantial libretto."⁵ Again, the idea would appear to have failed to gain any backing, or at least not under that title, and there is no mention anywhere that he ever had a musical produced.

Although singers were only occasionally associated with the Bostic sound on record after he remodeled his sound, the band often employed vocalists in club settings. Joyce Jackson was one such, who answered an appeal for auditions in August 1949. Bostic expressly said that he wanted a "fresh new face and voice."⁶ He first encountered her as a young shake dancer at a club in Washington, when she came up to his table for an autograph and he started to quiz her about her career. She mentioned she was also a singer, and offered to sing for him, which she did. Bostic listened attentively and afterward advised her to switch to singing full-time and abandon dance. A few weeks later when the orchestra was at the Royal Theater in New York, she sent him around a note to meet her in the wings and told him that she had decided to follow his suggestion and was all ready to go to work. Bostic agreed and took her on as a vocalist there and then. She toured with the band for a while. Although she made no recordings with Bostic, she made a few sides with John Peek's Band, notably "Lonely Blues" and "Baby Rocking Daddy," but eventually left the profession to raise a family. At one time it was announced that blues singer Maude Thomas was about to record "Gambler's Blues" with his orchestra, but no such recording has come to light.

Bostic often auditioned new bandmembers while on the road. Around the same time that Joyce Jackson joined, he also put the call out for a new trombonist. He set aside the first hour in each new town to hear auditions. As he commented at the time: "Who knows what future stars there may be who just need an opportunity. I plan to give it to one and hope other established band leaders will follow suit and thus inject some new life and ideas into the always colorful music business."⁷

As well as his usual work on tour, Bostic took part in several midsummer festival shows as part of a roster of upcoming talent. In August 1949 Francis Spencer, a local promoter in Kansas City, Missouri, began an annual showcase.⁸ Singer Roy Brown's star had risen quickly since the previous time they played together in January, to such an extent that he leapfrogged Bostic as the headliner. Herb Lance, Wini Brown, and "Chubby" Newsome were also on the bill. Lance was a baritone in the Billy Eckstine mold, whose most popular number was a version of "Close Your Eyes." Wini Brown was an interesting blues type singer, a protégé of Lionel Hampton. Bostic headlined a similar package the following summer which also featured vaudeville performers. This included comedy singing duo Apus and Estrellita, dancer Louis Hawkins, billed as the Boy with Educated Feet, and Lady Darlene, an exotic dancer. Bostic was full of praise for his fellow entertainers. The whole ensemble was described as the surprise hit show of the season, and sold out at all three cities where they played, namely, in Memphis, Lexington, and Louisville.[9]

For practically the whole of 1949 the band was continually on the road playing a host of one-nighters, across the Midwest and the South. The band also took its first extended tour of Florida, which was by request of several band members who lived in the state. Occasionally, they made it back to New York for some big shows. In March they returned to the Apollo Theater for a week, followed by another week at the Savoy Ballroom, where their headline show caused a lot of renewed excitement. Twice during their set Bostic left the bandstand to lead his men on a conga line around the dancefloor like a pied piper, blowing his sax in time-honored fashion.[10] They returned to one-night stands for most of the year and played only a few longer dates, such as a week at the Show Boat Café, Philadelphia, over the summer. A definite highlight of the year was the third annual *Pittsburgh Courier* Poll Winners' concert held at Carnegie Hall on April 9. Bostic was again prominent among the stellar lineup, which included Ella Fitzgerald and Erskine Hawkins. The show started at midnight and went on until 4 a.m. Undoubtedly, the appearance of the beleaguered Billie Holiday, after 3 a.m. drew by far the warmest response of the night. She had recently been refused a police card by the New York Police Department (NYPD) so was unable to play in Gotham night clubs. Even before she started her set, the audience gave her a five-minute ovation. It was a remarkable show and truly a night to remember for all present.[11]

In November 1949, the orchestra clocked up its first million miles on tour. Bostic reckoned the landmark was reached about eight miles outside Tampa, Florida. He stopped the car and took the rest of the band to the side of the road, where he treated them to an impromptu picnic feast to celebrate.[12]

Every musical act from the smallest to the grandest was touring in the middle years of the twentieth century. Some of the theater circuits across the country followed well-worn routes that vaudeville and stage performers had known since Adam was a lad. By the postwar period, conditions of travel and accommodation had largely improved, although hotels in the South were segregated, like most things. Many of the biggest outfits were used to a level of relative comfort, if not luxury, but even they had struggled in the early days. Unlike the big bands, such as Duke Ellington, Tommy Dorsey, and others, the Bostic band in its various incarnations seldom if ever traveled by train or chartered coach. Instead, being a generally smaller combo, the band had to make do with a small fleet of cars, usually numbering two or, more often, three. These generally consisted of Bostic's shiny Studebaker or his eight-seater Cadillac, another sedan, and a station wagon to house the instruments. It was necessary that the cars were in good order because they were required to cover a lot of terrain and extreme weather conditions. They had to withstand huge fluctuations in temperature, ice, snow, or hot desert sand. Brakes were well tested by steep gradients and the suspension ditto over some rough roads and dirt tracks. Over the years they endured all manner of trials, both natural and human-made, including snowstorms, thefts, car accidents, holdups, explosions, and absconding managers, with the threat of violence lurking in the background, to say nothing of the everyday casual racism which gnawed at the soul. Crucially, the gigs themselves were highly successful, so much so that the band was constantly in demand and returned to many venues numerous times. There was a huge appetite for entertainment, and nothing beat live performance. In those days there was no alternative but to appear live. Although many played regularly on radio, and a select few appeared in the odd screen musical, television had not yet taken hold, and even after it did practically every musical act spent most of their time touring. Bostic personally suffered many serious problems, including a near-fatal car crash in December 1951. The long years of constant touring culminated in his first heart attack in June 1956.

The band played all manner of venues, from huge plush ballrooms to tiny back street bars. Besides night clubs of every kind and theaters, they played town halls, army posts, civic auditoriums, movie houses, school gyms, citadels, college campuses, restaurants, labor temples, parks, resorts, country clubs and anywhere there was a demand. Bostic also made personal appearances at record stores and was sometimes invited to appear on radio in whichever place they happened to be visiting. No gig was too large or too small, and generally they said yes to everything offered. Naturally, the whole experience on the road was made up of highs and lows. In June 1948, just a week or two after appearing on Broadway for the first time, Bostic was the alleged victim of a holdup outside the Howard Theater in Washington, D.C., where they were playing. There was no knowing what to expect. Everyone was especially wary traveling in the South, where trouble might flare up from the slightest thing. Besides the everyday realities of staying in segregated hotels, there was sometimes the ridiculous prospect of having to use the back entrance to some venues where they were headlining.

In December 1950 the band ran into a heavy snowstorm in Minnesota and was caught in high snowdrifts. Its small fleet of cars got stuck, and they were helped by the combined efforts of snowplows and the state troopers, who escorted them for eight miles out of Minneapolis. Tenor sax man Count Hastings afterward recalled, "At a range of twenty miles or more we couldn't see anything but a snow haze. Thank God, we made it."[13] No matter how bad the weather, they still attracted capacity crowds. A similar snowstorm in Denver with sixteen inches of snow piled up and temperatures of fifteen below did not deter the audience of 800 hardy souls from turning up. Bostic fans were a dedicated bunch.

There were times when there was a potential risk to life and limb. Drummer Jimmy Cobb recalled a gig in New Orleans when someone got a gun out and two rival groups suddenly started shooting at each other across the street. Cobb described it as being like something out of the Wild West, and said that Bostic probably took refuge under the piano.[14] There were also the unscrupulous promoters to contend with, such as the time the band was left high and dry when a Maryland café owner absconded with the box-office takings and left Bostic holding the baby. The band was due to start a tour on the West Coast and Bostic paid the $2600 air fares for the orchestra members to fly them there at short notice. Fire was another hazard, particularly in old theaters. A matter of hours after their highly successful stand at one venue, the building burned to the ground. There were also many positive stories, such as the time on a Southern tour when all the lights went out at the venue where they were playing when a hot rod blitzed into the main power pole, but the kids were undaunted and pulled their cars up and danced by the light of the headlights and the moonlight.

To play fifteen nights nonstop was not unknown or even unusual. Over a period of several years, they might have just a few weeks off in between, and they played most nights until 1 or 2 a.m., with trips of 100 to 300 miles a day between dates. Nor was the pay the best, considering that everyone had to find their own traveling expenses. It was better than Lionel Hampton paid, but on balance not much. Benny Golson, who was with the band between 1954 and 1956, recalled that he made around $25 a night. However, pianist Chester L. Lane remembered that when he played a few dates a few years later, around 1959 or 1960, Bostic offered him $150 a day for two days in Denver. Lane turned him down on that occasion because he had just come off a long road tour and was not keen to travel again through snowstorms.[15] It was not a life that suited everyone, and many came and went over the years. Besides being a trumpeter, Stanley "Ace" Adams was famous as a songwriter. He co-wrote "Everybody's Somebody's Fool," which was a hit for Connie Francis. For a spell in the mid–1950s he toured with Bostic. However, the grind of constant travel began to get him down, so he decided paradoxically enough to become a bus driver instead, although he did not need to work because his songwriting gave him an income for life.[16]

For some of the young band members straight out of high school or college, it was a thrilling, once-in-a-lifetime experience that could never have been replicated elsewhere. Some expressly joined to enable them to travel and explore new places. Before he joined, eighteen-year-old Stanley Turrentine recalled that he already had experience of touring the South, but was frustrated that he was unable to tour the North. In that regard, he certainly got his chance with Bostic to explore not just the North but the whole country. Despite any and all inconveniences, Turrentine loved the whole ride. As he recollected: "I was a kid, so it was exciting. We would do 30 one-nighters in a row, without a break, and all the older guys were really helpful, teaching me, showing me things. I got to see the country, to know a lot of healthy people."[17]

14

The Bostic Sound

"The Bostic outfit rolls along like a well-oiled machine while he sets an uninhibited pace for his men with his sax-tooting, and glad-hands the patrons and they like it."[1]

The year 1950 was a vintage one for Earl and his band, who were on their way up. Constantly on the road, he joined forces again with Dinah Washington on some sell-out dates. Meanwhile, his records began to cause a sensation on jukeboxes around the country, and started to make an impact in the nascent charts based on record sales, as opposed to sheet music as they had previously. He continued to develop his unique sound further until he reached his apogee with "Flamingo," recorded just after Christmas, which encapsulated much of what he had been working toward in the previous two years.

At the beginning of the year, he again played on the same bill as Billie Holiday when he appeared at the Riviera in St. Louis during a week-long stay. She had a lot of unwanted media attention around that time, but at the Riviera at least she was the headliner. Earl and his band spent much of 1950 backing the great Dinah Washington, the "Queen of the Juke Box." They first played for her in November 1949, and over the next two years they took part in several joint tours, through to 1952. The orchestra played for her at a special party with 400 invited guests to celebrate her twenty-sixth birthday in August 1950, much to her delight. She remarked: "Now I know my party is going to be a smash success. Music makes any party and it's my luck to have one of the greatest combos in the business to brighten up mine."[2] For Bostic's part, she had always been one of the singers he most admired, and they got along splendidly throughout their time together. There were a few awkward moments. The most publicized was a misunderstanding during her birthday bash. He said he would do the show gratis, but Washington insisted the band ought to be paid. Her contention was that no musician should ever go unpaid, as it went against union rules. Bostic insisted he had already given his word, and that it was his way of honoring her. In the end they compromised. The band was paid $1000 and he donated the money to charity.[3] Nevertheless, overall, everything went swimmingly between them, and they were true professionals. The shows were always packed, and had good reviews. Nonetheless, Bostic may have been rueful that two of his men left his orchestra to go touring with her instead.

With his regular band, he took on several vocalists in that period, including Helen Young, who only joined for a short time but, unlike some of his singers, made it on to record. She can be heard to effect on "Portrait of a Faded Love," which showcased the bandleader in mellow mode. The song was written by Oscar Washington, Earl's old buddy from school days, who was now working as a science instructor at Washington Technical High School in St. Louis.[4] While visiting St. Louis, Bostic met up with Washington again and gave the song a tryout. He was so impressed with the result that he organized a recording of it, which was released as a single. On occasion, Earl still took the vocals himself, and was probably at his best on "Way Down," his own composition, which was also recorded in the same year. Here he appears to devote himself entirely to singing, and the sax heard is probably that of tenor man Count Hastings. Although not the greatest of vocalists, Bostic nonetheless did full justice to this surprising number, which showcases his tongue-in-cheek, rather sardonic humor. In its style the record could be described as the point where rock 'n' roll and rhythm and blues meet.

Helen Young was one of several new members who joined the orchestra around the same time, with the others being guitarist Al Casey, pianist Clifton or Cliff Smalls, and vibes specialist Gene Redd.[5] Casey had been a member of the Fats Waller band from the age of eighteen, and after Waller's untimely death led his own trio for a spell. Voted the best jazz guitarist by *Esquire* magazine for two years running in the 1940s, he worked with many of the greats over the years, including Louis Armstrong. When he left Bostic later in the 1950s, he played with another leading saxophonist in the same mold, King Curtis. Smalls, from Charleston, South Carolina, had spent four years with Earl Hines as arranger, trumpeter, and his favorite backup pianist. Gene Redd, who had started out with Cootie Williams, was a noteworthy addition to the Bostic ensemble. A writer and producer, he played not only the vibes but also the trumpet, and was employed as a musical director at King Records. One of the unsung but influential talents of the age, he worked with Milt Buckner and James Brown. Redd later managed Kool & the Gang, and his four children were all successful R&B artists. He added a key dimension to the Bostic sound and played on most of the outstanding records during his years with the orchestra. Witness his impressive playing on Franz Schubert's "Serenade." Bostic's skillful

14. The Bostic Sound

arrangement of the romantic classic saw him at his most soulful. Earl's own "Seven Steps" was a decent jump blues that proved a hugely popular hit in the spring of 1950.

Bostic covered much of the country again during the year. There were lengthy but highly successful tours right across the South and Midwest, with lots of returns to earlier glories. He was soon dubbed the king of the one-nighters. Extended excursions in the East proved just as lucrative. They broke many attendance records en route—for instance, at the Celebrity Club, Providence, Rhode Island. The band were invited to be the opening act at newly launched ventures, such as the refurbished Gem Theater in Petersburg, Virginia, and there was no space to be had at the Show Boat in Philadelphia. Among the audience at the latter were Joe and Dorothy Bostic. Joe was an ex-teacher who became a radio announcer and was

A collectible 7" EP *All Time Hits* issued by King Records in 1956.

sometimes described as a PR man. Although he was often mentioned in articles as being Earl's brother, they were unrelated. A story circulated that Earl had recently become a viscount after the death of a distant relative. When asked by a Pittsburgh newspaperman about his elevation to the aristocracy, he joked, "The new title and eight cents will get me on any trolley in Philadelphia."[6]

He had plenty to say about contemporary music and dance, and of his generation he was among the progressives. For example, he felt that modern dancers had failed to keep pace with the changing times, while jazz was continually moving ahead, with bebop. Meanwhile, in his opinion, dancers had not advanced much from the Lindy hop of the 1920s.[7] Things were beginning to change in that direction, and a new freer approach to dance forms was ushered in during the decade, often spearheaded by teenagers who attended his shows.

Earl also had his own ideas about where and when he should play, refusing to follow the established norms if he felt so inclined. For example, during the main holiday times the usual policy was to play the big cities, but Bostic felt that this was unfair to those who supported bands during the nonholiday period. True to his word, over Independence Day week in 1950, he announced that he would play Canton, Laurel, and Hattiesburg in Mississippi, and Ponchatoula and Napoleonville, Louisiana.[8]

Despite his hectic schedule, he did manage to get away on vacation, and in August 1950 he took off for a much-delayed break, said to be his first in three years. He and Hildegarde spent three weeks in Haiti. Although the Caribbean island nation has always had a volatile history, there were attempts by successive administrations to open the country to tourism in the postwar period up until the mid-1950s. In retrospect, the time before the advent of the dictatorship of "Papa Doc" Duvalier has been seen as something of a golden age in comparison to earlier and later eras. Bostic was attracted to Caribbean countries and during his time there it was reported that he made an extended study of traditional Haitian music and folklore, particularly that which served as the basis of rituals and ceremonials, which always fascinated him.[9]

His growing reputation was often fueled by the reception of his records, which began to take on a greater significance. Sometimes they dictated where and when he would play. A return engagement at Bop City, New York, in August was directly inspired by his success with Schubert's "Serenade." Again he engaged in one of his regular music battles, this time with an old confrere, Al Sears. The result was adjudged another win for Bostic.[10] He impressed the great swing pioneer Fletcher Henderson, music director at Bop City. Originally booked for only a single week, Earl proved so popular that he was unexpectedly re-signed by Henderson from September 14 for four weeks, with the stipulation that he had a specially featured spot in his ambitious new jazz revue spectacular. Bostic was required to play and read prepared lines at intervals during the show, entitled *The Jazz Train*, which was written and directed by Mervyn Nelson. Subtitled "A Musical Dedicated to the Negro People," the show took the form of an extravaganza chronicling not just of the development of jazz, but of black music and culture, with singing engineer Leslie Scott in the role of narrator. Each section of the train took the form of coaches dedicated to chronicling the different eras. All told, about a score of performers took part, including singers Irene Williams and Dotty Saulter, a comedy team, The Chocolateers, and several of Henderson's men with solo spots, notably trumpeter "Red" Allen. Although Henderson played the music in the revue itself, Bostic and his orchestra entertained during the intervals. By all accounts, they made the most of their opportunity.[11] The hour-long show was summed up as "Fast, funny and sometimes furious" and was a critical and commercial success. Al Salerno of the *Brooklyn Eagle* observed, "Earl Bostic, whose band plays a stirring session of bop and jazz between shows, also sets the hep customers shuffling with a very hot ... sax solo."[12] A revamped, recast version of the show later ran at the Paradise Club and introduced a young Harry Belafonte. Several years later the musical transferred to London, where it received rave reviews and was eventually committed to disc.

A Bostic lineup similar to that at Bop City returned to the studio in October 1950. This consisted of Count Hastings on tenor, Gene Redd, vibes, Cliff Smalls, piano, and Keter Betts, bass. Of the songs to emerge from that session, "Don't You Do It" featured vibrant work from Bostic and Hastings and displayed an appealing change of pace in his reevaluation of Franz Lehar's "Merry Widow Waltz." Both made a splash in the charts.

Bostic's music at times perturbed the purists in the postwar era, and his new, dynamic direction did not always meet with universal approval among the purveyors of taste. In many ways the wail of Bostic's alto sax was, like the primal scream of Little Richard, misunderstood. "Flamingo" predated "Tutti Frutti" by three years. Nevertheless, many traditionalists were similarly alarmed by it, and immediately dismissed it as a rasping buzz saw. It was in essence like the reaction to rock 'n' roll among some. Critics found as many negative adjectives as they could to disparage the new sound, hoping to strangle it at birth. And yet, had not people said similar things about jazz in 1917, when it was labeled the Devil's music? After all, even the inventor of the phonograph, Thomas Edison, memorably remarked that jazz might sound better if it were played backward. A later critic perceptively described Bostic's playing as "raw yet rich, aggressive yet persuasive," and his sound as "very masculine, very authoritative."[13] Bostic was a wayfinder who broke new ground for others to follow.

His sound was new and exciting. There was an expansiveness to it, and a sense of fun. It was of its time and yet ahead of its time, with its blurring of boundaries between different types of music in a way few others attempted. Ever since its invention by Adolphe Sax in the 1840s, the saxophone had a unique ability to create atmosphere and was one of the most versatile and expressive of instruments. Witness all the great jazz saxophonists, be they tenor, baritone, alto, or soprano. It could be earthy or cool, mournful or joyful, stimulating or restful. It conjured up pictures in the mind's eye: perhaps a smoky, late-night club setting with a few lonely drinkers drowning their sorrows at the bar, or a roadhouse joint full of dancers having a ball. It sounded as though it promised nights of adventure ahead, with a hint of possible danger. There was a sense of urgency, of anticipation in Bostic's sound, which was always driving forward. It was sophisticated, sultry, urbane, playful, and futuristic. It sounded go-ahead and optimistic, in tune with the fifties mood of bold scientific advancement encapsulated in the Truman and Eisenhower years—those days when the standard of living was at its highest, and despite the ever-present Cold War, there was a feeling of boundless confidence abroad, albeit underscored by a vague sense of unease. Against this background, the new music moved into the center stage of the collective consciousness. Bostic pointed the way forward. His flamboyant, evocative style and the way the sax interacted with the vibes suggested a different way of approaching the blues, with its strong backbeat, and the expressive alto always out front in place of the vocal. Seen as heresy by some at the time, his approach was soon adopted by others and became the template for the greatest discovery of the decade: rock 'n' roll.

15

"Flamingo" Takes Off

> *"His booting, biting saxophone tone, with its heavy rhythm backing, is not subtle enough for the modernist; is too striving for the traditionalist. Yet few could deny that Bostic swings.... His records have an atmosphere that makes the diehards tap their feet when nobody's looking."*[1]

Recorded and released in 1951, "Flamingo" was a million-seller and became Bostic's only gold record. It took off immediately in Europe, where it gave him perhaps his biggest hit. His unique arrangement came to define his sound. Beyond doubt, it made him as an international star, and afterwards his popular success seemed assured.

"Flamingo" was recorded in the first session of January 1951 in New York with a septet. The personnel, besides Bostic, consisted of Gene Redd on vibes, Count Hastings on tenor sax, Cliff Smalls on piano, Keter Betts on bass, with the addition of René Hall and Jimmy Cobb on drums—what might well be called a classic lineup. On some tracks there was a singer, Clyde Terrell. Of the other songs committed to disc that day, two gave newcomer Terrell a chance to show what he could do on songs of contrasting tempo and mood. "Rockin' and Reelin'" and "September Song" proved he was a competent vocalist, but he did not compare well to the departing Roger Jones. While the vocal tracks were forgettable, the two instrumentals stood out in bold relief. Bostic's inventive interpretation of the all-too-familiar standard "I Can't Give You Anything but Love" showed great confidence and a decided command of tone and mood. The ease with which he blows on this track is impressive, and the long, floating note to finish is simply stunning.

Clearly, the standout number of the session was "Flamingo." The song had been written by Ted Grouya and Herb Jefferies and given to Duke Ellington, who crafted a romantic version that proved popular on its release in 1941. Bostic's superlative reimagining a decade later took it in a completely unexpected direction, and more than anything it came to define his sound.

It was a big hit in France, and when released in England it took off to such an extent that it became an all-time best seller in British jazz. It was featured by several influential DJs, including Jack Jackson on his BBC show, and was also taken up enthusiastically by Radio Luxembourg. The sensation it caused meant that soon demand outstripped supply. King records had an agreement with Vogue records in Europe, and in England, Vogue was principally known as the jazz label which "made a healthy impact on the market."[2] In the United States "Flamingo" had not initially created such waves as it had in Europe, until it featured on radio broadcasts, after which it skyrocketed, and reached number 1 on the R&B charts. It spent 20 weeks on the charts all told, from November 1951 until May 1952. In Europe it took

"Flamingo" backed by "Sleep" was issued on the distinctive Vogue label in England, 1952.

off again later in 1952. After its soaraway success, Bostic always considered it lucky, and opened each recording session with it as his warm-up tune. He also started many of his gigs with the song.

Some of the success of "Flamingo" was attributed to the producer of the session, Ralph Bass. The producer fulfills a crucial role in the career of any popular artist; witness Sir George Martin and the Beatles. Nonetheless, perhaps producers' importance should not be overstated. Bass started out with Savoy records, and had only recently joined Federal Records, a King subsidiary. He had the knack of recognizing a potential hit when he saw it, and could identify what would work best to bring out the singular essence of any artist. He was instrumental in signing James Brown to King, and was even said to have "discovered" John Lee Hooker, although that was open to debate. Hitherto, Bostic's sessions had followed a similar pattern, with a jump blues, followed by a novelty R&B number, a standard, maybe a romantic ballad or classical piece. Bass changed things somewhat and concentrated on what he saw as Bostic's strengths, namely, his natural facility for illuminating melody allied to his growling style of attack on the saxophone. These he harnessed to a series of familiar songs to explore Bostic's remarkable and imaginative arrangements. It was this simple approach that contributed to the unique Bostic sound on record. The formula was not his invention, but Bass was shrewd enough to see it, and his approach provided the conduit for Bostic to fully realize his special sound in its full glory. Practically all his sessions thereafter were produced by Bass. After he left King in 1959, Bass spent almost twenty years with Chess Records of Chicago.

The next recording session later in the month employed the same personnel as before, and produced another gem in Bostic's arrangement of "Sleep." The song dated from 1923 and was written by Adam Geibel and Earl Burtnett, although it was originally issued under the pseudonym Earl Lebieg. The first recording of the waltz time number was by Fred Waring and His Pennsylvanians, and it became Waring's signature tune. A great many others took a stab at it afterward, but it was Bostic who breathed new life into it after years of neglect, and his bold reinvention was memorably cited by DJ John Peel as "one of the very greatest records of all time."[3] It was released before "Flamingo" and featured in the top ten of the many different charts, reaching as high as number 6 in the *Billboard* chart. Of the other songs recorded that day, most were standards which did not have the same impact but showed great merit. "Always" gave pianist Cliff Smalls a chance to shine, and Bostic's restrained playing on the perennial "I'm Getting Sentimental Over You" was well judged for the George Bassman opus, which has been covered countless times since the Dorsey Brothers first did it in 1932.

Throughout the year the Bostic band continued their sellout tours. In the spring and early summer, they were again with Dinah Washington and playing to capacity crowds. Beginning with a week at the Apollo, New York, they traversed the country with select dates at the Rainbow Room in Denver, via Atlanta, Georgia, and as far west as San Bernardino, California, among many others. The gig in Atlanta was typical of their shows, and drew an audience of over six thousand. With a 50–50 split of the take, they each made $3,200 for the night.[4] In many ways, Bostic and Washington had much in common. Like him, she had a devoted following, the esteem of fellow musicians, and her records sold well, but she divided the critics, some of whom accused her of selling out. She had a natural facility to adapt to all kinds of styles of music and was never tied to one genre. The same was often said of him. This fluidity was perhaps one reason why they got along so well and responded to each other's artistry. A special highlight during their tour was a backstage champagne party they gave for dancer extraordinaire Josephine Baker while playing at the Strand Theatre, just before beginning their coast-to-coast tour. Earl presented her with flowers and Josephine was visibly moved by the occasion, embracing both stars warmly. Over the whole of the summer the Bostic orchestra alone were a major attraction during their ten-week stay at the Surf Club in Wildwood, New Jersey.

In October 1951 the band returned to the King studios in Cincinnati, with a lineup unchanged from their previous session. The songs they recorded included two average vocal numbers which again featured Clyde Terrell. The other songs were also standards. "The Moon Is Low" was a less well known Nacio Herb Brown and Arthur Freed tune brought to vivid life by Bostic in full 1950s color. It was astute of him to see its potential, and he was the first jazzman to record it since the great Fats Waller eleven years earlier. "Lover Come Back to Me" presented a far different challenge, as did all those standards that become overfamiliar. Since its debut in the Broadway show *The New Moon* in 1928, this Oscar Hammerstein II favorite has been given the treatment by practically every popular singer and musician. Bostic simply did his own thing, applying his trademark sound. In terms of mood and tempo, it perhaps had most in common with Mildred Bailey's appealing, understated version. Critic Hugues Panassié noted Earl's instinctive ability to choose the right tempo for any given song, and was especially impressed with the bouncy tempo he often adopted.

The next joint tour package with Dinah Washington began in October at the Apollo. Earl signed up for dates with her to continue well into 1952, but for him, if not his orchestra, this was cut abruptly short by what happened next.

16

Accident

In December 1951, Bostic suffered a terrible car crash that might easily have proved fatal. Although amazingly he recovered within a matter of months, his passenger and fellow band member Cliff Smalls was not as fortunate, and faced over a year of inactivity followed by a long rehabilitation. Earl came back better than ever after his accident and went on to enjoy perhaps his best years.

He loved cars, and reputedly had more of them than Elvis Presley, although unlike Elvis, Earl was keen to drive all of his. Among his favorites was the Studebaker Commander, but for Earl, as for many other personalities of his time, the Cadillac became the ultimate status symbol, the sign that one had made it. This was as true for black entertainers as it was for white, only more so. Not only was it the ultimate fifties symbol of success, it stood for the height of luxury and having achieved a level of fame unmatched by all but a few. Perhaps Earl felt he had something to prove, and feeling like the master of the road in his Cadillac, he proved it. All that shiny chrome, with the tailfins and the sheer scale of it, the bright colors, made it the apogee of space-age design. The image of this car in front of a roadside diner can stand for all time as epitomizing the decade in shorthand. A materialist society seemed to judge success by the flaunting of its super-luxury "toys." Such a car was way out of the reach of the ordinary Joe, and that exclusivity must have made it so desirable and so satisfying once attained. Other cars did not come near to it, and even the equally iconic Chevrolet was dismissed by some as the poor man's Cadillac.

Bostic adored the overwhelming feeling of power and satisfaction he felt when driving these state-of-the-art cars with their precision engineering. Like many, the normally mild-mannered musician may have changed his personality somewhat once he got behind the wheel. He often said how much he loved driving, but there was a big difference between taking a leisurely drive in the country on a Sunday afternoon in the height of summer, and driving all day and night in all weathers crisscrossing the country on endless tours over huge distances with scant sleep. At such times a substitute driver would have been a good idea, but Bostic would have none of it. He insisted on driving himself, and, according to Coltrane biographer J.C. Thomas, "Once, he drove all the way from Los Angeles to Midland, Texas, more than a thousand miles and close to seventeen hours without allowing anyone else to sub for him as chief chauffeur."[1]

In the early hours of December 6, 1951, Bostic and his band were headed for Phenix City, Alabama, from their previous date in Jacksonville, Florida, almost 300 miles. They were traveling in two cars. Bostic, as always, was driving his Cadillac sedan in front with two other passengers, one of whom was pianist and trombonist Cliff Smalls, who was in the passenger seat. The other occupant of the car was not identified. Bostic had been driving all night and, as often happened, became drowsy, and he fell asleep at the wheel. Around 4 a.m. he crashed head-on into a gasoline truck, which pinned the auto's occupants. Burnie Peacock recalled, "The car was a total loss and one of the worst smash-ups I've ever seen."[2] The accident happened near Tifton, Georgia. Luckily for him, the other vehicle full of his musicians was following behind his and they managed to rescue Bostic and the others from the Cadillac before it caught fire. He emerged with a fractured pelvis, hip, shoulder, and arm. He was first rushed to the nearest county hospital, the Archbold Memorial Hospital in Thomasville, Georgia. There he was treated by Dr. Fred E. Murphy, whose medical skill in the immediate aftermath of the accident saved him from being permanently disabled. Earl's wife Hildegarde was contacted and flew to Georgia to be with her husband at his bedside. On December 15 he was taken to Jacksonville, then flown to New York via Eastern Lines, and transferred to the Hospital for Joint Diseases at 1919 Madison Avenue, New York. There he underwent numerous operations, the first just a few days before Christmas, carried out by Dr. Leo Mayer, a distinguished orthopedic surgeon who devised new methods of reconstructive surgery. Earl's pelvis was completely reduced to powder and had to be reconstructed. The effects of the accident lingered for a considerable time and according to one report there was a chance that he would have to be in a cast for up to two or even three years. In the event, that was not the case, although that prognosis proved sadly almost correct for Smalls.[3]

It was hardly the first or last traffic incident in which Bostic was involved. He had several near misses over the years, some of which were serious and might easily have been fatal. It was perhaps not so surprising considering all the territory they covered and the hours of driving involved. All the same, he was often fined for reckless driving. Earlier in 1951 alone he was twice arrested for driving offences. In April he was prosecuted in Fremont, Ohio, for driving on the wrong side of the road.[4] Then in July he was fined $10 for speeding at Somers Point, New Jersey.[5] A few

16. Accident 97

years after his near-fatal accident he knocked over a boy riding a bicycle, as he was driving four band members from Binghampton, New York, to a date in Lawrence, Massachusetts. Twelve-year-old David Kearns suffered severe head injuries, including a fractured skull, as a result of the accident, which occurred on November 4, 1955 at West Springfield, Massachusetts. The boy had just received the bicycle for his birthday. At the time, Bostic claimed he was wholly innocent of the charge.[6] He was found guilty in the District Court of being careless and negligent in operating a car and driving to endanger life. However. he appealed the fine.[7] The boy's father George Kearns filed suit for $50,000 against Bostic, and the case dragged out into 1956 and beyond. It was finally brought to the Superior Court in West Springfield. Just before the case went before a jury in May 1957, Bostic agreed to pay an unspecified sum described as "a sizeable settlement" for the boy's personal injuries and an additional $1000 in consequential damages for his medical care.[8] Bostic was later recruited to front a campaign to urge teenagers to drive carefully.

For Smalls, life was turned upside down. His recovery was much slower than that of Bostic, although he appeared to get the same or similar medical treatment from the beginning, and had the same surgeon. With his legs encased in plaster for over a year, he was rendered completely inactive and unable to do anything. The inactivity and feeling that the recovery would take a long time naturally got him down. The cast on his left leg began under the armpit. He was helpless to do anything after his wife brought him back from the hospital. As he remarked, in his own words, "so I laid in bed for all of '52, 'til March of '53."[9] Once he was able to move about and regained the feeling in his legs, it took him still longer to find the use of his fingers again and get back to his former self, let alone start to making his living again. He recalled:

> "The first time I got out of bed, they asked me where I wanted to go, and I said to the piano. But I had no strength at all in my fingers and I couldn't play, and the tears just started coming out of my eyes. The doctor came by and gave everybody hell, said they'd probably injured me for life. Even now, if I make a mistake, which I don't do very often, I tend to think back to that accident, and for a long time I'd find myself hating Earl Bostic. Of course, he didn't do it intentionally, but he never came to see me, not one time. His wife came, and brought my horn back to me, but she wasn't in the house a half-hour."[10]

It is hard to understand Bostic's neglect of Smalls in this way, and difficult to square with his usual attitude or his public persona. It seems out of character, and it almost looks as though he had gone into denial about the accident, as though he refused to believe it was his fault, rather as he did when he knocked over the boy on the bike. Publicly he made a great play of always helping other musicians and raising money for hospitals and good causes, which was no doubt sincere. He dropped everything to come to the aid of the hospital that had taken care of him after the crash. He once turned down a date in Atlanta worth $1500 in order to attend a charity dance in aid of the Archbold hospital. All the money raised at the gig went toward providing an annex for colored patients. When one of his ex-players, Arnett Cobb, was injured in an auto crash, Bostic was prominent among those who played in several benefits for him, even though he was no longer a member of his band at that time. Yet privately it seems he was not forthcoming to tangibly help or even accept any responsibility for causing a valued band member to suffer such injuries and furthermore lose his livelihood for over a year. Smalls filed suit against him, almost forced to do so by dint of his lack of funds. Bostic was driving, so it was a clear-cut case, and because he caused the crash, he was deemed liable. It was a great pity that it could not have been settled amicably before he was forced to admit liability. The case did not reach a conclusion until almost six years after the accident, when Bostic finally agreed to pay Smalls an out-of-court settlement amounting to $14,000.[11] Ultimately, Smalls's story was one of success against the odds. Having begun his career with Earl Hines, he later became an arranger for a diverse array of artists including Smokey Robinson. He even appeared playing the piano in Coppola's homage to jazz in *The Cotton Club* (1980).

Despite the main man being *hors de combat* from December 1951, the show had to go on. Bostic's band had commitments to fulfill and continued touring with Dinah Washington for the first few months of 1952 under his replacement, Burnie Peacock, a former Basie alto man. Peacock had previously been with "Lucky" Millinder and "Bull Moose" Jackson. After leaving Bostic, Peacock led his own band and did a tour of Korea during the war there. Bostic was overwhelmed by, and greatly appreciative of, all the hundreds and thousands of letters, cards, and messages that poured in to the joint hospital in New York to express good wishes for his recovery. All the same, he faced criticism in some quarters for not taking enough rest while driving or better still employing a full-time driver. He was doing well and could clearly afford it. One unnamed musician was quoted at the time as saying, "Earl had no business driving. He knows how fatigue gets the best of you after hours of playing. Why didn't he invest in a driver, period?"[12] Later, he did advertise for a full-time secretary and driver. It was never clear whether he took anyone on for the position, but it seems unlikely because he was almost always to be found ferrying the band around even years later—in fact, right to the end of his life.

Bostic was someone who thrived on work and activity. He was not the kind who could be idle for long. Needless to say, after the operations, the two or three months in hospital, and further time recovering at home,

16. Accident

he was keen to get back into the swing of work as soon as possible, even though it was against doctor's orders. By the end of February, he was even well enough to receive the delayed award for best alto sax player of 1951 presented by representatives of his agents, Universal Attractions.[13] Surprisingly, it was announced that he intended to reenter the recording studio in spring and that the next tour would start on the East Coast as early as April 1. By June the band, which had by then increased to an eight-piece, arrived in California for the next leg, and from then on, they kept going practically nonstop. It was almost as though the accident had never happened.

17

A University of the Saxophone

> "Working with Earl Bostic is like attending a university of the saxophone."[1]
> —Art Blakey

After his accident, Bostic returned to lead his band from the spring of 1952. It was around that time that he recruited an outstanding young sax player to the ranks, John Coltrane. One of the immortals of jazz, he stayed for the rest of the year. Just as it was said that working with Fate Marable on the riverboats was something akin to attending a jazz conservatory, so it was a similar experience working for Bostic, and those who passed through the Bostic "university" could fill a book of their own.

By all accounts, Bostic was blessed with a sunny disposition and was easy to work with. Practically everyone he met found him immensely likeable, easygoing, and eager to please. Fellow musicians, managers, booking agents, electricians, janitors, and company directors all attested to his personal appeal and unaffected personality. The experienced Joseph G. Glaser, manager to the stars and president of the Associated Booking Corporation (ABC), spoke for many when he said, "I think Earl Bostic is one of the nicest I have ever met. It is a real pleasure to do business with a man like him."[2] Bostic's round, open face radiated good humor and positivity. He emanated a real joie de vivre and there seemed to be no "side" to him. Intelligent and quiet-spoken, he was articulate both as public speaker and as musician. Most of the many who passed through his various bands over the years spoke well of his professional and personal qualities. The only real difficulties emerged over artistic rather than temperamental disagreements. Pianist Jaki Byard was one such who had the most problems. Byard was a bop stylist on piano; his heroes were Bud Powell and Charlie "Bird" Parker. "He [Bostic] didn't dig Bird," commented Byard, "Bird had no tone for him. And my guys on piano were Bud and Erroll Garner, who played behind the beat, while Bostic liked to go forward. We didn't get along too well."[3] Even so, and despite their differences, some sources maintain that Byard stayed with the band for at least two years from 1947, and possibly three.[4] It is worth noting that Errol Garner invited Earl on stage one legendary night at Pep's in Pennsylvania for what turned into an exciting jam session, as both artists "really got carried away."[5] Some musicians found their scope for self-expression too limited with Bostic. Unlike several outfits, there was little chance for anyone else to shine, because he took most of the solos going. Nevertheless, there were compensations, and the kind of training offered could not be had anywhere else.

Earl's reputation was high among his fellow musicians, many of whom witnessed his battles with Charlie Parker. Fellow alto saxist Lou

A young John Coltrane spent much of 1952 touring with Bostic, and admitted that he learned a lot from him, including the circular breathing technique. This is the cover of the 2017 reissue of the *Coltrane* LP first released in 1957.

Donaldson remembered: "Bostic was down at Minton's and Charlie Parker came in there. They played 'Sweet Georgia Brown' or something and he gave Charlie Parker a saxophone lesson. He [Bostic] was a swing player, melodic, and he could read anything. Great musician."[6] Bobby Booker recalled seeing the same thing happen at the Club Harlem on 145th Street: He recollected: "At the same place, once, I ran into Earl Bostic and Charlie Parker. They battled for hour after hour, I'm telling you. I will tell you something, people don't respect Earl Bostic. They've got to be crazy, because that man was something else!"[7] Earl did something similar with many others over the years, including Al Sears, Hal Singer, "Cleanhead" Vinson, and trumpeter Cootie Williams.[8]

Although these meetings between altoists were often seen as contests, and even likened to showdowns between gunfighters, this is in some ways misleading. Clearly, they all wanted to prove they were the best, but they were excited and fascinated by every new talent who came along and there existed a definite fellow feeling between altoists. Herb Wong has talked about the way in which alto saxophonists differ from the more romantic tenor counterparts. He explained, "Alto saxophonists seem to have their own private fraternity—an unspoken brotherhood—and altoists seem to listen to each other more intently than any other musicians I know."[9] This was certainly the case with Bostic, who was by all accounts a great listener. When he first encountered "Bird" he was captivated; he listened and watched closely over several nights. The same was true when he saw Coltrane and others. While they were all rivals in a way, first and foremost they were musicians who appreciated each other for their individual qualities.

John Coltrane was the most famous personality who played with Bostic, although he was willfully obscure at the time he joined. Born in North Carolina, Coltrane started on the clarinet in high school, but switched to saxophone and was presented with his first alto by his mother for his seventeenth birthday. His first sight of Charlie Parker was an epiphany for him. He made his first recordings while in the Navy toward the latter end of the war. According to several sources, he stayed with the Bostic band between April and December 1952, but the definitive reference work on his life and times states that he left by October. His time with the band has been covered in considerable detail, as has virtually every part of Trane's personal history. He joined the band in spring, just after Bostic had recovered from his accident, although they had been aware of each other for at least two years prior to that, since the days when Earl was a regular at Minton's. Benny Golson recollected the occasion of one of their first meetings: "Coltrane was with me, and we heard Bostic play in any key, any tempo, playing almost an octave above the range of the alto saxophone. We talked

17. A University of the Saxophone

with him and he explained the different fingering techniques on all makes of saxes, Martin, Buescher, Selmer."[10] The drummer "Specs" Wright, Coltrane's friend and ally, toured at the same time with Bostic. "Specs" died young at thirty-five, but packed a lot into his years, with stints alongside some of the great names in postwar jazz, including Sonny Rollins.

Coltrane remembered of his time with the orchestra: "I enjoyed it—they had some true music. He's [Bostic is] a very gifted musician. He showed me a lot of things on my horn."[11] Coltrane learned the circular breathing technique which Earl had down pat, and which he taught to several other band members over the years, even to one of his drummers. At that point Coltrane already had a dedication similar to that which the youthful Earl had displayed. The younger man also developed a surprising level of stamina that enabled him to go on playing for a long time while keeping the same level of intensity and fire going, something that he admitted to Roy Haynes he had learned directly from Bostic.[12]

During the time Coltrane and Wright were with them, the orchestra were at their busiest and had few days off. The band was booked solid and played to sold-out shows. After sensational stands in Cambridge, Maryland, New York City, and Washington, D.C., the band set new attendance records in Hartford, Connecticut, and Elizabeth, New Jersey. At the Richmond Civic Auditorium in July 1952, they attracted a crowd of over 4000. Not only was Coltrane featured on sax, but he also contributed significantly as a singer in a trio. They were widely promoted in press reports as "The Three Bs." The other two were Richard "Blue" Mitchell and "Pinky" Williams. Coltrane was also proficient on the guitar. Despite having seemingly little scope to express himself, Coltrane nonetheless was clearly a standout talent who was fast making a name for himself. He was frequently featured in photographs in newspapers publicizing forthcoming visits. Bostic rated him highly and was keen to place him in the forefront of all publicity regarding the band. "The Three Bs" were a popular addition and generated a lot of interest. Keen to get in as much practice as he could, Coltrane often jammed with some of the others in the band after hours, when most, including Bostic, had already gone home. Earl was not someone who liked to hang around for a long time afterward at that stage of his career. In the words of one witness, he preferred to squire all the ladies home in his eight-seat Cadillac.

They covered a lot of territory, and among other dates they played a fortnight engagement at the Glass Bar in St. Louis, Missouri, and made an overnight trip to Los Angeles to appear at a Shriners concert. This was followed by key dates in Ohio, and at Providence, Rhode Island. By August, constant touring was beginning to get Coltrane down, as he admitted in a letter home to his mother, when he wrote, "This tour is the longest one

I've ever been on and I'll be so doggoned glad to get home."[13] He stayed a while longer, but after September his appearances lessened, and by October he had, according to some biographers, already left. Others suggest he may have played a few dates in November. Later, he joined Johnny Hodges, a player he much admired, although he was eventually fired by Hodges because of his increasing unreliability over his drugs addiction. Despite all his problems, he went on to achieve not just greatness but immortality with his solo work, particularly with the seminal Blue Note LPs *Blue Train* (1958), *Giant Steps* (1960), *My Favorite Things* (1961), and *A Love Supreme* (1965). His outstanding career ended with his early death at the age of forty of liver cancer. All the musicians he had worked with over the years had an impact on his style, and it is difficult to tease out the different influences, but he always spoke well of his time with Bostic. Looking back, Coltrane acknowledged all he owed to his early experiences touring and the leaders he had learned from. He once commented: "I didn't appreciate guys like Bostic at the time because Bird had swayed me so much. After I'd gotten from under his spell, I began to appreciate them more."[14]

After Coltrane left at the end of 1952, he recommended Stanley Turrentine, who consequently took his place and stayed until 1954. Although not given anything like the attention that went to Coltrane, Turrentine was nevertheless a supremely talented player who enjoyed a remarkable and varied career. A native of Pittsburgh, he was only eighteen when Bostic asked him to join, and it was just his second touring experience after beginning with Lowell Fulsom. In later times, he talked with fondness of his time with Bostic and the lasting value of all the things he learned from him, not just in musical terms, but in the whole experience that gave him a great grounding in the blues and set him up for life. Turrentine went on to recollect: "And Earl Bostic used to tell me that if I was gonna play something it should mean something. You shouldn't just play something because it's on the right chord, you try to express what the song's about or what you feel about the song."[15] He learned a lot more from him too, not just about music but about the business side of things, which Bostic understood well. In those days most musicians just thought about playing but totally neglected to find out about business, much to their regret years later. Turrentine recorded an impressive run of LPs for Blue Note in the 1960s and 1970s, including several acclaimed collaborations with his wife, the organist Hazel Scott, both during and after their marriage.

At one stage, the orchestra almost became a Turrentine family affair. Stanley's elder brother Tommy (1928–1997) was also with the band over a similar period (1952–1955). Considered a hard bop trumpeter, he nonetheless found a central place with Bostic. He was also a composer, and later played with a wide range of artists including Charles Mingus. Tommy

Stanley Turrentine toured extensively with the Bostic orchestra for two years from the age of eighteen and was greatly influenced by him. He went on to enjoy a long and fruitful career during which he recorded many acclaimed LPs for Blue Note, including *Jubilee Shout*, first recorded in 1962 but not released in its entirety until 1986

made few recordings as leader but was well remembered for his collaborations with some of the greats, among them Max Roach and Lou Donaldson, as well as his own brother Stanley. The brothers came from a talented musical family. Their father Thomas Sr., played saxophone for Al Cooper's Savoy Sultans and, according to Stanley, their mother Rosetta "played great stride piano."¹⁶

Tenor man Benny Golson, a good friend of Coltrane, also worked with the Bostic band after Turrentine left (1954–1956). He became one of the few members to be fired. Initially happy in the band, as time passed and the tours continued, he became increasingly frustrated for various reasons. For one thing, he grew tired of having to play the same commercial material too often, and because Bostic was to the fore all the time, the rest of the band were left with little to do. Golson played several practical jokes on Bostic. Once he fiddled with Earl's perfectly tuned-up guitar that was on a chair ready for Earl when he needed it. Of course, when he came to play it, the tuning was haywire and Bostic was at a loss to understand what had happened. The others laughed and looked at Golson, so he was aware who had done it. Another time Golson charged from the back of the stage and pretended to throw his saxophone to the audience just as Bostic was starting his solo, which irked Bostic no end, because he would tolerate no interference with his solos. The final straw came in Seattle when Golson told a fellow tenor saxist, Walter Benton, that he could sit in on a session, something which he knew Bostic never allowed. When suddenly Benton started playing on stage, Bostic was aghast. After he discovered who was behind it, he gave Golson two weeks' notice. Nevertheless, despite his apparent discontent, he had nothing but praise for Bostic in after years. As Golson once remarked of him: "There was nothing he couldn't do. He was amazing. He was from another planet. 'Bird' would step back and listen to him."[17]

Drummer Art Blakey once famously remarked, "Nobody knew more about the saxophone than Bostic. I mean technically, and that includes Bird. Bostic could take any make of saxophone and tell you its faults and its best points. Working with Bostic is like attending a university of the saxophone."[18] Many concurred with his assessment. Pianist Jimmy Manuel recalled, "It was like being in school, Bostic made me aware of the work that is necessary to become a musician."[19] Around 1955 George Goldsmith, a drummer from Detroit (b. 1939–2004), spent thirteen months with the band. He joined straight from school at the age of sixteen when he asked to tour with Bostic, who agreed. Goldsmith had previously been in the band at Northeastern High School. Of his time with the orchestra, Goldsmith later commented, "It taught me a lot—gave me whatever foundation I had at that time. Benny Golson and other musicians came through Earl Bostic's band, and I considered it a privilege to have had that opportunity."[20] Another pianist, Joe Knight, remembered: "Everyone in the Bostic band got along with everyone else. We were a playful bunch of fellows. All Earl ever cared about was that each musician could sight read on the spot. We had more than 150 tunes in the book, and if you couldn't read them the first time around you were out of a job."[21]

For many, if not most, the band was a jumping-off point to great things. Drummer Jimmy Cobb (1929–2020) joined for a year (c. 1950–1951) at the start of his career, on the recommendation of Bostic's double bassist Keter Betts. It was Cobb's first experience on the road, and it was during his time with Bostic that Cobb first played with Dinah Washington. Cobb and Betts then left the Bostic band in 1951, and formed a trio with Wynton Kelly. Thenceforward, this trio formed the backing for Washington, and Cobb stayed with her for three or four years in total, becoming part of her management team. Individually, Cobb went on to play with Miles Davis between 1958 and 1963, and achieved immortality with his work on *Kind of Blue*, *Sketches of Spain*, and several other Davis classics. Betts himself had been recruited by Bostic after he saw him at a show in Washington, D.C., in April 1949 and stayed until August 1951. He once said that he accepted Bostic's offer not because he wanted to be in an R&B band, but in the hope of traveling and seeing the country. He certainly fulfilled that wish.

Earl was always keen to help youngsters get started, and many bandmembers joined straight from school or college right at the start of their careers, such as Freddy Cole, younger brother of Nat. Coming from such a talented musical family, Cole played piano from childhood, but it was originally his ambition to pursue a career in football, until a hand injury decided him to go for music instead. He was also a vocalist, with a pleasing voice, and was with Bostic from 1955 for a year. Other singers who worked with Earl included Dwayne "Fatman" Wilson around 1957. Then a teenager, Wilson also sang with The Shirelles.

Trumpeter Richard "Blue" Mitchell (1930–1979) hailed from Miami and was another who joined the Bostic band right after high school. He found great success with the Horace Silver Quintet and worked across genres, encompassing jazz, rock, R&B, and funk during the course of his impressive career. As leader of his own ensembles, he recorded prolifically for Blue Note and Riverside.

Pianist Wynton Kelly (1931–71) was one of the most accomplished and in-demand accompanists of his generation, and came to early prominence with his work for Miles Davis. Blessed with a warm and engaging personality, he struggled to escape being typecast as a sideman and never made it as a solo artist. His career was hampered by alcoholism and he died of a seizure at only thirty-nine.

The Bostic orchestra was a broad church, and encompassed everyone from traditionalists to hardline bop disciples to R&B progressives to near avant-gardists. It was a tapestry of talent and experience like no other. There were some whose careers stretched back to the dawn of the twentieth century, and teenagers just starting out. Several had been centrally involved in bands led by Fats Waller, and others had helped to shape the Fats Domino sound. Eras and genres overlapped, and all seemed to be harmonious in what was a musically exciting era. A résumé of all those who passed through the band at different times would fill several pages. They included Eldridge

Morrison, Skippy Williams, Ike Isaacs, and Sir Charles Thompson. Trumpeter Eldridge Morrison led the most famous interracial big band in Indianapolis in the 1940s. Williams played tenor sax and was also an arranger, and took Ben Webster's place in the Duke Ellington orchestra. He went on to play with a host of famous names including the great Thelonious Monk, before forming his own trio. Bassist Ike Isaacs, who was with Bostic between 1951 and 1953, spent two years with the Carmen McRae Trio and became McRae's husband. He later worked with Erroll Garner. Pianist and organist Sir Charles Thompson (1918–2016) had long experience with many artists including Coleman Hawkins and Dexter Gordon. He usually played with small combos and spent most of his career freelancing. He joined Bostic in the late 1950s. After he left, Thompson went on to lead his own band and embarked on international tours. He had been dubbed Sir by Lester Young, and lived to the remarkable age of ninety-eight.

The roll call of the many other jazz luminaries Earl worked with included trombonist John Ewing (1950–1951), drummer Kenny Dennis (1953), multi-instrumentalist Ray Carline (June 1947 at the Club 845), and trumpeter John Anderson (who recorded with Bostic in 1958). Bassist Vernon King was one who viewed bop as a passing phase, and always preferred to hear the melody. After three years at the University of Illinois, he was inspired by slap bassist "Pops" Foster to pursue music instead. He joined the Horace Henderson band and for many years toured extensively with that and other groups across the country. He lived to regret his decision to decline an invitation from Nat Cole to join his trio when they were just starting out. In all, King spent around five years with Bostic.[22]

Among other notable saxophonists who spent time with the orchestra was tenor man Teddy Edwards (1924–2003), who began on alto but was encouraged by Howard McGhee to switch to tenor. Born in Jackson, Mississippi, Edwards was one of the first significant jazz musicians to migrate to the West Coast in search of sun and a more harmonious life. This move seemed to diminish his status in the eyes of the New York critics, but he maintained a strong reputation in Europe. He was with Bostic during 1959 and always played with plenty of thrust, in the manner of Earl.

It was not only important names in jazz who contributed to the orchestra. Drummer Earl Palmer and guitarist Ernest McLean joined in the late 1950s. Palmer worked with everyone from Elvis to Sinatra. An integral part of the Fats Domino sound, Ernest McLean was once described as the best musician in Dave Bartholomew's band. Quiet by nature, he was not a natural self-publicist, which perhaps helps to explain his undeserved obscurity. These and all the other musicians added to the unique tapestry, folklore, and reputation of the band over the twenty-plus years that it existed.

18

A Thousand Saturday Nights

> "Earl believes that gradually there will be a merging of all styles of swing, rhythm and blues, Dixieland and progressive jazz. Although the rock 'n' roll and bop craze is now the fad, the merger will overcome it and the blend will include all beats."[1]
>
> —Karl Zanco

The early 1950s saw Bostic at the peak of his critical and commercial popularity. Between 1950 and 1953, he had more hits on what was then known as the Sepia Hit Parade than any other artist. Moreover, he was still getting good reviews in the music press, and his live shows were often the hottest ticket in town. He had by then fully developed his unique sound that brought him legions of fans, and in 1954 he was voted the top R&B instrumentalist in the annual *Billboard* poll. This was just before the rock 'n' roll explosion which he had helped to detonate years before.

The band recorded three sessions in 1953, the first in Los Angeles and the other two in Cincinnati. The first, in June, once more gave prominence to the standards, among them Ray Noble's "The Very Thought of You." "Memories" by Egbert Van Alstyne and Gustave Kahn dated from 1915, and as presented by the Bostic ensemble in suitably relaxed mode gave much of the limelight to pianist Luis Rivera. Earl's own composition, "What! No Pearls" was inspired by Glenn Miller's "String of Pearls." He worked his magic on contemporary melodies which took his fancy— witness "Melancholy Serenade," which was attributed to Jackie Gleason and first recorded with an orchestra bearing his name in 1952. However, it seems likely that beyond coming up with the basic melody, Gleason had little input thereafter. Nonetheless, for many years it served as the theme tune to his hit CBS television program *The Jackie Gleason Show*, a fifties staple, which ran on prime time on Saturday nights and in turn led to the sitcom *The Honeymooners*. A curiously sad tune for a light-hearted variety show, the theme's juxtaposition with the show was in itself a sign of the times. It made the comedy appear more sophisticated. Bostic's version brought something hitherto unheard in the original, which was sedately played, and his certainly had far more swing to it and a lot more soul. As *Billboard* summarized: "Sinuous rhythm and bluesy interpretation make the side a natural for late-hour play."[2] He sometimes invited entries to add words to his numbers when he felt those were needed. For instance, he advertised for lyrics for "Velvet Sunset," announcing that the winner would receive fifty percent of all royalties and a co-writing credit. Needless to say, he was inundated with entries.[3]

The next session, in August 1953, yielded four absolute classics. His satisfying arrangement of the languid Gene Gifford–Ned Washington classic "Smoke Rings" was arguably among his best. The song was first recorded by the Casa Loma Orchestra in 1932. Writing of this and some of his others from this time, critic Hugues Panassié observed, "These are pretty, yet swinging performances full of singing phrases. Bostic does not use any growl here but plays it with a very pure, clean, and beautiful tone."[4] "Deep Purple" dated from 1933 and as recorded by Bostic twenty years later proved to be one of his most popular. There have been countless instrumental interpretations, and there was the famous vocal reworking by the brother and sister duo Nino Tempo and April Stevens, which scored a memorable hit in November 1963, but of the instrumental versions in that period Bostic's stands out. "Jungle Drums" was based on another old song that dated from 1928. It began life as "Canto Karabali" by the Cuban composer Ernesto Lecuona, who also wrote "The Breeze and I." An appealing early version was recorded by Carlos Molina and His Orchestra and released on the Victor imprint in 1932. Bostic took this charming rumba and reinterpreted it in his own inimitable style, with his familiar growling sax striding out front with the melody, and the vibes to the fore. The number made a striking return to the public consciousness many years later when it was used to effect by John Waters in his paean to the fifties, *Cry-Baby* (1990), starring Johnny Depp. Bostic's own compositions were not forgotten, including the vibrant "Cracked Ice," which kept the dance floors full. His personnel on these definitive sides consisted of "Blue" Mitchell and Stanley and Tommy Turrentine, with Edward Richley on vibes, Alexander Sample on piano, Charles Grayson, guitar, Bob Breston, bass, and Granville T. Hogan on drums. Little is known of most of the session musicians. Drummer Hogan stayed with Bostic for several years.

The orchestra's next session, in October, emphasized the more sweetly classical side of their repertoire, including "Danube Waves" and "My Heart at Thy Sweet Voice." "Danube Waves" was a famous Romanian melody by Josef Ivanovici that dated back to 1880. It was later adapted with lyrics and became better known as "The Anniversary Waltz." Camille

18. A Thousand Saturday Nights   111

Saint-Saens's "My Heart at Thy Sweet Voice" was a famous aria from the opera *Samson and Delilah*. Two gems were "Off Shore" and "Poème." Bostic was one of the first to record the plaintive "Off Shore," which was composed by the harmonica player Leo Diamond and released the previous year. The reflective "Poème" was written in 1893 for piano by Czech composer Zdenek Fibich, who later incorporated it into his symphonic idyll *At Twilight*. It was adapted posthumously by violinist Jan Kubelik, who gave it the title "Poème," although with added lyrics it is also known as "My Midnight Madonna." Unsurprisingly, it was always a mainstay in the songbook of every light classical orchestra, and several swing bands gave it a try, including Tommy Dorsey. Bostic retains the integrity of the romantic melody but incorporates some playful touches nonetheless. March 1954 introduced the mambo into proceedings, which Bostic enthusiastically ran with on "Mambostic" and "Mambolino." His later recordings that year resulted in more hit records. His innovative approach was evident on the nocturne "Liebestraum" by Franz Liszt, which went back to 1850. Record reviewer John Hardin was so impressed by Bostic's interpretation that he spent thirty minutes listening to its nuances and found himself fascinated. He remarked, "Earl treats this old classic with care and makes the listener of popular dance music enjoy each bar of this arrangement."[5] Charles King's dreamy "Song of the Islands" (composed 1915) was a natural to receive the Bostic treatment. In his hands, the understated, rather mysterious-sounding melody becomes more vital and surely got everyone tapping their feet. The following day (October 9) came "Sweet Lorraine." Another song dating from the Roaring Twenties, this was resurrected by Bostic in his inimitable driving style. There had been a notable recording by pianist Teddy Wilson in 1935 but Nat Cole had by far the biggest hit with it in 1956. Bostic's lively interpretation was arguably the finest instrumental version and was played with all his customary verve allied to a strong melody line. Not only was it a great swinger, but it had the familiar bouncy confidence, and there was a surety of touch to it, almost a swagger. Hearing this, it felt as though he was truly going places, that his imagination was striding ahead, and that he had ideas which he had not yet begun to explore. Above all it was the sheer joy of his playing, which was reciprocated by that of all the couples who danced to it with the same abandon on dance floors across the nation.

His dates across the country in that period centered on theaters, ballrooms, and night clubs. In common with many artists, he also played at movie theaters, which often incorporated some leading jazzmen on stage in what was essentially a variety bill prior to the big feature film of the night. For instance, in February 1953 he was one of the headliners in a show at the Earle Theater, Philadelphia, that featured two other jazz greats,

Coleman Hawkins and Roy Eldridge. Hawkins was dubbed the king of the tenor sax, and trumpeter Eldridge, nicknamed "Little Jazz," was often cited as a prophet of bebop. They all took their work where they found it, in a lineup peppered with vaudeville-style comedians before the B-movie feature began. In this instance, the film they all preceded was *The Ring* (1953), a boxing drama about a Mexican teen overcoming bigotry. Among all the different entertainers on display, Bostic received much of the attention. Local correspondent Barbara Wilson praised his unflagging energy and was especially taken with his warm and soulful rendition of the standard "Smoke Gets in Your Eyes." She observed approvingly that the band "treat all the old numbers … with a loving touch and don't clutter them up with dissonant chords."[6]

He was also invited to participate in some significant jazz festivals, including the 9th Cavalcade of Jazz, an open-air concert held at Wrigley

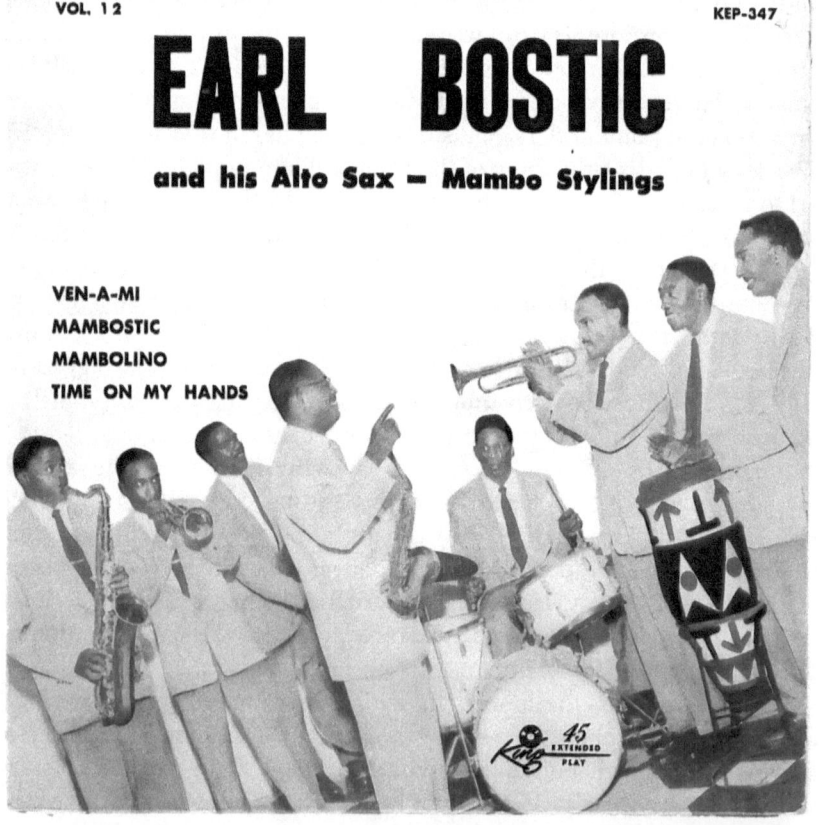

Earl and his orchestra on the cover of the 7" EP *Mambo Stylings* (1955).

Field, Los Angeles, in June 1953. Produced by Leon Hefflin Sr., the other artists featured included Satchmo, Nat "King" Cole, and Lloyd Price. Unfortunately, the event drew less than half its 19,000 capacity. This was chiefly attributed to its reputation in recent years and the riotous behavior of drunks brawling in the stands, who spoiled the whole thing for the real music fans.[7]

Throughout that time, Bostic was in such demand that he frequently signed contracts four months in advance. In August 1953 he was nominated as top band leader in the night club field. This followed his terrific stands at clubs in New York, and before long he was setting attendance records all along the West Coast, which he had not previously played to the same extent. His records were jukebox hits along with all the other rising stars, Fats Domino, Clyde McPhatter's Drifters, and more. All this was before Elvis Presley burst onto the scene. Bostic's love of melody allied to the strong backbeat enticed listeners and many considered this was much of the reason for his great sales, but it was also his unique arrangements and what Steve Hoffman called his "undeniably sensual feel."[8]

Records created the buzz, but there was no question that the live scene was where it was all at, and Earl's orchestra was praised wherever they played. A North Carolina correspondent acclaimed: "His torrid rhythm section ... is bolstered by Gene Redd's hot vibraharp and on terse rhythmic passages numbers five men with drums, piano, guitar, bass and vibes working. The alto-tenor-trumpet upfront stylings ha[ve] also drawn plaudits wherever the group has been heard, in person or on recording."[9] In September 1954, his was voted the top combo of the year. The following month he played a prestigious date at the legendary Basin Street in New York, along with Dave Brubeck and Carmen McRae, in what the critics lauded as "a well-rounded and enticing show." Bostic kept the audience in thrall. As one reviewer observed, "His topper and final number, the carefree 'Let's Ball Tonight' was the wildest sax performance we've ever seen. Bostic was supreme. A great show-man and crowd pleaser."[10] By then, his reputation as the leading instrumentalist in popular music was well established and his salary had already reached six figures. He still used singers on tour, and Sonny Carter joined the band around that time. He made it onto disc, and was heard on "There Is No Greater Love."

Earl was in some ways frustrated that having a small band, usually six or seven, limited his scope to experiment musically, and ideally, he would have preferred a bigger outfit. Moreover, he did not think the age of the big band was over, contrary to the prevailing opinion. He once remarked: "There can be no substitute, either artistically or economically, for the small band in the smaller night clubs, for recording backgrounds to name artists and the small dance halls, unable to accommodate enough patrons to justify large band fees. However, I am positive that big bands will once more be the vogue."[11] Nonetheless, his band was always exciting to see live because the members had plenty of chance to improvise and put a lot into each performance. From the beginning his orchestra packed a punch, no matter if it was only a quintet. To use a boxing analogy, they punched well above their weight. Bostic always relished the theatrical aspect of the show. Stanley Turrentine recalled having to walk the bar: "I used to follow him. He'd say follow me and the whole band would have to, except the rhythm section. We'd get up there and walk the bar. Fortunately, I never had to crawl on the floor and roll over like I saw a lot of cats do. But I did all that stuff. I walked the bar and worked the crowd into a frenzy. That was part of the times."[12] Bostic always enjoyed personally taking the band up and down the theater aisles in his pied piper fashion, just as he had from his earliest days in Tulsa. Some venues were too small to try it, but he did not stick fast, and when possible, he led the band on the sidewalk in the vicinity of the club or theater where they were playing. It was a good way of getting free publicity. They even had a special permit from the police to enable them to play on the sidewalk around the 421 Club in West Philly.

It was an exciting time, and everyone was caught up in it. Although this was before the official start of rock 'n' roll, it was clear something new was happening, and Bostic was one of those at the forefront. After all, he had been rocking since 1948. Renowned columnist Bill Soberanes was impressed and surprised by a typical Bostic night out at the Primalon Ballroom in San Francisco's Fillmore district. He wrote: "We witnessed a night of dancing by people who just let themselves go to the mood of the music. We had never seen anyone dance quite like this before in a section of San Francisco which has a distinct, different, and colorful flavor."[13] The early 1950s were sometimes considered staid, but that was far from the truth on the streets and in the dance halls, not to mention the juke joints and roadside diners. Dave Dexter recalled: "I was a producer at Capitol Records then, and I'd walk across the street to Music City and all these little kids from Hollywood High were already dancing to Bull Moose Jackson and Earl Bostic. I suppose those records were classified as rhythm & blues then, but they sure sounded like rock."[14] The lines were blurring between genres of music, so that one of Bostic's labelmates, a so-called hillbilly artist like Moon Mullican, incorporated as much from jazz pioneers such as stride pianist James P. Johnson as he did from the country tradition. Jerry Lee Lewis in turn took his cue from Mullican. There was a new feeling abroad that nothing was as cut-and-dried as it had been. The old certainties and demarcations between types of music no longer seemed to matter so much. Journalist Pete Hamill was a teenager at the time and summed up the feeling of his generation: "So when I drove slowly through traffic in Biloxi,

18. A Thousand Saturday Nights

Miss.... I remembered being in a black nightclub there in '54, watching a great R&B band led by an alto sax man, Earl Bostic, and how I realized that night that jazz and the slow blues belonged to us all, black and white, Northerners and Southerners; it didn't come from academies but was bred in the heat and smoke and passions of a thousand Saturday nights."[15]

19

The Nation's Favorite College Band

> *"Popular music always will be our greatest seller, but modern swing, modern jazz and commercial bop are gaining in popularity by leaps and bounds. The ages from 16 to 30 are my best fans."*[1]
>
> —Earl Bostic

As an ex-university man, Bostic had a natural affinity with students and was one of the earliest black artists to play on the college circuit. His band was always a great draw, so much so that at one time it was dubbed "the Nation's Favorite College Band." His shows were equally popular with men and women on army posts up and down the country, as they frequently missed out when many of the name bands were touring on the regular circuits. Although his itinerary was full already, Bostic even gave up time to help with fundraising for schools and hospitals. His branching out in this way paved the way for others and further helped to break down barriers.

Servicemen and women stationed on army posts, air bases, and other military installations across the country were often disappointed to miss out when popular bands were touring on the regular circuits in their area. The established circuits tended to see artists travel between theaters, community halls, and clubs, often revisiting some venues several times. However, it was not always possible or feasible for service personnel to get leave to travel, in some cases long distances, to the town where the act was appearing. While playing a one-night stand at the Church Street auditorium in Orlando, Florida, in 1949, Bostic received a note from the commanding officer of the local GI Air Base to the effect that the men had never received a visit from any bands playing in the area in the last six months. Ever ready to help, Bostic and his band entertained the men royally in a two-hour show prior to their scheduled gig in town that night.

19. The Nation's Favorite College Band

It was a similar story in his home state of Oklahoma, and in 1950 they played no less than three times for the infantrymen of Fort Sill within a matter of months because the demand was so great, and still they wanted more.[2] From then on, dates in camps and military installations became a more regular feature of tours. Whenever an opportunity arose to play shows for servicemen and veterans when they visited a particular city, they tried to oblige. For instance, during a residency at the W.C. Handy Theatre in Memphis in July 1950 along with his company the Harlem Revue, Bostic transferred the whole show to entertain the patients of the Kennedy Veterans Hospital.[3] At times some of his shows were free to all enlisted men—for example, his gig at Carson's Mountaineer Theater in Colorado, which was near Camp Carson.

In the fall of 1948 Bostic broke more new ground when he was invited to play college campuses in a tour that took in the University of Illinois and in Ann Arbor, the University of Michigan. The following year he embarked on an even more ambitious tour of twenty colleges and seats of learning. In April 1950, he toured yet others, including Howard University, South Carolina State College, the Tuskegee Institute, and Tennessee State College over a two-week period.[4] Hitherto, although white bands had long since played the circuit, their colored counterparts were not considered, but Bostic struck out on his own. His orchestra had a definite appeal to all races, and in that way did much to change perceptions. On account of his status, the bookings attracted widespread attention, and other agencies took a keen interest in watching how the band was received. The tours went well and showed the way in which things were beginning to change for the better. Of course, the booking agents saw it from the mercenary angle, in terms of the potential for revenue, but Bostic was thinking of the wider benefit and the chance to open things up. The scheduled itinerary of dates across northern California later that year (1950) included Vallejo Junior College, Monterey Peninsula College, and Fresno State University. In October 1951 they were invited to play the formal dance for the Alpha Phi Alpha society held at Claflin University in Orangeburg, South Carolina.[5]

Remembering his own beginnings, Bostic was always willing and eager to help school and army bands. For instance, he helped the American Legion and the Civic League in Tallahassee, Florida. Students and the faculty at the Lincoln High School in Detroit had decided to organize a concert to raise funds to buy new uniforms for the school band. The sum mentioned was $2500. Slighting remarks about the frowsy appearance of the band prompted the principal, Prof. E.A. Kershaw, to do something about smartening them up and thus improve morale. The Bostic band gave a concert in the gym. Bostic was a big name by then and much in demand, but he always had time for people. As soon as he heard about it, he was quick to offer his support. He recalled, "I once played with my high school band in Tulsa and I know what a morale builder uniforms were for us. This is what I call a practical way to help these youngsters and I'm glad to lend a small hand."[6] He was a big favorite with the students of his own Alma Mater at Xavier, and "Tut Strut" was a top seller on campus there.

Bostic signed deals for several smaller tours with specific aims in mind. In the spring and summer of 1954, he signed with Van Tonkins, a promoter of one-nighters, for a joint tour with R&B singer Christine Kittrell. This was a specific deal that took in colleges and army camps at which the sites were provided free by the venues, which also dealt with ticket sales. In return, the hosts received 20 percent of the take, and Bostic 50 percent with a guarantee of $500, out of which he paid Kittrell, and Tonkins took the remaining 30 percent. The Fort Ord Soldiers Club seated around 4000 and charged $1 for tickets. Student shows cost $1.25, with the public admitted for $1.50.[7] Van Tonkins previously promoted the big dance bands, but after a poor run of returns for a Dorsey Brothers show in Fresno, he became convinced that R&B acts were where the money was, and decided to invest in them instead. Several years before, Tonkins had been assessed a massive fine by the musician's union of $20,000 for underpayment and exploitative treatment of his group The Teenagers.

Bostic's date at the Chico State College in April 1954 was a tremendous success, and typical of their campus shows. At the hour-long concert, the 500 students in the auditorium responded with great enthusiasm and had a lot of fun. By now, he had his stage show down to a tee, and knew exactly what he was doing. As one witness, Phil Guthrie, commented, "Bostic had the youthful crowd under control from the beginning." The familiar strains of "Flamingo" opened proceedings as usual and set the tone for the show, which received a more spirited response than many of those present could recall. Among the other songs, they played the old favorites "Cherokee" and "Avalon," with the latter featuring an imaginative obligato solo by trumpeter "Blue" Mitchell. Part way through the set, Bostic put his saxophone to one side to play the guitar, showing his skill on that instrument and somewhat surprising the audience. As he often did, he introduced the band members, which then included Stanley Turrentine, and they traded licks, to the delight of all present. They ended with a rousing rendition of "Let's Ball Tonight," which went down a storm. Guthrie concluded: "The crowd loved it. Applause at times drowned out the final chorus, and the enthusiasm was so great that a few of the college pre–Pioneer Day celebrants tossed their ten-gallon hats around the auditorium."[8]

By the late 1950s and early 1960s, the college circuit was well established as a thriving concern, and a great many more artists regularly played on campus. Bostic was often invited to play special benefit shows and dances by fraternities and college clubs, for instance, the Winter Germans Concert at Chapel Hill, North Carolina, and the Fullbacker's Club of Dillard University in Louisiana.[9] In May 1955 they played the universities of Oregon, Portland, and Seattle.[10] He played a joint date with Bill Doggett at the Arizona State College in Flagstaff (January 10, 1959).[11] Bostic provided the music for the grand Monarch Costume Ball at the University of Florida in Gainesville (March 14, 1959) with its medieval theme.[12] It was the highlight of the Kappa Sig's Star Crescent weekend. He was also chosen to play the formal dance during Greek Week at the University of South Carolina, which took place at the Columbia Township Auditorium in February 1961. While he played the Friday-night dance, another current favorite, Dave Brubeck, played in the same vicinity the night before. Brubeck and Bostic had played together on the same bill several times, including at the University of Kentucky Coliseum just a year earlier.[13]

The Clemson University in South Carolina had already played host to several big names, including Tommy Dorsey and Clyde McPhatter and the Drifters. Nonetheless, when Bostic visited, he made a vivid impression. Audiences were enraptured when he played a long Valentine weekend of dances to different audiences in February 1961, at which time it was said that his "mellow saxophone ... sent the dancers into a land of phantasy." One of the happy auditors set the scene: "Earl hit his peak at the 'come-as-you-are' Saturday afternoon concert in the Field House. The gym was filled by the troops donning their 'go-to-hell' hats, supported by tennis shoes, and accompanied by their dates in their form-fit toreadors and sweaters. The students had the spirit and Bostic had the sound."[14] At the Winston-Salem Teacher's College, North Carolina, in 1962, students had tremendous fun dancing to the music of Bostic at the Victory dance for the football team homecoming. Playing the music for the football team was something which he had done many years before, during his own salad days.[15]

20

A Gentleman of Dignity

> *"[Earl Bostic] has always been one of their favorites for his distinctive styles of music and for public deportment as a gentleman of dignity. He is a great credit to his race and to the musical profession all over the world."*[1]
> —Edith McCormick, President of the International Fan Club of America

As good as he was on record, Bostic was something else live. That was the verdict of all who ever saw the band at their best in a live setting. He ventured more on the public stage than he did on disc, and it was often the case that his men got more chance for their own solo spots, because they were not limited by time or other constraints. The mid-1950s found Bostic at the top of his game, riding high in the charts, and among his other laurels he was voted the top R&B artist in the *Down Beat* poll. Fully booked up for the whole of 1955, and most of 1956, he continued to work at a terrific rate, but in June 1956 the pace took its toll, when he was felled by a heart attack.

Fellow alto sax man Lou Donaldson marveled at what Earl could do on sax, and once challenged him as to why he never put any of that down on record. Earl revealed that he did not want anyone to copy him. He also advised Donaldson what reed to use, and said that he used a Meyer #6 mouthpiece with a #2½ reed.

Latin American rhythms were suddenly all the rage in the mid-1950s, and like many musicians of the age, Earl got caught up in the trend. He recorded some mambo-inspired records aided by several accomplished Latin sidemen. "Mambolino" and "Mambostic" stood out among these, incorporating the Bostic sound with embellishments. He brought out several long players in which the bossa nova and cha-cha-cha featured prominently. Although successful, there was sometimes a sense that the rhythms were superimposed to an extent and did not always arise naturally from the songs themselves. It was something of a craze, and once the vogue ended, those records tended to date quickly. Undaunted, Earl further announced that he was aiming to try out a mambo version of "Say, Hey," the hit inspired by baseball star Willie Mays. In the event, it was not recorded.

He had several high spots during his tours, which took him to an array of places with a host of different audiences and expectations. For instance, some were straight-ahead jazz venues such as the Blue Note in Chicago. While he might once have been welcome there, since his experimentation and move toward R&B, it was perhaps more surprising to see him not only invited back but lauded on repeated returns. He appeared there regularly, and in 1955 his "No Name Jive" got across in a big way. The Black Hawk in San Francisco was another place where he was always warmly received, and he played there for well over a decade. Others were

Bostic Blows, King 7" EP (1956).

restaurants or cocktail lounges, where the music was just the background to a convivial evening. No matter the nature of the venue or the audience, his band was always great value, and no one would ever die wondering.

His tour of the South in 1955 was widely lauded as one of his most successful to date. This included several firsts, notably his debut at the Celtic Room in Nashville, Tennessee, as previously outlined. He broke new ground in other directions, for example, by venturing into uncharted territory when his tour reached Ogden, Utah, after three years of attempting to get a chance. A major innovation was his two-week stand at the Club 1042 in Anchorage, Alaska, in May 1955. It was about as far north as it was possible to go. The night club owners were keen to encourage new bands to visit and paid the round-trip air charter for the whole orchestra.

Earl's ambitions at one time strayed once more to a possible Broadway show. It was reported that Victor Vito, beautician and hairdresser to the stars, had come up with an idea for a Broadway musical, *High Sweep*, for which Bostic was lined up to write the incidental music, but it would seem the production never materialized.[2]

Among Bostic's hobbies and outside interests, he was a keen collector of coins, which were said to be his first love. He owned several thousand rare U.S. coins, beginning with a five-cent piece dating from 1793, up until the latest issues of 1955. His collection also contained many uncirculated items. He started collecting in the 1940s and took time to study the subject diligently so that he knew all about the coins he had in his collection, to such an extent that he became one of the leading authorities on the subject.[3] As he once commented, it began as a hobby "but now it has developed to the state where it is a serious business." He estimated he had amassed around 5000 coins worth about $40,000. It was reported that he once offered $6000 for an ultra-rare 1913 Liberty "V" nickel, of which only six were ever minted.[4] One of the few times he reportedly lost his temper was when sports journalist Sam Lacy doubted the veracity of his story about the Liberty Head coin. More than anything, it seemed to be the insinuation of Lacy that Bostic could not possibly know about such things, but he patently did, and was vouched for by acknowledged experts. Earl once averred: "I can spot a genuine coin in a single glance, and come pretty close to telling you its value within a few cents."[5] His drummer Earl Palmer got interested and took up the hobby, largely thanks to him. Bostic eventually sold a fair proportion of his extensive collection at auction in a famous sale conducted by Stack's of New York, which took place at the Carl Fischer Concert Hall in December 1956, and for which an extensive catalog was issued. The auction catalog itself is now a sought-after collector's item in numismatic (coin-collecting) circles. As one of the most active and famous coin collectors, he was approached by a national magazine to write about his collection and interviewed several times.

Alongside coins, Earl collected stamps, and again had several valuable specimens. It was reported that he once had a rare stamp collection, valued at $4,500, pilfered from his hotel room, for which he offered a $250 reward.[6] His stamp collections must have been substantial, because his deal to buy a motel complex was financed through the sale of one collection to a collector in San Francisco. Photography was another hobby he pursued. One of his most expensive interests was automobiles, and his collection kept on growing. They were his pride and joy. By the later 1950s he had turned his attention to the Chrysler range, and among other models he had an Imperial, a Windsor, and a Town & Country. Practically all the high-end manufacturers were represented, and he picked many up on his travels; for instance, he once bought a Plymouth station wagon during a passing visit to Philadelphia.[7]

Earl was 5'11" and weighed 178 pounds, and was once described by Marion Brown as a "very well-hewn man."[8] According to one interview, he tried to keep active and was said to enjoy cycling and swimming. He loved good food, and his years in New Orleans had led to a lifelong love of Louisianan and Cajun cuisine. He sometimes felt the need to lose weight, although an all-citrus diet he undertook while staying in Orlando backfired when he gained twenty pounds in eight days.[9] He was a light smoker, as were most people in that era, but he was apparently not a big drinker and was usually described as sober. This seemed to go back to his early years on the riverboats with Fate Marabel, for whom alcohol was a complete no-no. With his round, horn-rimmed glasses, the distinctive pencil moustache, and ready smile, he was one of the most recognizable figures in popular music. Success did not change him. As one who knew him well remarked, "Earl is still the swell guy that he started out to be—never too busy to be considerate to all."[10] He took pains with his appearance and was always a natty dresser, with a penchant for flamboyant ties. He gave generously to a variety of charities, and his ultimate hobby was listed as helping other musicians.

Independent and self-contained by nature, he preferred to do as much as possible himself. This probably went back to his childhood. From an early age he got used to being self-reliant and self-motivated. Hence, he was not only the bandleader, soloist, composer, multi-instrumentalist, and chief arranger, but chauffeur, business manager, one-man PR team, and did anything else that needed doing. Not someone who could delegate easily, his overriding need to do everything perhaps sometimes left other band members feeling frustrated. Blessed with an equable temperament, he was patient, tolerant, and seldom riled. There were only a few instances of him losing his cool—for instance, if anyone dared to interrupt him or take the limelight away from him during his solos, which were sacrosanct, or if anyone ever doubted his word. He tended to call everyone "pardno," his jokey way of saying partner.

Bostic was savvy where money was concerned. Alongside his investments in property, he often played the stock market, which earned him some lucrative returns. At one time, he made a lot from some AT&T shares. He usually reinvested in other ventures, especially his coin collection. On occasion he would help out band members with short-term loans, but he was not a soft touch and insisted on being repaid. Enthusiastic by nature, he was interested in people. His varied career and wide experience contributed to an engaging personality, and he was often described as a good conversationalist.

He was sometimes invited to advertise products, either related to the saxophone or for popular beverages, and was particularly associated with

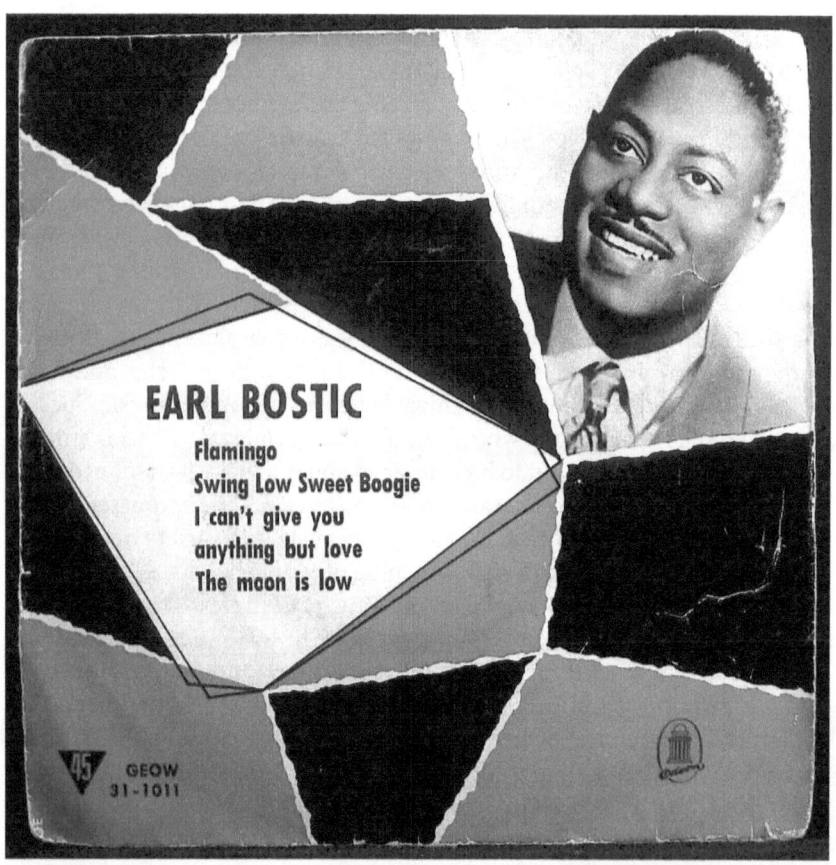

A seven-inch EP issued on the Odeon label in Germany (1955).

Royal Crown Cola. As a leading personality at the height of his fame, he was recruited to front nationwide campaigns, the most notable being the National Safety Council's crusade to persuade teenagers to drive carefully. It was a cause he understood all too well, as he said, from "when you've been as close to death as I was after that accident." Moreover, he felt that he was able to influence the young. He concluded his remarks by saying: "Whenever a performer plays before a house or dance hall packed with teenagers, he should close his performance with a word of caution about safety-first while driving away from the affair. Just a little appeal like that could help save a human life."[11]

Earl was as ever busy in the studio and his records were doing good business, gaining him many admirers and an ever wider following in places where he never visited. One of the best LPs of the year was his fourth, *Dance Time*, which arguably showcased him at his versatile best. There were plenty of the swinging hits to the fore, including "Where or When" and "Harlem Nocturne," along with the standards such as "Sweet Lorraine" and "The Sheik of Araby," the latter an old favorite stretching back to his days with "Hot Lips" Page. A more unusual but engaging choice was the poignant classic "Roses of Picardy." Several reviewers were mesmerized by his dazzling skill and eclecticism. His poise, finesse, imagination, and assurance made this one of his most satisfying long-playing records. It clearly showed that he could never be neatly pigeonholed, and this was his strength because it meant his sound appealed right across the spectrum. *Billboard* concluded: "Actually, this one is hard to categorize, and there should be sales to r & b, jazz and pop customers, not to mention teen-age rock and rollers."[12]

Meanwhile, the everlasting tour was going like a train. Highlights in 1956 included a big charity concert in aid of the Doll League at the Zenda Ballroom in Los Angeles in April. Described as a star-studded event for the good cause, the show also included the renowned interpretative dancer Archie Savage, who created a buzz with his artistic interpretations of the Bostic sound.[13] The demand for Earl's services was greater than ever, and the orchestra members were making money hand over fist. He was partway through a long tour all along the Pacific coast that sometimes brought in $50,000 over the course of a single week, and had just struck a deal to extend his bookings further. Unfortunately, the pace became too much for him to sustain, and in June 1956 he collapsed on stage while leading his band at the Fort Ord Soldiers Club in Monterey County, California. He was swiftly admitted to the Good Samaritan Hospital in Portland, Oregon.[14] Initially, nervous exhaustion from overwork was cited as the cause of his collapse, but it soon became apparent that he was far more seriously run down. The band were due to play in Fresno the following night, but that and the remaining twelve gigs were canceled.

Dance Time (King, 1957).

For the rest of June and most of the remaining summer of 1956, Bostic was said to be hospitalized with pneumonia and all bulletins stressed that he needed a good long rest. Despite their severity, his problems were perhaps underplayed in the press, and possibly shrugged off by himself. Rumors that he had suffered a heart attack were initially laughed off, but he later admitted that it was true.

All the doctors advised him to take it easy and not take on any new work for at least three months. Such news was anathema to the restless Bostic. Nevertheless, he seemed to take the medical advice seriously, and apart from a ban on touring, he also kept out of the studio for a while. Thinking of his health, it was at that point that he decided to forego life on the East Coast in favor of the West. The idea was that being away from New York would mean he could enjoy a less hectic life, and that the Californian climate would be a boon to his health. By September, three months after his heart attack, he had lost twenty-five pounds, and it was widely reported that he had laid aside the saxophone almost completely, as per doctor's orders.

Even before his attack, Bostic had started to invest in property in Los Angeles. In 1954 he bought a housing development worth an estimated $75,000 and a twelve-unit apartment house. By November 1956, the Bostics sold their Long Island home where they had lived for the past eight years. They moved out to sunny California, where Earl and Hildegarde settled in a home worth about $50,000 in the exclusive Baldwin Hills locale. The area was sometimes known as the black Beverly Hills, and attracted many other famous entertainers, including Ray Charles and Nancy Wilson. Earl made several further investments in the city, notably a forty-unit court in an upmarket part of town.[15] No matter how far up the social scale one went, some things never change, and the reaction of some of his new tenants on finding out that their landlord was an African American was to immediately move out.

After his health scare, it was reported that he might switch careers and move into personnel management instead, but there was never any serious suggestion that he would leave music. As if to convince him, in November 1956, he was voted the winner of the best alto saxophonist of the year in the annual *Pittsburgh Courier* poll, almost a decade after he had first won the award.

21

Moving Spirit of the Alto Sax

"I'm telling you; Earl Bostic was the greatest saxophone player I ever knew ... the man could play three octaves. I mean play 'em, I don't just mean hit the notes."[1]
—Lou Donaldson

Bostic was highly influential on his time, as he was to upcoming generations. By the mid-1950s he had his imitators both in the United States and especially in Europe, where "Flamingo" had caused such a sensation. The saxophone was suddenly front and center in some of the biggest bands of the era, as jazz, rock 'n' roll, and rhythm and blues coalesced to produce a new kind of popular music that informed the decades that followed.

One of the most significant hits of 1955 was "Rock Around the Clock" by Bill Haley and the Comets. Haley freely admitted that the band modeled themselves on the approach of Bostic and other rhythm and blues bands. Their brand of rock 'n' roll took a great deal from the different strands of their influences, from country music to R&B. The tenor sax of Rudy Pompilli was a crucial part of their sound, and although he did not play on the original hit, he was prominent in a reworked version. The song made a memorable impression as the introductory music for the era-defining movie *The Blackboard Jungle* (1955). Pompilli began his career working in jazz bands, and was surely one of the most influential players in rock history. He was arguably heard to best effect on "Rudy's Rock," which became his signature tune. Bostic had always kept the jazz instrumental alive throughout the whole period almost singlehandedly, and once others took him up on the idea that the sax should be in the spotlight, it gained a following like never before. In April 1952 the first official record released by Sam Phillips's iconic Sun Records was by a teenage saxophonist, Johnny London, in whose sound the abiding influence of Bostic was clearly discernible. His direct influence on some of the artists of the age can be heard in the tenor playing of Lee Allen, especially on his acclaimed *Walkin' with Mr. Lee* (1958). The same is true of Red Prysock, "Tiny" Bradshaw, Sil Austin, Arthur Blythe, James Moody, and Sam "The Man" Taylor, to name just a few. It is notable that Bostic's influence stretched across the new genres. Prysock, for instance, is considered a rocker, and as a direct tribute to Bostic, he recorded "That's the Groovy Thing," which appeared on his *Rock 'n' Roll* (1955), arguably his finest LP, released on the Mercury label. Bostic also arranged for tenor man "Tiny" Bradshaw (1907–1958), who was often thought of as an R&B artist but whose appeal, like that of Bostic, crossed boundaries.

The tenor sax was essential to burgeoning areas of new sounds, for instance in the great R&B doo-wop hit "Why Do Fools Fall in Love?"

The appealing cover art of the highly collectible 10" LP *Bostic Meets Doggett* (Parlophone, 1957), on which Earl played with organist Bill Doggett, a similarly pivotal figure in R&B.

(1956) by Frankie Lymon and the Teenagers, with its memorable sax solo by tenor Jimmy Wright. Although not part of the group per se, Wright was an influential and well-known musician in his own right who had his own orchestra going back to the 1940s. Among the later artists, the soulful style of King Curtis perhaps drew most frequent comparisons to that of Bostic. Plas Johnson, famous for his timeless version of the "Pink Panther" theme, had first been inspired to take up the saxophone by Bostic's innovative style. He observed, "I love the way Earl Bostic did this real raucous growl through a melody."[2] Such devoted jazzmen as Cannonball Adderley and Sonny Rollins also acknowledged a debt to Bostic and those who went before. Perhaps surprisingly, he even informed the work of such avant garde figures as Sun Ra and his Arkestra, through the individual playing style of alto saxophonist Marshall Allen.

Bostic's name was often linked with that of organist Bill Doggett, a similarly pivotal figure in the history of popular music. They had much in common. Both came from a jazz background and were two of the greatest progenitors of rhythm and blues. Doggett began as pianist and arranger for the Ink Spots. He had stints with Louis Jordan's Tympany Five, then switched to the Hammond organ, inspired by "Wild" Bill Davis. The addition of a saxophone to the basic trio made all the difference, and Doggett found his signature style for dance audiences. He and Bostic were keen to work together on something special, but the meeting took a long time to set up, principally because they were each booked solid with touring schedules. It took two years to arrange, but eventually they managed to be in the same place at the same time in April 1956. The results of their recording session appeared initially in single format as "Bo Do Rock" and "Mean to Me." There was also issued a 7" EP and a 10" LP with an attractive light-hearted cover design featuring cartoon versions of Bostic and Doggett shaking hands: an evocative artifact of its time. The record was split evenly between the two, with them playing together on some songs and individually to the fore on others. It was long feted in R&B circles as the meeting of two of the greatest talents of the genre at their zeniths, and was immediately lauded by fans and music lovers alike.[3] An instant classic then, and one of the greatest of collector's items since in any format. The 10" LP is especially sought after.

Bostic was popular and influential internationally. As such, he had several imitators. In Europe, two of the most notable were Geoff Taylor from England and Earl Cadillac of France. Taylor (1929–2009), who was originally from Ilford but who settled in Manchester, first came to prominence when he was spotted by Steve Race and was voted one of the *Melody Maker* new stars of 1952. He was soon christened the English Bostic. As Taylor commented, Bostic's sound was exciting and stood out: "It definitely had something, plenty of drive and all that." Taylor insisted he was not trying to mimic his hero, but to give his interpretation of the music.[4] The national and local jazz scene was strong in Europe in the 1950s and 1960s, and there was a lot of interest in the old time American jazzmen, particularly those pioneers from New Orleans that gave rise to the Trad Jazz boom that was especially popular, not to say cherished, in England. However, the scene was clearly demarcated, and not only between traditional and contemporary jazz. As ever, there appeared to be a fair degree of snobbery at play. The jazz critics were often at their most pedantic and fastidious in England, and were more damning of any mavericks or new stylists than their American counterparts. This division where Bostic was concerned was vividly demonstrated by the reaction to Taylor's set in Manchester, when half the audience walked out as soon as he started playing. Jazz afficionados and armchair critics alike were never going to accept him into the fold, or anyone else who emulated him. After his first successes, Taylor was initially prompted to turn professional, but found the going difficult and decided to remain an amateur. He restyled his sound and his later music veered far more toward swing, leaving the driving Bostic influences to one side.

Earl Cadillac was the nom de plume of Hubert Rostaing (1918–1990), a clarinetist, tenor saxophonist, and former member of Django Reinhardt's Quintet. Rostaing recorded or was the orchestra leader for several films including *The Tenant* (1976). As a saxophonist he released several records under his Earl Cadillac alias in the 1950s directly inspired by the Bostic approach, delivered with a soupçon of French élan. His romantic style was heard to excellent effect on such numbers as "Andalusia," "Paris Canaille," "Zon, Zon, Zon," "Il Suffit d'une Mélodie," and Glenn Miller's "Adios" among others.

It was not only the younger generations who began to imitate his style. Even some of his contemporaries and seniors in the business did the same. One of the most notable was the veteran Jimmy Dorsey, who made a striking recording of the old 1930s song "So Rare" that sounded for all the world like a Bostic record, or at the least one arranged by him. They say imitation is the sincerest form of flattery, and hearing this rendition for the first time must have made many double check the artist's name on the label. It was a testament to how far he had come that he was now influencing those who had been around for a good deal longer than him. Dorsey recorded the song in November 1956, and it was his first session in four years without any input from his brother Tommy. Among the songs that day, "So Rare" caused the most problems, because Dorsey was unhappy with the arrangement as written by Howard Gibeling, and appealed for help from Neal Hefti. Between them they came up with something directly inspired by Bill Doggett's monster R&B smash of that moment, "Honky Tonk," allied to the sound of Bostic. The finished record was released in January 1957 and gave Dorsey one of his biggest ever hits, reaching number two on the *Billboard* charts, the highest ranking for a Big Band record in ten years. It sold half a million copies and earned Dorsey a gold record. Sadly, it came rather late for him because he was already ailing and died just a few months later, aged fifty-three, a matter of seven months after his brother Tommy. It is a great recording which sums up a whole era in flux. The arrangement seems pure Bostic, and said as much as anything that the Big Band era was embracing rock 'n' roll if not R&B. It may have been a case of "If you can't beat 'em, join 'em," but however it came about, it was an outstanding record. It has a bold sense of drama that is missing from some of the numbers by the big bands of the later period, and what Dorsey's biographer calls "the eloquent, yearning zest in Dorsey's saxophone."[5] This version stands as a lasting testimony to Dorsey's artistry and a tribute to Bostic's abiding influence.

Bostic was not just in demand in the United States and Canada, but had several lucrative offers for world tours. Unfortunately, for whatever reason, they never came to pass. In 1957 it was reported that he turned down a possible twenty-date tour of South America worth $50,000.[6] At that point he was still recovering from his heart attack and was reluctant to extend his travels too far. He made it known that he also desired to spend a restful time over the Christmas season with his wife and family. He returned to visit his mother in Tulsa whenever he could, and also caught up with his other cousins spread across the country. He always got along well with his in-laws, especially his father-in-law, a highly personable soul. Earl expressly said that he did not wish to fly long distances in light of his health. As far as possible, he tried to arrange it so he had his annual vacation around the Christmas and New Year period. Later, he received an offer of $60,000 from the government of Sweden for an extensive tour of Scandinavian countries. He declared himself open to the whole idea in principle: "I'm ready to go anywhere—America, Sweden, Italy or France—just so long as they'll put up the right kind of dough."[7] He often said he wanted to take an extended vacation in Europe, hopeful of adding to his coin collection, but again he abandoned the idea. He remained popular across Europe, especially in Germany, and as far afield as Japan. There was the example of the Japanese jazzman Sadao Watanabe (b. 1931), who played the alto sax and often recorded bossa nova numbers. He highlighted Bostic as one of his earliest key influences.

Among other comparable saxophonists of the era was Tab Smith (1909–1971), who had a number one hit with Tony Bennett's "Because of You" and recorded great versions of "You Belong to Me" and "Pretend." His

21. Moving Spirit of the Alto Sax

sound was a slightly more mellow variation on the Bostic approach, and he was widely regarded as one of Bostic's chief rivals. He recorded mostly for United Records, although unfortunately after the label closed in 1960, he practically retired from the music business. His formative influence was the great Johnny Hodges. Smith had, like Bostic, served his apprenticeship with Fate Marable on the riverboats just a short while earlier than Bostic. Clarinetist and tenor sax man Jack McVea (1914–2000) wrote the riff of the famous hit "Open the Door, Richard." Earlier in his career he played baritone sax for Lionel Hampton. Remembered as the leader of the resident house band for Black & White Records, McVea sometimes took a leaf out of the Bostic play book—witness his honking rendition of the old favorite "Oh, How I Miss You Tonight."

Despite Bostic's widespread popularity, or perhaps because of it, few jazz critics had anything good to say about him. His commercial success was a major stumbling block to any kind of even grudging appreciation among the arbiters of taste. In their view jazz was art, if not religion, and he sold out. Those who did champion Bostic in the purely jazz fold were sometimes themselves seen as eccentric, if not beyond the pale. The French critic Hugues Panassié, for instance, once wrote that "Earl Bostic is, to my mind, one of the greatest saxophonists jazz has ever known."[8] Panassié (1912–1974) was a charismatic but sometimes controversial personality who remained true to the New Orleans school, but who has been seen by some as a divisive figure. Nonetheless, despite his perceived faults, he had the overriding virtue of an independent mind. He was not so swayed by the prevailing orthodoxy of jazz criticism that lauded the bebop artists as demigods and treated the popularists like lepers. Moreover, he was a prolific author as well as a record producer, and highly influential.

Among the banks of critics who tended to pore over records like connoisseurs of vintage wine, the British were sometimes predictably snooty where Bostic was concerned. Such publications as *Jazz Monthly* viewed him with studied disdain. Even in the popular music press, Bostic was sometimes a contentious figure. He was clearly the bête noire of Humphrey Lyttelton, then the resident jazz reviewer for the newly founded *NME (New Musical Express)*. Lyttleton lambasted Bostic as one of the "transient freaks" of popular entertainment, and accused him of gimmickry, along with every other musical sin under the sun. Worse, he vilified his followers as morons. Derision from a respected figure in trad jazz circles carried more weight than it might from a less high-profile personality, and he was in a prime position to influence young people. Nevertheless, his comments sparked a heated debate and many readers took him to task for his intolerance. No doubt the controversy he stirred up boosted circulation. Not everyone was wholly derogatory about Bostic. A rival publication, the much older *Melody Maker*, was far more open minded. Long known as the musicians' bible, the magazine had a strong reputation for covering jazz. It once featured an interesting measured appraisal of Bostic in its *Family Favorites* series by the great Jack Hutton, a jazz trumpeter who later became a dynamic editor during the heady days of the 1960s.

Gerald Lascelles, writing in society magazine *The Tatler*, provided an appreciation of the way that Bostic had found a route to success. He observed that he kept things to essentials and that was the key to his popularity. Lascelles, a younger son of the Earl of Harewood and a cousin to Queen Elizabeth II, was, seemingly like every other educated Englishman in the 1950s, an expert on jazz. He noted: "Less than two years ago Bostic's work would have been classified as rock 'n' roll. It has that accentuated beat which the undiscerning would dismiss as tasteless; but though the music does not overflow with taste, it has those essential ingredients that make for enjoyable jazz, while still retaining that simplicity which apparently spells commercial success."[9] Elsewhere, Lascelles conceded that although Bostic was dismissed by the literati as an exhibitionist, he admitted that despite this "I rejoice in the fact that he gets up and blows without repression."[10]

The key thing was that with his music, Bostic sailed over the heads of the critics and doubters and reached the people who mattered: the record-buying public and the ordinary people. As Rudolph Nureyev once remarked, "The only critic is a full house."[11] Earl's dances were sold out wherever he played. Moreover, he was popular in those places where he was only ever heard on records. Many a romance was nurtured by the Bostic sound. Mrs. Lenanton of Southampton, England, recalled: "When we were courting my husband was really 'gone' on Bostic. On nights that we didn't see each other he would phone me, not to talk but to play Bostic records to me for about an hour! I think if I had not liked those records my husband would not have wanted to marry me."[12]

Two of the foremost critics of the time in Britain were doyens of the literary world, the poet Philip Larkin and the novelist Kingsley Amis. These friends set themselves up as commentators on jazz as an art form and wrote in the national press on the subject. At least they had their own ideas and were less influenced by what others thought. Amis wrote about Bostic in his column in *The Observer* in 1956 and portrayed him in a positive light. Larkin was the more individualistic if not idiosyncratic of critics, which reflected his contrary personality. He made his preference for the older style and dislike of bebop apparent. John Coltrane was one he found difficult to warm to, whereas the critics raved about him. However, Coltrane's old mentor Bostic was a different matter. Bostic harked back to the 1940s and as such reflected much of what Larkin appreciated in jazz.

John Kenyon, a colleague of Larkin's, once recalled an evening he spent with Larkin at the house of a mutual friend, John White:

> Larkin slumped rather tiredly in a corner until John casually put on Earl Bostic's "Flamingo," at which he suddenly levered himself to his feet and began shuffling silently round the room roughly in time to the music, his bulk accentuated by a low ceiling, which caused him to stoop. John and I watched in stupefaction. (I remember thinking he must be drunk, and was afraid he was going to fall on us at any moment; but he wasn't and he didn't.)[13]

Whatever else the critics might say of him, Bostic achieved the seemingly impossible, and managed to get the ungainly and lugubrious Larkin, one of England's finest poets, to dance.

22

The King of King Records

> "He just likes people. And it seems that people like Bostic, too, as he has been acclaimed by newspapermen and disc jockeys all over the nation for his honesty in relation to his work. He is truly a musician's musician."[1]

Bostic recorded more prolifically than any other artist on the King roster, with the possible exception of James Brown. For this, he was dubbed the King of King Records, although workhorse might have been more apt. The sheer number of hours he spent in the studio was staggering, and inevitably led to a falling off in the standard of material. This decline probably inflicted more damage to his latter-day reputation than anything else. Nevertheless, his live show was a different proposition entirely, and he continued to receive plaudits for his exciting work on stage at such hip venues as the Blue Note in Chicago and the Black Hawk in San Francisco. As the alto sax man of choice of *Playboy* magazine in their annual polls, he was invited to be part of a landmark jazz festival held in August 1959 in which he took his rightful place among the greats over the course of a weekend which Leonard Feather called "The Greatest Three Days in Jazz History."

After his health scare, Earl did not retire as first suggested, but his work schedule was lessened considerably in the following year and his live appearances became more sporadic. It was reported early in the new year of 1957 that he had opened his own publishing firm in Hollywood, and intended to take work on a more casual basis for one-nighters in small towns locally along the West Coast. He was always amenable to play at charity balls and benefit nights, particularly those for the Elks and the NAACP.[2] Among those for the Elks, he played in Sacramento in March that year, which drew an excited younger audience. In October for the Brotherhood of Sleeping Car Porters in Los Angeles, he showcased some of his newest material, and the night was described by the dance organizer as "an event to be remembered for a long time."[3] Earl and Hildegarde purchased life membership in the NAACP, and he volunteered his services

22. The King of King Records

for the annual Special Activities Committee dances held in the city. He also sponsored events, and was one of the cosponsors of a meeting at the Shrine Auditorium at which the Rev. William Borders addressed a cheering crowd of some 5000 souls and recalled with pride how 27,000 black citizens had converged on the Lincoln Memorial in Washington, D.C., in the Prayer Pilgrimage for Freedom in May 1957.

At the end of 1957 Bostic was voted overwhelmingly by the International Fan Club of America as the artist people would most like to see come out of retirement. The club president, Edith McCormick, spoke in glowing terms of the qualities of the man and his music. By the time of the poll, he was back once more into the swing of things, with an increasing number of obligations stretching well into 1958. In October 1957 he returned to the Apollo in New York. As a sign that popular music never stood still, he was second on the bill to the in-vogue vocal group the Del-Vikings, although he was ahead of five other acts, including Slim Gaillard. Earl did several such shows with some big contemporary hitmakers, among them The Platters, Jesse Belvin, and Frankie Lymon and The Teenagers.

In the new year of 1958, Bostic surprised many in the business when he terminated his agreement with his agents, Universal Attractions, after ten years with them, and was signed up by Joe Glaser of the Associated Booking Corporation (ABC). This was a long-term contract scheduled to run until 1965 with the option to renew. Over the years many different agents had tried to lure him away from Universal, including one who offered him a house if he signed up with them. All had been rebuffed, so it was unclear what tipped the balance in favor of ABC and what was different or exciting about their offer. Perhaps Glaser was just more persuasive or maybe it all came down to money. At one time a boxing promoter, Glaser was the manager for some of the most famous names in music, among them Louis Armstrong and later Barbra Streisand. It was announced that Earl had several new ventures lined up, including a television appearance on the West Coast, and the tour of South America was discussed again.[4] The pace of his work gathered momentum as the year rolled on and he returned in earnest to the live music scene. He was fully booked up from the spring onward. At the Mocambo in San Francisco in March he received nightly raves and was praised for the most consistent success since his return. To consolidate his advance, he played an impressive two-week engagement at the Blue Note in Chicago that saw his stock rise further. This was followed in quick succession by one-nighters at the Brass Rail in Milwaukee, the Zanzibar in Buffalo, the Surf Club in Baltimore. And so it went on.[5] It was probably around that time that a teenage Frank Zappa was drummer with his high school R&B band the Black Outs, and acted as a warm-up act for Bostic and Louis Armstrong.

Bostic was a hard worker, and may even have been seen by some as a workaholic, although he would likely not have admitted it. He seemed to be one of those who was not happy unless he was busy. Those jazzmen of that era were often like that. They had amazing stamina, and kept up a solid pace throughout the year, hardly seeming to take a day off. He loved what he did and could not look upon it as work. Not that he needed to do it, and especially not at such a rate. Over a period of ten years from 1947 he had sold over five million records. By the mid-1950s, he was making about half a million dollars annually. He could well afford to slow down and coast along for a while. Perhaps there was always the nagging insecurity that many successful people retain. Those who have come from a relatively poor background who get to the top seem sometimes unable to relax. They have a suspicion that it might all end tomorrow unless they keep working as hard as ever. Outwardly, he did not seem to be a worrier, but his later belief that California was about to fall into the sea suggests that perhaps he was not as happy-go-lucky as he appeared. There is no doubt he took a lot on, arguably too much, but also that he thrived on activity. Throughout his life he was busy, whether as a leader and multi-instrumentalist for his own band or as composer, sideman, or arranger for others. He recorded prolifically, and more so as time went on; King Records kept him in the recording studio for days at a time. The long road tours were incredibly popular but must have been exhausting for all concerned. Witness his horrific car accident in 1951, which could easily have been fatal and required operations followed by rehabilitation for months on end. The peripatetic lifestyle was not good for his health, nor were the endless recording sessions. It was hardly the best thing for a man prone to heart problems. Like many, he appeared to play down his health difficulties. Perhaps he also found it hard to say no to people and maybe took on far too much, whether as a favor to friends or because he was accommodating by nature and liked to please. Above all, he gave it everything when he was playing. He did take vacations, more so as the decade progressed, and tried to take six weeks annually. Usually, he and his wife took off around Christmas. Even then he visited places that interested him culturally and musically. Some of them even sounded like busmen's holidays.

From when he started at King Records in 1948, he was kept busy, but far from slowing down after he had been there a while, his workload increased alarmingly in the late 1950s. Not that he was alone in that. Boss Syd Nathan was described as a squat Little Caesar type, always chewing a fat cigar, who apparently knew little about music but had an uncanny knack of making money. Many found him intimidating, but his instinct for discovering talent could not be denied, and the King roster was one of the most varied and impressive for any company, let alone a smaller

22. The King of King Records

First release of *C'mon Dance* with Bostic (King, 1958).

label. One of the label's foremost stars was Moon Mullican, an interesting artist from the country tradition who overlapped with different genres. So-called hillbilly music was issued on the maroon label and R&B on blue. Others were also frequently in the studio, and James Brown was one who recorded almost as often, but Bostic was the mainstay, especially in the 1950s. Bostic was once introduced to Brown, who was being shown around the studios just after he was signed up, and who watched during one of Bostic's sessions. The two were a study in contrasts: Bostic the model professional who fulfilled all obligations to his record label, and Brown constantly in legal battles for violating his contract. There is a lot to be said for the middle ground. Earl's loyalty to the company might also partly be explained by their avowed policy to stand up to any kind of discrimination, and determination to strike a blow against any Jim Crowism. The King staff came from all kinds of backgrounds, and race was immaterial.

In addition, the company oversaw the whole recording process from start to finish in the same place, so any given song could be recorded and released within the week.

As the decade progressed, much of the attention of record companies began to move away from singles and toward long-playing albums. This involved a lot more work for artists, and Bostic's workload increased considerably, particularly when he signed up to deliver a set number of records in a short space of time in 1958. In these years he was not touring so often, and the thinking was that he had more time for studio work. Prior to this he had recorded about four times a year, usually three or four songs a time, roughly a dozen or so in total. After 1957 not only was he employed to record new material, but also to re-record whole albums, in stereo, which were promptly released under the same identifying numbers and titles as the originals. To an extent, all these actions combined to undermine his later reputation. They obfuscated his original and better releases for the sake of quick, ready sales, but this was false economy on the part of the label. The constant demand for product to satisfy the record-buying public led to an inevitable loss of quality. The same could be said for many successful artists. They had to follow up their success with more success, and this led to an inevitable leavening of material. After all, for every "Long Tall Sally" that Little Richard released, he was also induced to record a "Baby Face." Instead of one or two albums in two years there might be seven, but they came at a cost, and by their action King Records arguably did a disservice to their most loyal employee. Bostic was, as ever, willing. Yet at times, a tired feeling pervaded on some of the later records, and it was not surprising.

The situation he encountered in the spring of 1959 is a case in point. He was faced with the prospect of recording ninety-six sides for eight LPs. As such, his time was hardly his own. It was reported that a week before the convention of the Machine Operators of America (MOA) in April in Chicago, Bostic cut eighteen sides in one day, then twelve the day after that. During the week of the convention itself, he did eight more on the Monday, six on Tuesday, and a further six on Wednesday, with eighteen more over the following week. Even then he was not finished, because he was required to return to the studio in Cincinnati to do another twenty-four sides for the remaining two LPs, produced in mono and stereo.[6]

The zenith of the year 1959 for Bostic and his Sextet was their appearance at the landmark *Playboy* Jazz Festival in Chicago, held over the weekend of August 7 to 9, 1959. This was in the wake of his election to the *Playboy* All Star Band in the annual reader's poll for 1959. The three-day festival was the first of its kind, and set a precedent in the long term. The event was dubbed by no less a personage than Leonard Feather as "the

22. The King of King Records

Greatest Three Days in the History of Jazz." Nor did anyone quibble with his assessment. After all, some of the biggest ever names played at the festival. It was an interesting time with many of the old big bands still in their prime, including Duke Ellington, as well as some of the finest interpreters of song of all time, such as Ella Fitzgerald, Bobby Darin, and Nina Simone. With the Miles Davis Sextet, Coleman Hawkins, Sonny Rollins, June Christy, Dave Brubeck, Dizzy Gillespie, and Stan Kenton on the bill, among many others, who could ask for more. The Saturday evening headliner was Count Basie, followed by Joe Williams, Ahmad Jamal, and later the Jack Teagarden All Stars. After all that, Bostic rounded out proceedings with a rousing finish. His setlist included "Cracked Ice," "Flamingo," "Back Beat Boogie," "You Go to My Head," and a special composed for the occasion, "Jazz for the Playboy." Mort Sahl acted as MC, and commented, "This is the best session yet. I know, I've worked all of them from Monterey to Newport."[7] For once, Bostic was where he deserved to be, among the elite entertainers, and he even attracted the attention of the hip jazz critics. Dom Cerulli, writing in *International Music*, observed: "Earl Bostic varied his group's usual rock and roll presentation to offer a set of swinging, often bluesy, tunes."[8] The concert went down in jazz history and was recorded for posterity. It was released to great acclaim the following year as *Playboy's Jazz All Stars* over four long-playing records.[9] The recordings give a rare, tantalizing glimpse into the flavor of his live style and show that he was a true entertainer. His vast experience and complete mastery of the saxophone, allied to his quicksilver musical mind, made him a great draw live, where he was free to explore his imagination. The vibrant "Jazz for the Playboy" sounds spontaneous, and his amazing high notes clearly meet with approval from the crowd, and not a little astonishment. He had the instinctive ability to weigh up his audience. As Stanley Turrentine once remarked of him: "I don't care how many thousands of people he would be playing for, it seemed to me that he'd just look them over from the stage and know exactly what to play."[10] Considering how many live shows Bostic played over his career, it is a great shame that this is one of the few recordings of a gig known to survive. Despite its immediate and resounding success, it would be another twenty years before the festival returned. To underline how hectic his schedule was, the following day he played a gig at Edgewater Park, Celina, Ohio. The tour did not stop there, because they were busy throughout September 1959 with six days at The Castle, Eggert Road, Amersham, and so on into October and November. Thereafter, they were booked solid until Christmas and beyond.

23

Farewell to the Fantastic '50s

As the 1950s came to a close, Bostic could look back, if he was of a mind to, with a sense of accomplishment upon his busiest and most productive years. Not that he had much time to reflect. The fruits of his hard work in the studio were well received in their day, and several of those records deserve reappraisal.

Arguably, one of Earl's best albums of the entire late 1950s period was *Sweet Tunes of the Fantastic 50s* (1959) with its space-age cover. This proved to be one of his most popular. The record was warmly welcomed on release, and several publications featured it as album of the week. Beginning with a masterful, relaxed "Because of You," the album contained some charming evocations of the era, such as his rendition of the Leroy Anderson favorite "Blue Tango." "April in Portugal" was written in 1947 and originally titled "Coimbra" after the city. Derived from Fado, the Portuguese folk music of melancholy and loss, it was recorded by many in the 1950s, notably Les Baxter, and the great Amália Rodrigues, the Queen of Fado. Bostic's jazz-blues arrangement sounded effortless. His upbeat, rather jaunty rendition of the monster hit "Unchained Melody" was a major departure from the slow, almost dirge-like original which made its debut in the Chino prison film *Unchained* (1955). Similarly, his snappy take on "Love Is a Many Splendored Thing" (lasting all of one minute and forty-five seconds) made a striking contrast to the usual slow and sugary romantic approach. George Harris praised Bostic's treatment as "refreshing and uninhibited."[1] The album was at once curiously nostalgic and timeless. After all, he had enjoyed some of his best years in the decade that was then coming to a close. Although King later attempted to cash in on the record's success, the follow-up *Volume 2* could not replicate the same feeling. One of the discarded songs from the session, "Arrivederci Roma," appeared many years later, on *14 Hits* (Gusto Records, 1985). It has some of the same elusive charm of the earlier record.

The Fantastic 50s led to a whole series in which Earl reinterpreted popular songs of a specific era, beginning with the 1920s, then the 1930s and 1940s. Most were recorded with a sextet or septet, and personnel varied

23. Farewell to the Fantastic '50s

Space-age artwork aptly featured on the cover of *Earl Bostic Plays Sweet Tunes of the Fantastic 50s* (1959), one of Bostic's most popular records in that era, which gave rise to a series of LPs dedicated to the hits of different decades.

but included at different times his great fellow alto saxophonist Benny Carter, along with bassist Herb Gordy and Roland Johnson on vibes. With such talent involved, the records have obvious quality and deserve a better reputation. *Sweet Tunes of the Roaring 20s* captured the romantic escapism of that decade. Operettas were the order of the day, often set in a fairy tale Europe, or Broadway musicals, and these were some of the biggest sellers during Prohibition when melody was king. Bostic often mined the light classical repertoire, and made the most of the lush romanticism of its leading lights, for instance, in Franz Lehar's "Frasquita Serenade" and Sigmund Romberg's "Deep in My Heart." Reimagined through the perspective of the 1950s, "Softly as in a Morning Sunrise" becomes a cha-cha-cha. His natural swing brings something hitherto unheralded to

Austrian Robert Katscher's "When Day is Done," and he clearly relishes the satisfying melodic theme of "I Kiss Your Hand, Madame" from the German film of the same name. Each song gains something from the Bostic treatment, and as a contemporary *Billboard* review commented, "All are in a bright, danceable vein."[2]

When it came to *Sweet Tunes of the Swinging 30s*, Earl opted for a big band style arrangement, with the brass section much in evidence. From this decade often considered the golden age of songwriting, several of the best are represented, including Cole Porter and Jerome Kern. Although musicals still predominated, several of the numbers had links to sound films. The album is uniformly good, and among the highlights his attractive reading of "I Cover the Waterfront" makes an ideal opener to set the mood. The song predated the film but was tacked on to it just before release. Earl is at his most expressive here on Ray Henderson and Lew Brown's "The Thrill is Gone," which originated from a 1931 Broadway revue. *Sweet Tunes of the Sentimental 40s* rounded out the miniseries of albums, and although released in 1960 belongs with the others. The cover featured Bostic blowing his sax against the backdrop of the iconic photograph of U.S. troops raising the flag at Iwo Jima in 1945. This was another decade he knew intimately. Again, his approach was arguably most successful on the romantic favorites, expressly so on "Polonaise" and the evergreen classic "La Vie en Rose." Both this and the previous LP have been given little attention, perhaps because of overfamiliarity with the material, but they are quite rare now and worth seeking out.

Several of his other records harked back to his own early years. One example is *Bostic Rocks Hits of the Swing Age*, recorded with a sextet that included Tiny Timbrell on fender bass guitar and Wallace Snow on vibes, along with drummer Earl Palmer, who was with Bostic during most of the period from 1957 to 1959. This lively album included several familiar numbers from his days with Charlie Barnet, including "Pompton Turnpike" and "720 in the Books," on which he excelled. He was still playing fast at this stage—witness his virtuoso "Air Mail Special"—and gave a smoldering interpretation of the Chick Webb–Benny Goodman classic "Stompin' at the Savoy." Another standout was his blistering version of Jimmy Forrest and Duke Ellington's "Night Train." The preoccupation with standards and the whole commercial impulse for his recordings at this stage of his career have in many ways done much to harm his reputation. However, several of these records deserve a higher regard than they have been given. Despite the extra hours spent in the studio, his inherent and accumulated skill of a lifetime, allied to his individualistic approach to the material, not to mention the caliber of his fellow musicians, ensured a level of quality was maintained. Most of Earl's LP releases continued to garner

23. Farewell to the Fantastic '50s

Bostic and His Band Play Sweet Tunes of the Swinging 30s (Parlophone, 1959).

excellent reviews on issue. In reviewing *Bostic Showcase of Swinging Dance Hits*, Albert Anderson wrote how much he admired Bostic's imagination and flexibility, and further remarked, "His musicianship is almost perfect, with delicate phrasing of soulful chords and in some torrid jazz passages when needed."[3]

Earl was incredibly popular across the board in the era: with DJs, fellow musicians, and people in all walks of life. Bill Dupree, an influential DJ at WLIB in New York, was fulsome in his praise of the hard-working Bostic, and put him in the same category of importance as Duke Ellington and the other greats. Even Marilyn Monroe, that icon of the age, was a big fan of Earl's music. She was incredibly clued in to the culture of her time, and once remarked: "Jazz I'm insane about. Louis Armstrong and Earl Bostic—it just gets stronger all the time."[4]

24

"Hello Sixty"

"Music has been a great source of self-satisfaction to me. I enjoy my work wholeheartedly."[1]

—Earl Bostic

For Bostic, the 1960s began on a positive note, as he was voted one of the most popular alto-saxophonists in the *Playboy* poll. It was an accolade he won for several years in a row. Worryingly, his health problems returned, and in July 1960 he suffered his second heart attack. After that he was forced to take things easy for a while, but before long he was playing and touring again, albeit on a smaller scale than previously. He became a doyen of the nightclub and cabaret circuit in a more intimate show. He began to experiment again musically and was moved to record two radically different bona fide jazz records.

January 1960 found Bostic contemplating his next tour. On the 11th of the month his band played for the Rinky Dinks' fundraising party held in the plush ballroom at the Beverly Hilton in Los Angeles. Then it was back on the road again, and he followed with a run of dates in Arizona. His gig at Bob's Place in Tucson had little local publicity and drew a scant audience. Nonetheless, he was still popular with teenagers, and one of his Sunday afternoon sessions at San Bernadino drew a good crowd of eager students from nearby Elsinore High School.[2] For the first half of the year he continued at a pace similar to that of 1959, with several longer residencies in upmarket clubs. He also continued to play the college circuit and in November 1960 appeared at the Dallas Arts Festival.

In the middle of his tour of the East in the week of July 22, Bostic suffered a heart attack while appearing in Norfolk, Virginia, possibly at the Ebb Tide. He was immediately flown by air ambulance to New York. At first the severity of his collapse was played down, and, in the words of booking agent Joe Glaser, Bostic had suffered a "coronary deficiency." Glaser went on to say that the tour would continue as planned, and that the next scheduled date at the Minor Key Club in Detroit, Michigan, the following week would go ahead. It soon became clear that Bostic's problems were far more serious, and at least one of the specialists he consulted in New York said outright that he ought to quit. Consequently, the tour was immediately canceled and Bostic took it easy for a while. Indeed, some accounts stated that he was practically idle for the next three years, but that was not the case. He spent several weeks recuperating at home, and it was reported that he had decided to take a long vacation, possibly to Europe. There were even claims that he was just about retired from the music scene.[3] However, true to form, it was not long before he was back in harness. After his return to touring in August, he did not get a break until Christmas, and resumed in January, with no real vacation until June 1961. There was no doubt that his years of constant traveling and prodigious recording schedule contributed to his parlous state of health. Nonetheless, music was his life and he was unable to stop. He found it equally difficult to do things by halves because it was not in his nature, and he continued to put his heart into his music.

In light of his time away from the big touring circuits across country, his profile was not as high as it had been in the mid-1950s, and it is noticeable that news of his illness was not as prominent in the newspapers. Meanwhile, Hildegarde featured regularly in the gossip and society columns because of her hectic social life and charitable works with the Rinky Dinks. Quite apart from the public dances and fundraisers she organized, her famed Sunday "hen sessions" held at their home with many of her friends became a regular thing in the locale.

Chester L. Lane remembered that Bostic asked him to play with him around that time and said that Earl had been advised by his doctors not to play so much, and to quit touring altogether. Hence, he assembled a slightly bigger band at one stage, a ten- or twelve-piece orchestra, with the idea that they would take on more of the work so that he would not need to blow as much. At first Earl went along with the notion, and told the men to take over for him. After a few days he was back taking all the solos and lining up new dates for tours.[4]

He returned to recording, although it was nowhere near at the same rate as he had in the late 1950s. Nevertheless, in March 1960 he re-signed for a new deal with King Records. There was an increasing emphasis on longer format albums in the market, although singles sales still held sway in the charts. King continued to release a steady stream of his singles, mostly of standards or simply reissues. One of the most appealing was his own composition "Hello Sixty," which owed much to the rock 'n' roll approach. LPs of the period were generally linked together by a theme—for instance, *Earl Bostic Plays the Hit Tunes of the Big Broadway Shows* (1960) and *Bostic Plays Bossa Nova* (1963). Singles were still released on

10" format played at 78 rpm at the beginning of the decade, but increasingly these disappeared and gave way to 7" played at 45 rpm. Seven-inch EPs with attractive cover designs cost slightly more but were also popular. These records added only a little to the Bostic luster, and several might easily be dismissed as easy listening. The same could be said for a great many long-established artists in the early 1960s who tended to rest on their laurels. Nonetheless, his contemplative versions of "If I Loved You" and "Bewitched" displayed an undoubted charm and imagination. His surprising take on "All the Things You Are" drew praise from many quarters and was hailed as "refreshingly new."[5] After his health problems, he seemed to have noticeably slowed his tempo and softened his attack, so much so that his later sound had at times an elusive wistful quality to it, and could perhaps be best described as soul-jazz. His own songs were always the most distinctive and rewarding in this regard: for instance, "Make Believe," a beautifully-crafted track which again employed a slower tempo than some of his classics but nonetheless had the undoubted Bostic magic. An air of reflection pervaded, something like nostalgia, and on many of these records the vibes of Roland Johnson were much in evidence.

Musical Pearls (1960) contained some surprises, and was in some ways a study in contrasts. The standards were well in evidence again, for instance, "Don't Blame Me," but alongside the familiar he introduced new departures such as "Feeling Cool," which has the feel of a teen beach party track. He again sought inspiration from the light classical canon with the broody "Dark Eyes." The song started life in 1843 as a Russian romantic poem and was later set to the music of an obscure composer, Florian Herman. It was long favored by jazzmen, and Jack Teagarden recorded a fine, swinging version. Bostic's arrangement once more made good use of the fender bass guitar of "Tiny" Timbrell and the vibes of Roland Johnson. Along with the motoring "Let's Move Out," Earl included, dedicated to his wife, the previously unheard and suitably romantic "Hildegarde," a song he had written several years earlier, and "Tut Strut," which in some respects sounds like a precursor to an opus by funk maestros The Meters.

By Popular Demand (1961) went over old ground, with reworkings of some of his old hits and ubiquitous standards. Less familiar but more intriguing was his understated version of "The Key" from the William Holden–Sophia Loren film of the same name. This had already appeared on a previous release. In some ways, Bostic sounded more at home on *Hits of the Fantastic 50s Vol. 2* (1963), particularly on "Love Letters in the Sand," which was issued as a single. The LP was released in response to the great popularity of *Vol. 1*, although overall it was not nearly as successful. He continued to reinvent the half-forgotten classics of a bygone age, such as the Argentine tango "El Choclo," which dated from 1903. He gave it the vogueish bossa nova treatment, although it was his searing sax work that immediately drew the attention, and any extras were superfluous.

In terms of status, he was still up with some of the other big names in popular music. On New Year's Day 1961, he was on the bill of a hit show starring Ray Charles and his Raelettes at the Hollywood Palladium. In April, Bostic played the Spring Jazz Festival at the Memorial Hall in Dayton, Ohio. His orchestra was preceded by the great Louis Armstrong who headlined the concert, which was scheduled to last ninety minutes but went on for three hours. Bostic had a sextet on that occasion, within which were two trumpeters.[6] He followed that with dates at the Starlight Lounge, Kansas City, Missouri. On the eastern leg of his tour, he was in demand at nightspots around New York City and New Jersey. He was the honored guest artist at the seventh annual dance of the Jersey City Park Police. In between, he was among the celebrity guests at the wedding party of Dinah Washington to her sixth husband, Dominican Rafael Campos. She also stayed at Bostic's motel not long afterward.

In mid–August 1961, one of Earl's personal and exciting new sideline projects came to fruition. This was his restaurant, which he named the Flying Fox, situated at 3274 West Santa Barbara in the View Park area. At first it was reported that he intended to call it the Flamingo after his famous hit, but he decided against that. Hildegarde and the other Rinky Dinks were on hand for the grand opening. Earl appointed Jimmy Jackson manager of the club. Rumors that he was going to compose a song for the occasion proved unfounded. The restaurant turned out to be a big success and brought in a steady income. The same was true of his other investments such as the Bostic motel and his apartment block. He was a shrewd investor and gifted some of these to his wife. Significantly, the Flying Fox was also given to her. He consolidated some of his other holdings, such as the Edrich Motel at 4924 Washington Boulevard, with its heated swimming pool and complete en-suite kitchens. In those days such features were definitely state-of-the-art.

Having experimented with a larger band, he took the opposite route and went back to a sextet, then a quintet. During 1961 and 1962 he continued to play in smaller nightclubs and select spots. His shows had a more intimate feel and were perhaps less frenetic than those in the mid–1950s heyday. At the same time, although he had to all intents and purposes slowed down, there were few months of the year when he was not playing somewhere. His nightclub shows and longer residencies led him to experiment with a return to his jazz roots. He began to be noticed again by the critics and even viewed in a positive light. He was regularly invited to return to the scene of previous triumphs, such as the famous Black Hawk in San Francisco, where he played in December 1960 and again in April

1961. The latter show was broadcast live on radio. The Lighthouse in Los Angeles was long renowned as being at the vanguard of modern jazz. Sunday nights were given over to well-known groups, and during Bostic's turn he made a great impression. The *Down Beat Yearbook* reluctantly reported: "Earl Bostic scored on his night there this summer, to the consternation of jazz purists."[7] Over the course of the next two years, Bostic would give the critics even more to think about, when he came out with two outstanding records which proved beyond doubt that he was still a force to be reckoned with in the jazz firmament.

25

A New Sound

> "Someday I hope to be able to pick out some real good men, guys I know and want to play with, and go into a studio and cut some of the things I'd really like. You know; pure, clean, free, unrestricted. Just go."[1]
> —Earl Bostic, 1963

After several "quiet" years, Bostic returned to the limelight in 1963 with a new approach heralded by the release of his LP *Jazz as I Feel It*. This was followed a few months later in early 1964 by *A New Sound*. On both records he assembled a great little group comprising some of the most exciting talents of the time. These fulfilled a long-held ambition he had to cut loose and do things entirely his own way, devoid of any commercial constraints or obligations. The reaction was incredibly positive and gave rise to renewed interest in him. The recordings might have come too late for the jazz critics, but led to a degree of respect for him that had hitherto been lacking. In any event, he began to be seen in a new light, and undoubtedly, these reinvigorated his career. They were further acclaimed when re-released fifty years later.

For a long time, Earl had wanted to branch out and record with a bunch of hand-picked men. Increasingly, he was trying a more experimental pared-down approach live, with no more than a quintet and sometimes just a trio. His longing to do something radically different and unencumbered by the weight of expectation came along in the summer of 1963 when he approached several of his choices. On August 23 the new lineup assembled at the famous World Pacific Jazz studios in California, where many another classic was born. Besides Bostic the quintet comprised organist extraordinaire Richard "Groove" Holmes, Joe Pass on guitar, and Shelly Manne and Charlie Blackwell alternating on drums. Bass duties were shared by Jimmy Bond and Herb Gordy. The seven tracks that they recorded in the first session consisted of many new, totally untried songs. Earl summed up his approach and expounded on his philosophy of the blues. "The blues has it all; basic rhythmic quality, genuine lyric content, essential and basic chord structure, and maybe above all else, personality. The true blues lends itself to a musician's own personality and as for myself I like its easy melodic passages, its characteristic harmonic flavor of dissonance and harmonic passages."[2]

Above all, he showed a rejuvenated spirit, and had clearly lost none of his zest or ability. Gone was the obscure tired feeling that sometimes pervaded his later work, to be replaced by a resurgence of his power and playfulness. He showed also that he could work well in an ensemble without always needing to dominate. Hence, "Groove" Holmes, Pass, Manne, and the others all had their chance to shine. Holmes enjoyed some of his distinctive quicksilver passages, particularly on "Ten Out" and "Telstar Drive." Of all the numbers, Earl's remarkable playing on the latter

Jazz As I Feel It, recorded in August 1963, marked a sea change in Bostic's approach, heralding a more experimental and free-flowing sound.

has perhaps produced most comment over the years. All in all, it was a major surprise to many that he could reinvent himself this way. A switch to another label, even the hipper than hip Blue Note, would surely not have been out of the question if he had continued recording in this rich vein.

The fruits of the first session were issued under the title *Jazz as I Feel It* in November 1963. The second session was recorded a few weeks later in September at the same studio and released in March 1964 as *A New Sound*. These marked a true renaissance in Earl's career. The sleeve notes of the records were written by producer Hal Neely, a trumpeter from Nebraska, who wrote of Bostic: "This is a particularly articulate and quiet-spoken man. Soft in manner and voice, deep in basic philosophies and prideful of the opportunities of this land, he has prepared himself well and is a credit to his fellow musicians."[3]

At the heart of both these recordings is Bostic's exciting, revitalized alto playing, combined with the heady rhythm of Holmes on organ and the ever-evolving musings of Pass on guitar. These three appear on all the songs, augmented by the peerless Shelly Manne on drums for four tracks on *Jazz as I Feel It*. Earl's choice of personnel was inspired, and these were clearly musicians he admired, who were on a wavelength similar to his. Richard "Groove" Holmes was at the forefront of what became known as soul jazz in the early 1960s, although much of his work cannot be categorized; he was equally hailed as a rhythm and blues artist and in the 1970s his oeuvre was far closer to funk. He was highly influential, like his near contemporaries Jimmy Smith, Jimmy McGriff, and "Brother" Jack McDuff, in a surgency of interest in the organ in jazz and popular music. The Hammond organ was central to the sound of many popular blues and R&B groups, particularly in England in the 1960s, notably The Animals, The Zombies, and Procol Harum. Holmes recorded many well-received albums for Prestige and Pacific Jazz. As his guitarist, Earl chose the great Joe Pass, who emerged from years of chronic heroin addiction with his first record, the seminal *Sounds of Synanon*, named for the pioneering center where he was rehabilitated. Famously, he had no instrument of his own and amazingly played with a borrowed guitar on the album, issued in 1962. He went on to record prolifically both as leader and sideman, especially for pianist Oscar Peterson. It was interesting that several of Earl's guests, including Pass and Holmes, were long associated with bebop, and generally considered as hard bop stylists.

Shelly Manne was one of the most adventurous and prolific drummers in jazz. Some critics chose to term him a West Coast musician, which itself was made to sound derisive, and although considered an experimental, avant garde artist, Manne was another who straddled genres and styles. Over the course of his freewheeling career he played with practically everyone from Chet Baker to Bette Midler, and his soundtrack credits are voluminous. He later crossed paths with "Groove" Holmes when they played together on *Six Million Dollar Man* (RCA, 1975).

Earl eschewed the famous and ubiquitous standards and instead concentrated on songs and composers that were little-known. The writers included Herbie Mann, Sam Most, Joe Puma, and Lillian Lynch. There were several new ones that Earl penned himself, such as "Fast Track" and "Apple Cake." Three bassists played on the sessions: Jimmy Bond and Herb Gordy on the first and Al McKibbon on the second. Bond worked with the Art Pepper Quintet and bluesman Lightnin' Hopkins. Herb Gordy was a frequent collaborator with Earl. Two tracks on *A New Sound* were by King labelmate Johnny Pate, namely, "Blues for the Ivy Leagues" and "Que Jay." Both received interesting interpretations by Earl; the first was given an

A New Sound, released in early 1964, followed from the high standard set by *Jazz as I Feel It*.

unusual slow tempo arrangement that set the experimental mood of the record.

Earl won widespread praise from many critics. As one commentator remarked, he still "delivered every solo with a sense of boisterous elan."[4] He was further applauded both for exploring new material instead of the hackneyed standards of yore, and for the quality of the personnel he chose as sidemen. Albert Anderson called the record "a vibrant session of fine music." He concluded: "Bostic, whose sax tone at its highest register sounds like a squealing trumpet, is at his best playing spontaneously, and this is what he does on this disc."[5] British critic Mark Gardner was similarly impressed, commenting, "He plays hard as you might imagine, but his improvising is by no means routine. I cannot help feeling that, had the fates been different, Earl would have loomed large in the jazz histories."[6] A recent commentator lauded *Jazz as I Feel It* in a review for *Flophouse Magazine* as "flawless, blues-drenched and pure dynamite."[7]

Bostic's work on these two recordings has continued to inspire. Perhaps one of his most significant re-releases of the last thirty years was *The Complete Quintet Recordings* (2015), which gathered both albums on one CD for the first time. This certainly helped to resurrect interest in Bostic among record buyers and musicians alike, many of whom had probably never heard of him before, and several who were not even alive at the time he died. It also came as a surprise to those who associated him only with the more commercial material. In 2016, Spanish saxophonist Dani Nel·lo was moved to organize a tribute concert in Barcelona to Bostic, which was directly inspired by these two albums. He approached the renowned Dutch sax maestro Benjamin Herman, who, along with Hammond organist Abel Boquera, guitarist Dave Mitchell, and drummer Anton Jarl, took part in the second annual Sax-o-Rama Rhythm & Blues Jazz Meeting held over the weekend of January 30 and 31, 2016, in various clubs in Barcelona. The Bostic night was, appropriately enough, the Saturday at the Jamboree Jazz Club. Herman has been cited as "one of the most original musicians on the jazz scene in the Netherlands who explores influences beyond jazz boundaries." He described working on the tribute as "an enjoyable and instructive challenge."[8] At the time of the concert the publicity material for the Jamboree club lauded Bostic as "the perfect example to establish the connection between the spirit of jazz and the soul of rhythm and blues. His passionate, warm and rhythmic sound never detached itself from the reference that John Coltrane was for him."[9]

Earl retained much of his popularity during the 1960s despite not being so much in the public eye. For instance, in the annual *Playboy* poll for 1963, he was voted a credible third, behind Cannonball Adderley and Paul Desmond, and ahead of the ultra-cool cats Ornette Coleman and

Sonny Stitt.[10] Naturally, the critics sneered at the mere mention of *Playboy* for all its perceived negative connotations. Throughout the year, Bostic was again a mainstay of the cabaret circuit on the West Coast. He was a frequent guest at Gene Norman's Crescendo on Sunset Strip, generally for month-long stays. Norman, who set up Crescendo Records, began the club in 1954 and sold it in 1964. Famed for its integrated audience, it was a mecca for the smart set, and played host to most of the big names in popular music in that time, incorporating jazz greats such as George Shearing and hip folk groups including The Limelighters, along with new comics, among them a then little-known Woody Allen. During his stay at the Crescendo in August, Bostic shared the bill with Cuban pianist and bandleader René Touzet and doo-wop group The Rivingtons, famous for their novelty hit "Papa-Ooo-Mow-Mow." When he returned in November, the Ink Spots, Nancy Wilson, and comedian Dick Gregory were also in the lineup with Bostic. After his success at the Crescendo, he received an invite from Tommy Sands of the Sahara for an extended stay lasting from August to the end of September. Regular dates in between included the Why Not Club at Canoga Park, and the Crossbow Inn, North Hollywood. Among other highlights, he played the opening session at a new youth club in Reseda, the Precious Moment Club, which attracted big crowds for its monthly dance contest and especially for Bostic's set on Sunday night.[11]

His only engagement away from California in that period was in Buffalo, New York, as part of the trio of pianist Jimmy Manuel under the name Jaman. The gig at Frank and Teresa's Anchor Bay restaurant took place over three nights from June 14. Although his recordings were few, Manuel was a fine musician who made a unique contribution to jazz. This date seemed to captivate Earl's imagination more than his regular work in the West. He still felt that New York and environs was the hub for jazz innovation, and he had missed the buzz of the place. It was perhaps this interlude and his work on the two acclaimed LPs that sparked his longing to return to the East just over a year later.

The year 1964 was even more low key for him than recent years had been, and he played only a few dates, although they tended to be of longer duration. He began the year with sellout shows at the Crescendo, followed by a sensational run at Caesar's Supper Club. He was at his busiest in the summer months, and his stint at the Royal Tahitian club in Pomona, which began in May and ended in July, attracted a lot of interest and big crowds every night. The club was only extant for seven years (1960–1967) but attracted some of the biggest names in showbusiness in that time. While Bostic was playing one room, Duke Ellington entertained at the outdoor garden concert, and Rex Stewart could be heard serenading the dinner guests in the supper room. Between his other dates, Earl appeared again at some of the same haunts, including the Crossbow, and at Henri's Whip in Long Beach. When the summer ended, he took time off from performing and did not return until November. Inspired by his work with Jimmy Manuel and on his two experimental records, he formed a trio and explored a focused, more pared-down sound when he played a single date at the White Horse in Redondo Beach.[12] Around the same time, by way of a tribute to him, pianist Bud Powell covered his "No Name Blues" on the CBS LP *A Portrait of Thelonious*.

Bostic's last released LP was *The Greatest Hits of 1964*, which mostly covered the themes of popular films of the time, including *Charade*, *Lawrence of Arabia*, and *From Russia with Love*. His spirited version of "More" in vintage Bostic mode later induced Stanley Turrentine to record the song. A standout for different reasons was "Dominique," a surprising version of the unlikely worldwide novelty hit by Belgian artist The Singing Nun from the year before. Bostic brought out an elusive melancholy aspect of the rather sunny song. There was something valedictory about his arrangement, which is unlike any other interpretation of the jaunty original. Perhaps he was thinking of Sister Laetitia and his early days when he started out. An air of regret, or at the least nostalgia, permeates many of his later sides, which might itself have reflected his feelings looking back over his life, things he might have done differently, and even intimations of his own mortality since his second heart attack. The unusual and curiously haunting "Dominique" was one of his last released singles. Although no personnel were given for this, it seems likely that Roland "Vibes" Johnson was part of the group. In view of the two albums that preceded it, there was perhaps a degree of disappointment that he did not continue in true jazz vein rather than going back to the conventional, tried-and-tested formula. There were few surprises on *The Greatest Hits of 1964*; nevertheless, it had much of the same wistfulness of his later work, and his long-time fans delighted in hearing his interpretations of the theme from *Days of Wine and Roses* along with all the rest. Interestingly, his posthumous release *The Song Is Not Ended* (1966) included elements from both parts of his repertoire. In time, he would surely have got around to covering the Beatles and other popular artists of the 1960s. Perhaps he could have been persuaded to try something different, such as an LP on which he showcased his skill on guitar and other instruments. More pertinently, it would have done a great deal more for his long-term reputation if he had further explored his meditations on jazz on future releases.

In any event, it was likely that his two experimental recordings, *Jazz as I Feel It* and *A New Sound*, strongly indicated his future direction. Both were records to be proud of, and proved to be of lasting value. More such albums could have made him an increasingly interesting figure as time went on. After all, many jazz musicians went on recording well into their old age with no loss of form. Sadly, for Bostic, it was not to be. Nevertheless, these sides remain as a tantalizing prophecy of what might have been.

26

Interrupted Melody

> "What interests me most is playing new songs I know almost nothing about. Put 'em on the stand and just play. That's wonderful!"[1]
> —Earl Bostic, 1965

Early in 1965, Bostic left the West Coast and made a surprising move back East, this time to Detroit. He then returned to touring and was soon booked solid. Sadly, his seemingly happy marriage broke down because his wife wanted to remain in California and filed for divorce. After that his health took a drastic turn for the worse, and at the end of October, he suffered a third and fatal heart attack after playing the first night of a weeklong date at the Top of the Plaza at the Midland Tower Hotel in Rochester, New York.

The Bostics had been together for almost twenty-three years and had known each other since they were teenagers. They were long considered the model of a contented couple in jazz circles. Jazz was hardly known for its stable marriages, but they seemed to be a notable exception, and were thought of in the same way as the Basies. However, behind the scenes, Earl's seemingly serene domestic life was actually in upheaval. Toward the end of 1964 he and Hildegarde were drifting apart. By the turn of the new year, they were already estranged and no longer living together. The situation came to a head when he started a road tour in February 1965. Although they had no children, they appeared to be reconciled to that, and since he made over some of his property to her in 1956, she was in many ways financially independent. To an extent they led separate lives, Earl with his music and Hildegarde with her business and social life with the Rinky Dinks. Perhaps part of him missed the old days and longed to return to the thrill of touring, to once again be at the center of where it was all happening. The real problems began when he read a book about the science of earthquakes, and especially the effect of the San Andreas Fault. He became convinced that Los Angeles—if not the whole state of

California—would suffer an environmental catastrophe and be swallowed up into the sea in the not-too-distant future, possibly within the year. His ideas were also tied up with a feeling of impending doom, in the wake of the race riots which raged over six days in the city in mid-August. As a consequence, he wanted her to sell the Flying Fox restaurant and their other interests there and move back East with him. She was adamant that she would never agree to that. "I came to California because Earl was afraid the cold would affect his heart condition," she declared. "I have made the Flying Fox Restaurant and a motel successes; I don't intend to leave them. He said he wasn't coming back I said I wasn't leaving." In the suit she filed later in the year she accused her husband of "inflicting grievous mental suffering on her." Despite years of apparent harmony, things quickly went awry between them. Their assets began to be evaluated by assessors; the value of their shared house in Baldwin Hills was estimated at $75,000. She summed up her attitude at the time: "I expect to live in the manner to which I have become accustomed," she stated, and was unequivocal, further declaring, "There won't be any reconciliation. I think I've done as much as a wife should. He wants me to give up everything and move away from here because he's afraid of the earthquake and I don't intend to leave here."[2]

Earl remained just as adamant about what he was going to do, and he moved back East along with his mother. Perhaps surprisingly, he did not decide to live in New York, but intended to settle in Detroit. The attraction of that city for him was that some of his favorite cousins lived there, including Gus Reed along with Mabel and Marie Wilson, as well as several old friends from Tulsa. Gus (also called Augustus) Reed was married with two grown sons, Curtis and Augustus Jr. Earl spent a hectic time looking for a house to buy at short notice.

Despite all the turmoil of that year, Bostic still had time to remember those who had helped him along the way on his route to success. Even with the worry over his disintegrating marriage preying on his mind, he took time out to find out where Sister Mary Laetitia of Xavier was living. He eventually tracked her down to the St. Elizabeth Convent in Cornwells Heights, near Philadelphia, and sent her $100. She used the money to buy new benches at Xavier University to enable students not to have to go long distances between classes. "I knew she wouldn't spend it on herself," he remarked, adding, "I'm going to make an effort to send her more because she needs it in her work."[3]

Bostic and his trio began their eastern road tour in February 1965, commencing with a week at The Castle Rest Lounge in Eggertsville, New York. It was a long-established venue on their itinerary where they had played many times before, and they returned twice during the year, first in April then again in September. There was something of a buzz created by this because it was his first big tour after a long gap, and everyone was excited to see him again. They visited several nightspots in Pennsylvania, including Pittsburgh and Philadelphia. There were many repeat dates, such as at Lennie's in Boston, Pushnik's Waterfall Room in Lebanon, Pennsylvania, and Florento's Supper Club in Syracuse, New York. Most were for one- or two-week stays, but some were one- or two-night stands. Clearly he had been missed, and throughout the tour, the demand was as great as it had ever been, if not more so.

In August, they played at the Top of the Plaza, a relatively new but then state-of-the-art venue on the 14th floor of the Midland Tower Hotel in Rochester, New York. The first indoor shopping center of its kind, the Midland Tower had only been constructed in 1962, but the Top of the Plaza soon garnered a reputation for attracting top-flight jazz artists. Over the years it played host to such big names as Buddy Rich and Sarah Vaughan. The plush restaurant and concert room had panoramic views of the city. It was large enough to accommodate a lot of people but retained a feeling of intimacy with the star performers. The center did much to rejuvenate the downtown area at that period. Bostic's visit was his second. Regular concertgoers were in their element to find such a talent in their midst, who had not been seen regularly in New York for several years. Each night was sold out and the excitement of the audience was palpable. One who was there recalled the electric atmosphere: "The crowds were enthusiastic. They were 'wall-to-wall' people the three nights we were there. Bostic is a good performer. He plays the sweetest saxophone with hardly any effort.... The crowds spoke for themselves."[4]

After Rochester, the road tour moved on to return dates at Pushnik's, Florento's, and The Castle over the late summer and into the fall. On September 13 they played a one-nighter at the Polynesian-themed Aku Aku Club in Toledo, Ohio, a hot attraction which drew lots of other big-name jazz and cabaret artists. From October 11 to 24 they were resident at Baker's Keyboard Lounge in Detroit. The club had been hosting jazz concerts since it opened in 1934 and is still doing so to this day. During their residency he was interviewed by local music correspondent Ken Barnard, and it was evident from Earl's remarks that he was back doing what he wanted to do, enjoying it as much as ever. It had given him a new lease of life. Since November 1964 he had pared his ensemble down from a quintet to a trio, consisting of organist Maurine Marrett and drummer Buddy Henry. Music was still everything to Bostic, and he just desired to go on playing for as long as possible. He revealed that he had given up on composing so that he could concentrate on playing. "Anything that takes me away from playing, I don't want to do," he observed. "I love to play. I have to play. I don't know anything I'd rather do than play."⁵

It was while they were playing in Detroit that Earl received news that his wife was filing for divorce at the Superior Court in Los Angeles. In her suit dated October 13, she charged him with cruelty and asked for "reasonable support" because she claimed she was "without funds to support herself," although this latter appeared to directly contradict most other statements she made. Whatever the truth of the matter, it was sad that after so many years together it all seemed to be ending in acrimony.⁶

By the time they arrived in Rochester on Sunday October 24, Bostic was drained. Unsurprisingly, he was still feeling the after-effects of the long seven-hour drive from Detroit. Buddy Henry remarked; "Earl was very tired. The drive took a lot out of him." The audience on the Monday night was described as small but enthusiastic. Bostic appeared to have retained all his old verve and playfulness. He joked with the audience between numbers, and one who was there said that "several times he lifted his horn high above his head" during his set. The band played lots of requests and sang "Happy Birthday" for a young man from Oregon. Bostic remarked wryly that he remembered Portland all too well because he had suffered a heart attack there a few years earlier. He recalled how well the staff of the Good Samaritan hospital had taken care of him. He was warmly received by the audience and the night had been a great success.⁷

The next morning, he began to feel unwell, and at around 10 a.m. suffered a heart attack in his hotel room. He was immediately rushed to the Highland Hospital, Rochester, where he was described as in "fair condition, resting comfortably." His wife was contacted and flew to New York, arranging to get some of the leading heart specialists to treat him. It was at that point that they reconciled. Although his condition had appeared to stabilize, he took a sudden turn for the worse on Wednesday night, and died on Thursday morning October 28, 1965, aged fifty-two.⁸

The day before Earl died, booking agent Maxie Maxwell called on him hoping to reminisce with him over old times. However, when he got there, he was not allowed in to see him because his condition was so serious. Earl died the following morning. Maxwell remembered him fondly. He wrote: "Earl was always a gentleman, soft-spoken and very easy going."⁹

On short notice, the thirty-three-year-old local Rochester musician Joe Romano took Bostic's place leading the band from the Tuesday onward at the Midland Tower Hotel. Romano stayed on to finish the gig for the remaining days. The show was advertised by way of a tribute to Bostic. Romano (1932–2008) was described as "a swinging, fluid player on alto and tenor" and was mostly associated with Woody Herman, whose band he had joined in 1956 after army service.¹⁰ When the week ended on Saturday night, the trio were due to play next the following week at Lennie's in Philadelphia, and were booked for several dates after that. However, without their main man the band members were left high and dry without any funds for transport. Hence, the tour ended abruptly.[11]

Earl's funeral took place at the Mount Sinai Baptist Church, Los Angeles, on Tuesday November 2, and he was afterward interred at Inglewood Cemetery. The honorary pallbearers were Louis Prima, Chet Baker, Teddy Edwards, Leonard Feather, Edgar Hayes, Plas Johnson, Joe Pass, Rex Stewart, Gerry Wilson, and the comedian Slappy White. All had known and admired him for many years and most had worked with him at key points in his career. The service was conducted by the Rev. C.B. Williams, who called it "a moment of tribute to a great artist who made his contribution." There were several hymns, and Sam Fletcher sang "When I've Done the Best I Can," after which the service finished with the Lord's Prayer. Afterward, Rex Stewart reflected: "I was happy the funeral was quiet and dignified. It was fitting and proper for the dignity of the man."[12] Earl's grave at Inglewood is marked by a simple flat stone set in the ground with the inscription of his name and the dates of his birth and death. The year of birth is given erroneously as 1912.

Bostic's widow Hildegarde received a certain amount of unwanted attention at the funeral, principally because of the divorce that immediately precipitated his death. The fact that she appeared unmoved at the funeral service also drew much comment at the time. Afterward she was rather on the defensive, and commented: "My husband and I had a good marriage. He was a good provider, and I did everything for him that a wife could do." She continued, "I had three specialists there, and the best medical equipment that money could buy. None of them were enough to save his life."[13]

After his death, Hildegarde stayed on in Los Angeles for a while, but in 1969 she sold the Flying Fox club and her other interests in the city, at which time she went to live in New York. She was left a wealthy widow, and maintained her love of fine clothes and an active social life. Atlantic City was one of her favorite vacation spots to which she returned for many years in succession. At one time she started a catering business. Unsurprisingly, she had several suitors, including Earl's one-time bassist Ike Isaacs, who was previously married to singer Carmen McCrae. Al Williams, of the famous dancing group the Four Step Brothers, also courted her. Of them all, Isaacs seemed to be the most likely to persuade Hildegarde to take a walk up the aisle. However, despite his pleadings she did not succumb. She already had everything she wanted and never married again. In 1972 she was the victim of a hit-and-run incident when her leg was broken in two places. Over the years she suffered from a range of health issues

Earl Bostic Blows a Fuse (Charly RnB, 1985), one of several notable posthumous releases that helped rekindle interest in Earl's music.

which led her to seek a quieter life away from the social whirl, and by the early 1980s she relocated to Denver, Colorado. Eventually, she returned to her home city of New Orleans, and died there in October 2002 at the age of eighty-seven.[14] Both the two main women in Earl's life outlived him by a long way. His mother Druzella died in Los Angeles in March 1985 in her ninety-first year and was buried at the Evergreen Cemetery.[15]

Epilogue
The Song Is Not Ended

> "A great artist, superb showman and all-around good fellow, Bostic ranks tops in his field of endeavor."[1]

After Bostic's sudden death, one of the first posthumous releases issued in 1966 was defiantly entitled *The Song Is Not Ended*. The LP garnered some fine reviews at the time, including one from William Laffler, and put Bostic's name back in the spotlight. It showed he had lost none of his drive or his ability to reach the high notes, as he does in the impressive cadenza at the end of "Red Sails in the Sunset." At times he gave strong indications of where he was heading musically, most noticeably on "Shangri La" and "The Song Is Ended." On "Shangri-La" he ambitiously attempted to replicate the rippling effect of Robert Maxwell's harp. His arrangement of "The Song Is Ended" incorporated the electric organ to augment his sax and the vibes to create a still more experimental jazz sound following on more closely from his *New Sound* recordings. The next stage might have been a move toward the soul-funk territory that Richard "Groove" Holmes and others explored in the following decade. Indeed, it is likely that Holmes is the organist heard on the record.

Nonetheless, fame was a fickle thing, and as the influential DJ Kal Rudman remarked in the same year, "I hope Bostic is not already forgotten, because many of us loved his music and grew up on it listening to many R&B and pop record radio shows in the fifties."[2] This was only a relatively short while after the height of his fame when he was the bestselling instrumentalist.

Over the following years, Bostic was often reassessed and his reputation gradually grew, but it was a slow process, and those who believed they held a monopoly on what constituted taste in jazz succeeded in all but stifling any mention of him in a positive light. Consequently, he has remained an obscure figure to most. In time, he has come to be seen as the pathfinder, a bridge between prewar swing, early R&B, and postwar rock 'n' roll.

Fellow musicians always recognized his worth and the unfairness of the lack of attention he was given. Dr. John, for instance, once remarked: "I've always felt that Louis Jordan and 'Cleanhead' Vinson and Earl Bostic were the most underrated guys. They killed me."[3] Clarinetist and saxophonist Garvin Bushell rated Earl highly when considering the greats who he had seen during his seven decades in jazz, and Hank Crawford loved him for his power. Hal Singer maintained that "Bostic was the greatest sax player he had ever heard, with the ability to recognize a good melody and swing, play with equal facility over four and a half octaves and with a distinctive tone."[4]

DJ John Peel always championed Bostic, and encapsulated the difficulty of standing up for him against a wall of disdain. On a radio show broadcast in September 1999, Peel recalled the humiliation of his sixteen-year-old self at the hands of what passed for the jazz cognoscenti of his boarding school, the self-appointed arbiters of taste:

> "It's the first jazz or jazz-related record that I bought.... I thought it would give me a certain amount of prestige and enable me to become a member in good standing of the jazz club at the school, which was called the High Society, run by a rather snooty boy called Comyns. I've often wondered what became of him. I took along my Earl Bostic record and it was very much scoffed at, as I was, and I was rejected as a result of owning this record. But it still sounds like a great record to me. In the reviews at the time, all the jazz magazines used to dismiss Earl Bostic, saying that his tone was too broad, and his vibrato was too broad or something—I forget what it was. I used to think, whatever it is that they don't like about it, I think I would like that and I was absolutely right."[5]

Bostic had a wide influence on different genres of music. He made a decided impression on the phalanx of instrumentalists at work in the 1960s, including the reggae ska band The Skatalites and popular quartet The Viscounts, who were moved to record two of his hits, "Harlem Nocturne" and "Night Train." The musician Graham Bond, founding father of English R&B in the 1960s, similarly cited Bostic as his earliest and most important influence. Clearly, he was an inspiration to many saxophonists, not just those of ostensibly similar approach such as King Curtis, Clarence Clemmons, Junior King, and others, but also the more unexpected, for instance, alto and soprano saxman Greg Osby (b. 1960), who specifically pinpointed Bostic as one of his most important influences. He lived on through the direct impact he had on the many musicians who played with him, not least Stanley Turrentine. Moreover, Earl paved the way for the experimentations of John Coltrane, Eric Dolphy, Albert Ayler, and others. His influence permeated in many saxophonists for several decades after his death, among them "Rusty" Bryant and "Ace" Cannon, whose delicacy of tone was striking. Earl's abiding impact extended to Andy Mackay, whose lush saxophone was so central to the evocative sound of Roxy Music. Bostic was often hailed by other musicians, not just saxophonists, for example, jazz drummer Eddie Marshall, and Rolling Stones drummer Charlie Watts credited him as the one who opened the world of jazz to him as a teenager. Bostic continues to inspire young players today, for instance, Gary Gregg, saxophonist with Chaise Lounge, a jazz combo, who paid tribute to Bostic on the track "The Earl" from their album *The Lock and Key* (Modern Songbook Records, 2017). He even informs the work of such promising artists as the Dutch tenor saxist Gideon Tazelaar, who studied at Juilliard and is currently making a big name for himself.

A young David Jones, long before he became better known as David Bowie, was also influenced by Bostic. Bowie's first ambition was to be a saxophonist, having been inspired by Bostic's "Flamingo" and Lee Allen's sax solo on Little Richard's "She's Got It." He once said, "Those are two things that were total inspirations about what I wanted to do with my life." Thus inspired, his father bought him a saxophone on rent-to-own, and David even used a plastic mouthpiece in an effort to sound as much like his hero as possible. Bostic's name was later invoked by Bowie as one of the key influences that went into his memorable *Let's Dance* album.[6]

Bostic's music was sometimes used to effect on the soundtrack of films, notably Jim Jarmusch's *Permanent Vacation* (Cinesthesia, 1980). The sensational "Up There in Orbit" was intentionally the only found music utilized by the auteur director, who expressly wanted to invoke the feel of the fifties to suit his protagonist, an adolescent drifter, who ironically was a Charlie Parker devotee. Similarly, "Jungle Drums" was perfect for the mood of John Waters's stylish, tongue-in-cheek *Cry-Baby* (1990).

In 1993 Bostic was inducted into the Oklahoma Jazz Hall of Fame, although it is perhaps telling that few similar accolades came his way. He was never inducted into the Rock 'n' Roll Hall of Fame, for instance, nor even the more recently established R&B Hall of Fame, and despite his undoubted influence it seems doubtful that he ever will be. Memories are short. Similarly, Bostic's records have seldom been given much attention as collector's items. The received wisdom is that he is not worth collecting because of the ubiquitous overlapping releases by King and the fact they are too readily available. Largely, the company was to blame for the way they treated him. Nonetheless, he can be rewarding for the collector as much as for the lover of period R&B and rock 'n' roll.

Meanwhile, his more feted near-contemporaries have frequently been lionized. Clint Eastwood's *Bird* (1988), based on the life of Charlie Parker, was largely drawn from the remembrance of Teddy Edwards, a one-time member of the Bostic ensemble. There was no such tribute to Bostic, nor did anyone expect one. Parker died at the age of thirty-four, and Coltrane at forty, and since death their reputations have soared, to such an extent that Coltrane was canonized by a congregation in San Francisco known as the Yardbird Temple. In their jazz-inspired theosophy, "Bird" was transposed as John the Baptist with Saint John Coltrane as the divinity incarnate. On the same scale of values, Bostic might equate to a minor prophet in a vestry window at best or Judas at worst, depending on who is writing the text. In any event, it is unlikely that anytime soon anyone will be setting up a Church of Saint Earl Bostic the Divine. The man himself had no pretensions to claims of sanctity, but was content to be a great entertainer who lighted the path for others. It might come as a surprise that Pharoah Sanders, seen by many as the spiritual heir to Coltrane, was in turn influenced in his early days by Bostic, as he readily acknowledged.[7] As Albert Ayler once declared, "Maybe [Coltrane] was the Father, Pharoah was the Son, and I was the Holy Ghost."[8] One wonders where this leaves Bostic, who influenced all three.

In many ways, Bostic remains enigmatic, both as an artist and a man. For certain he can never be pigeonholed. Labels are meaningless. His music defies neat categorization and his complete mastery of his instrument was sans-pareil. Whatever else may be said of him, none can deny his talent. Even his detractors acknowledged it. He was never a tortured artist struggling against a spiral of drugs and other demons. Whatever vices he had went largely unrecorded. By all accounts he seemed a generally placid, easygoing, and well adjusted individual, with plenty of failings like everyone else. A phenomenally hard worker, he was reliable and eager to please his audience. Granted, he may have lacked the searing intensity or artistic vision of a Coltrane, and perhaps his adherence to the commercial route was his undoing. He even acknowledged this himself, and his two free-flowing quintet recordings late in his career gave an indication of both where his heart lay, and the route he might wish he had taken earlier. The first part of his life in jazz made him a respected and admired figure: in a word, promising. It was only after he changed direction from 1948 that perceptions of him began to change too. Once he found his sound, he stayed close to the same formula for most of the rest of his career, and it is perhaps for this apparent lack of adventure that he has paid the price in terms of his latter-day standing. Notwithstanding, he is important not only for the big names he played with, but for the many and varied talents who learned their craft with his orchestra over a period of more than thirty years. As such, he was essentially a bridge between eras and a nurturer of young talent, as a roll call of names who played for him testifies.

26. Epilogue

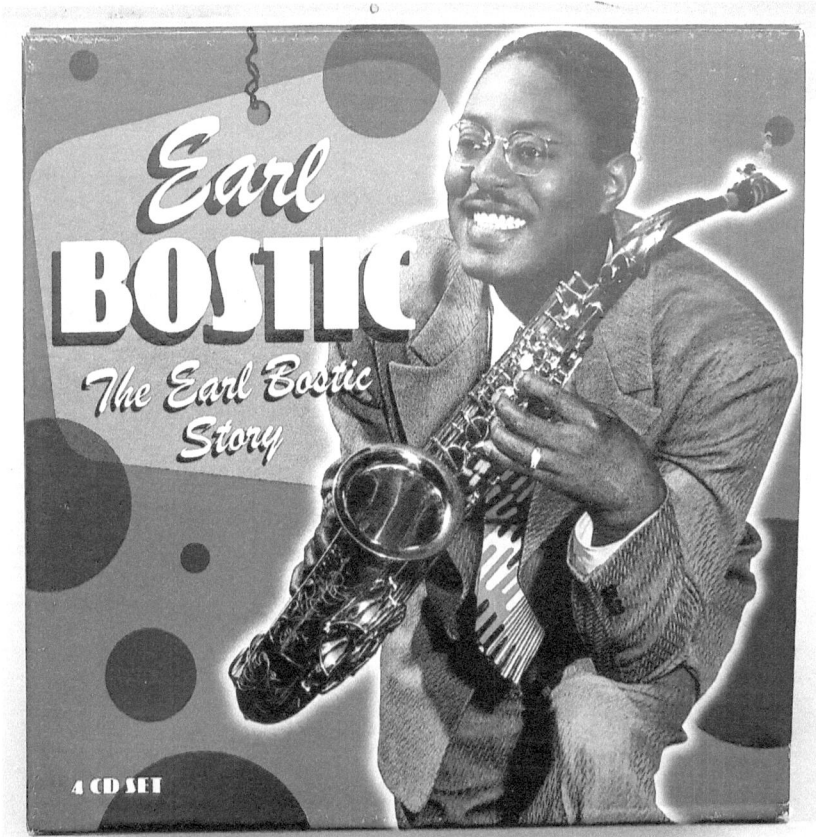

The first-class four-CD box set *The Earl Bostic Story* was released by Proper Records in 2006.

He was a true entertainer who lived for music. As Victor Schonfield once wrote, "His greatest gift was the way he communicated through his horn a triumphant joy in playing and being, much as Louis Armstrong and only a few others have ever done."[9] In the final analysis, if Earl's music is still played and enjoyed, not purely for its nostalgic properties, but for dancing, and to marvel at his sublime ability to blow the alto sax like no one else before or since, then his song is clearly not ended.

Appendix A

Collecting the Earl

It has been said that Bostic's records are not worth collecting. The reasoning seems to be that there are too many of them, they are easily available, and that because of the way they were released it would be an impossible task to sort them out. While it is true that King released and then re-released his records consistently, he is nonetheless a collectable artist. Moreover, a good representative collection would be straightforward and would not break the bank.

As ever with records, it depends what the impetus is for the collection. Some might wish to concentrate on original issues of singles and/or LPs, and the key thing as ever in these matters is condition. It is always worth paying that little bit more for something in the best condition available, bearing in mind that these records by their nature are becoming scarcer. Half the fun of collecting is deciding one's own parameters, and everyone's collection is unique in that regard. If you are new to the hobby, do not be put off by disdainful reviews or the opinions of self-proclaimed experts. I never give advice as a rule, but I would always say, go for what you like. Whatever aspect appeals to you, pursue that. From my own perspective because I am interested in visuals and design, I find 7" EPs appealing, and they take up a lot less room than 12" records. Their heyday was the early 1950s until the mid to late 1960s, a period they capture vividly in miniature. Everyone has their own ideas, and their own finite financial resources, and clearly not everyone wants to start a collection as such. Anyone wishing to dip a toe in the water regarding Bostic could do worse than look out for the two EP collections issued by See for Miles a few years ago. These can be had for a remarkably low price like many CDs these days, and present great value considering the extensive liner notes and combined fifty-two tracks, which it would be difficult—not to say expensive—to find in their original format.

Anyone wishing to collect originals would not find much difficulty, although some of the first records might prove elusive. Bostic's earliest recordings on Gotham, Savoy, and other labels do turn up for sale. Singles are a straightforward matter and hopefully this appendix will help provide a checklist. The first LPs released by King were 10" records consisting of six tracks in total. Although classed as long players, they were more akin to EPs, or extended play records, and most played at 78 rpm. Some of the earliest of these were released in 1951, so they are becoming much harder to find in excellent condition. The first three had no title as such but were released as "Earl Bostic and His Alto Sax," with similar artwork but in different colors.

Dating from 1956, his 12" LPs are more readily available, but the problem is that these were often re-recorded and re-released using the same titles and numbers with entirely different personnel. In this case it is as well to examine the cover designs closely, as these can be a giveaway for date, and generally to avoid stereo versions altogether. The vinyl LP at 33 rpm soon became the most desired format for many because it was the ideal length and did not require turning the record over after one song. That was a real luxury after fifty years of playing shellac discs on wind-up gramophones. Usually consisting of a dozen songs, the LPs cost between $3 and $5 on release, and on that basis at least have held their value and often doubled it. One of the first was *The Best of Bostic* (1956), which naturally enough kicked off with "Flamingo" and took in several other highlights including "Jungle Drums" and his sublime rendition of "I Can't Give You Anything but Love."

Long-playing records in those days tended to be cobbled together rather than conceived and recorded as a single entity, as was more usual later. Record companies were not generally concerned as much with aesthetics as they were with cashing in on their artists. Even so, some of the designs are appealing, and the ones which conjure up the period most evocatively are for me the best. *Earl Bostic for You* (1956) had tracks all different from its predecessor, and notably included "Sleep" and "Cherokee," which were the lead-off numbers on sides A and B, respectively.

The rather whimsical cover of *Alto-Tude* depicted Bostic with sax in hand hovering horizontally in midair over a turquoise background representing the sky, with a yellow globular sun, and has a lot of charm. *Dance Time* (1957) with its revolving pocket watches on the cover is perhaps one of his finest records and shows him at or near his best. The earlier version of the LP has a stylized sax on the front. Most of the tracks were from previous recordings. "Harlem Nocturne," "Sweet Lorraine," and "Where or When" are among the highlights, but the whole record stands up remarkably well for its consistent quality. The front of the first version of *C'mon Dance with Bostic* (1958) features a shot of teenagers jiving and is entirely redolent of its era. The cover of *Dance Music from the Bostic Workshop* (1959) shows Earl seated at the piano with the saxophone atop. However, this is rather misleading because he does not play the keyboard on the record. On *For You* with his arms raised, he looks as though he is addressing a prayer meeting.

There are lots of avenues that might be explored. For instance, some might like to concentrate on European releases. Those issued on Vogue in France and England probably already have their admirers, because Vogue is a highly collectable label. The records tend to differ only slightly in terms of tracks, but the cover designs are invariably different and each reflects its own country's visual ideas—for instance, the stylized bottles in red, white, and green that adorn the front of *Earl Bostic His Alto Sax and Orchestra* (Vogue, 1954). The English Parlophone versions also attract collectors, because yet again the label was an iconic one. In the 1930s it was renowned for British dance bands, but it was the association with the Beatles that ensured it a place in recording history, so much so that it was brought back to life in the 1990s. In Germany and France, Bostic's releases appeared on the Odeon label, some of which might be mistaken for classical records when judging by the covers alone. President Records also issued some EPs in France in the 1950s. It is worth looking out for oddities from Japan and elsewhere. The Japanese releases were issued by Angel Records. As to other artifacts relating to Bostic, flyers and posters do crop up from time to time.

Some of the significant posthumous releases included *That's Earl, Brother* (Spotlite Records, 1985), which covered much of his early work with Lionel Hampton, "Hot Lips" Page, and Rex Stewart. This includes liner notes by Tony Williams. Dating from the same year is the appealing *Earl Bostic Blows a Fuse* issued by the excellent Charly Records, containing an entertaining survey of Earl's career compiled by musician Danny Adler. The Proper Box set of four CDs making up *The Earl Bostic Collection* is the definitive collection and boasts a forty-four-page booklet with an exhaustive appreciation by Joop Vissar, along with numerous rare photos. Also among the most recent releases of note is the two-disc compilation *The Earl Bostic Collection* (Acrobat Music, 2015), which is a good résumé of his career and is complemented by the inclusion of an interesting essay by Paul Watts.

Photographs are much less evident generally, and anything signed is likely to be the most highly valued of all.

Appendix B

Bostic as Composer

"The Model" (E.E. Bostic), c. 1931.
"I Love Swing" (E.E. Bostic), December 1, 1938, New York (Unpublished).
"The Major and the Minor" (E.E. Bostic), c. 1941.
"My Desire" (E.E. Bostic), March 6, 1941.
"Small's Special" (E.E. Bostic), April 8, 1941.
"Let Me Off Up Town" (E.E. Bostic, Redd Evans), April 16, 1941.
"My Blue Dream" (E.E. Bostic, Eugene Hall), October 1941.
"This Mess Is Messy" (E.E. Bostic), December 3, 1941.
"Harlem Serenade" (E.E. Bostic), May 22, 1942.
"Trylon Swing" (E.E. Bostic, Irving Mills), American Academy of Music, January 11, 1943 (New York).
"All On" (L. Hampton, E.E. Bostic), December 15, 1943.
"Paradise Shuffle" (E.E. Bostic), Leeds Music Corp., July 18, 1945.
"That's the Groovy Thing" (E.E. Bostic), 1945. (First recorded March 1946 with Jimmy Shirley on guitar.)
"Brooklyn Boogie" (L. Prima, E.E. Bostic), Enterprise Music Corp., February 22, 1946.
"That's the Heat You Gotta Beat" (E.E. Bostic, B. Mason, Evelyn Harris), Essgee Music Publishing Corp., March 24, 1946.
"Let's Ball Tonight" (E. E. Bostic), Essgee Music Publishing Corp., March 1, 1947.
"Away" (E.E. Bostic), Essgee Music Publishing Corp., March 1, 1947.
"Cuttin' Out" (E.E. Bostic), Essgee Music Publishing Corp., July 24, 1947.
"I'm the Guy That Loves You" (E.E. Bostic), Essgee Music Publishing Corp., August 4, 1947.
"My Special Dream" (E.E. Bostic, Eugene Hall), Essgee Music Publishing Corp., August 19, 1947.
"Bostic Bounce" (E.E. Bostic), Essgee Music Publishing Corp., October 2, 1947.
"845 Stomp" (E.E. Bostic), Essgee Music Publishing Corp., October 2, 1947.

Appendix B. Bostic as Composer 175

"Blow Cat" aka "Blow Man" (E.E. Bostic), Essgee Music Publishing Corp., October 2, 1947.
"Bostic Rhumboogie" (E.E. Bostic), Essgee Music Publishing Corp., October 2, 1947.
"September" (E.E. Bostic), c. 1948.
"Artistry by Bostic" (E.E. Bostic), Andrea Music Co., December 7, 1949.
"No Name Blues" (E.E. Bostic), Lois Publishing Co., January 10, 1950.
"Slightly Groovy" (E.E. Bostic), Andrea Music Co., January 11, 1950.
"Scotch Jam" (E.E. Bostic), Lois Publishing Co., January 11, 1950.
"Joy Dust" (E.E. Bostic), Andrea Music Co., January 11, 1950.
"Wild Man" (E.E. Bostic), Andrea Music Co., January 11, 1950.
"Bostic's Boogie Blues" (E.E. Bostic), Andrea Music Co., January 11, 1950.
"Wobbling Duck" (E. E. Bostic, Charles McCormick), Andrea Music Co., January 11, 1950.
"Nay, Nay, Go Away" (E.E. Bostic), Lois Publishing Co., January 24, 1950.
"Serenade" (E.E. Bostic), Lois Publishing Co., April 7, 1950.
"Seven Steps" (E.E. Bostic), Lois Publishing Co., June 21, 1950.
"Way Down" (E.E. Bostic), Lois Publishing Co., November 10, 1950.
"Serenade to Beauty" (E.E. Bostic), Andrea Music Co., December 12, 1950.
"Don't You Do It" (E.E. Bostic), Lois Publishing Co., Cincinnati, March 26, 1952.
"Earl Blows a Fuse" (E.E. Bostic), Lois Publishing Co., Cincinnati, March 26, 1952.
"Earl's Imagination" (E.E. Bostic), Lois Publishing Co., Cincinnati, March 26, 1952.
"Wrap It Up" (E.E. Bostic), Lois Publishing Co., Cincinnati, March 26, 1952.
"Swing Low Sweet Boogie" (E.E. Bostic), Lois Publishing Co., Cincinnati, April 16, 1952.
"Velvet Sunset" (E.E. Bostic), Lois Publishing Co., Cincinnati, May 20, 1952.
"Steamwhistle Jump" (E.E. Bostic), Lonat Publishing Co., Cincinnati, February 17, 1953.
"What! No Pearls!" (E.E. Bostic), Lois Publishing Co., Cincinnati, July 20, 1953.
"Cracked Ice" (E.E. Bostic), Lois Publishing Co., Cincinnati, March 22, 1954.
"Mambolino" (E.E. Bostic), Armo Music Corp., Cincinnati, June 21, 1954.
"Mambostic" (E.E. Bostic), Armo Music Corp., June 29, 1954.
"Ubangi Stomp" (E.E. Bostic), Armo Music Corp., June 29, 1954.
"Apollo Theatre Jump" (E.E. Bostic), Andrea Music Corp., May 5, 1954 (Unpublished).

Appendix B. Bostic as Composer

"Bostic's Jump" (E.E. Bostic), Andrea Music Co., May 5, 1954 (Unpublished).

"Hot Sauce Boss" (E.E. Bostic), Andrea Music Co., November 26, 1954.

"United Nations Stomp" (E.E. Bostic), c. 1955.

"The Bo-Do Rock" (E.E. Bostic, Bill Doggett, Ralph Bass), Armo Music Corp., Cincinnati, May 7, 1956.

"Too Fine for Crying" (E.E. Bostic, Charles Trammell), Earl's Publishing Co., February 19, 1957.

"Exercise" (E.E. Bostic), Earl's Publishing Co., April 9, 1957.

"A Gay Day" (E.E. Bostic), Earl's Publishing Co., August 7, 1957.

"Just Too Shy" (E.E. Bostic, Robert Farlice), Earl's Publishing Co., August 7, 1957.

"Answer Me" (E.E. Bostic), Earl's Publishing Co., August 19, 1957.

"Make Believe" (E.E. Bostic, Lexie Williams), Earl's Publishing Co., August 19, 1957.

"The Wrecking Rock" (E.E. Bostic), Earl's Publishing Co., August 19, 1957.

"Pinkie" (E.E. Bostic, Ralph Bass), Armo Music Corp., Cincinnati, May 28, 1958.

"Sweet Pea" (E.E. Bostic, Red Holloway), Earl's Publishing Co., May 28, 1958.

"Wee-Gee Board" (E.E. Bostic), Earl's Publishing Co., May 28, 1958.

"Ducky" (E.E. Bostic, Johnny Gray), Armo Music Corp., Cincinnati, February 10, 1959.

"Gondola" (Earl Bostic, Ralph Bass), Armo Music Corp., Cincinnati, February 10, 1959.

"The Key" (E.E. Bostic), Earl's Publishing Co., February 10, 1959.

"Up There in Orbit" (E.E. Bostic, R. Bass, J. Gray), Armo Music Corp., Cincinnati, February 10, 1959.

"Who Cares" (E.E. Bostic, R. Bass), Armo Music Corp., Cincinnati, February 10, 1959.

"White Horse" (E.E. Bostic), Earl's Publishing Co., October 9, 1959.

"I Hate to Go" (E.E. Bostic, R. Bass), Armo Music Corp., October 13, 1959.

"Tut Strut" (R. Bass, N. Nathan, E.E. Bostic) Armo Music Corp., December 15, 1959.

"Hildegarde" (E.E. Bostic), Earl's Publishing Co., January 27, 1960.

"Let's Move Out" (E.E. Bostic), Earl's Publishing Co., February 7, 1960.

"Stop Your Crying" (E.E. Bostic, Charles Trammell), Earl's Publishing Co., August 29, 1961.

"Apple Cake" (E.E. Bostic, C. Neely), Earl's Publishing Co., 1963.

"Fast Track" (E.E. Bostic, C. Neely), Earl's Publishing Co., January 29, 1964.

"Telstar Drive" (E.E. Bostic), Earl's Publishing Co., January 29, 1964.
"Star Gazer" (E.E. Bostic), Earl's Publishing Co., July 15, 1964.
"Inquiry" (E.E. Bostic), September 3, 1964.
"Touchstone" (E.E. Bostic), September 3, 1964.
"Let's Dance, Little Girl" (E.E. Bostic), Earl's Publishing Co., November 18, 1964.
"The Repeater" (E.E. Bostic), Fremont Music Co., June 30, 1965.

APPENDIX C

Discography

Note: All are U.S. releases unless stated otherwise.

Singles

10" 78 RPM

That's the Groovy Thing/Tippin' In *Gotham* 104 (1946).
The Major and the Minor/All On *Majestic* 1056 (1946).
That's the Groovy Thing Pt. 1/Part 2 *Gotham* 111 (1946).
The Man I Love/Hurricane Blues *Majestic* 1055 (1946).
Cuttin' Out/Here Goes *Gotham* 151 (1947).
My Special Dream/I'm the Guy That Loves Ya *Gotham* 152 (1947).
Bostic's Jump/ Hot Sauce!—Boss *Gotham* 155 (1947).
845 Stomp/Earl's Rumboogie *King* 4198 (1947).
Bostic's Jump/Hot Sauce!—Boss *King* 4204 (1948).
Temptation/Artistry by Bostic *Gotham* G-160 (1948).
Bostic's Boogie Blues/Bar Fly Baby *King* 4229 (1948).
Joy Dust/Slightly Groovy *Gotham* G-162 (1948).
Joy Dust/Slightly Groovy *King* 4247 (1948).
Where or When/Disc Jockey's Nightmare *King* 4266 (1949).
Liza/Scotch Jam *Gotham* G-172 (1949).
Blip Boogie/Watch Where You Walk Boy *King* 4277 (1949).
From Midnight to Dawn/Earl's Blues *King* 4302 (1949).
Choppin' It Down/No Name Blues *King* 4343 (1950).
Serenade/Wrap Your Troubles in Dreams *King* 4369 (1950).
Seven Steps/Portrait of a Faded Love (Vocal by Helen Young) *King* 4387 (1950).
The Man I Love/Apollo Theatre Jump *Gotham* G-248 (1950).
Way Down/Merry Widow Waltz *King* 4420 (1950).
Serenade to Beauty/Tiger Rag *Gotham* G-255 (1951).
Rockin' and Reelin'/I Can't Give You Anything but Love *King* 4437 (1951).
September Song/Sleep *King* 4444 (1951).
Always/How Could It Have Been You and I *King* 4454 (1951).

Flamingo/I'm Getting Sentimental Over You *King* 4475 (1951).
I Got Loaded/Chains of Love *King* 4491 (1951).
Lover Come Back to Me/The Moon Is Low *King* 4511 (1952).
Linger Awhile/Velvet Sunset *King* 4536 (1952).
Smoke Gets in Your Eyes/For You *King* 4570 (1952).
You Go to My Head/The Hour of Parting *King* 4586 (1952).
The Sheik of Araby/Steam Whistle Jump *King* 4603 (1953).
Cherokee/The Song Is Ended *King* 4623 (1953).
Deep Purple/Smoke Rings *King* 4674 (1953).
Cracked Ice/My Heart at Thy Sweet Voice *King* 4699 (1954).
Jungle Drums/Danube Waves *King* 4708 (1954).
Mambolino/Blue Skies *King* 4723 (1954).
These Foolish Things/Mambostic *King* 4730 (1954).
Ubangi Stomp/Time on My Hands *King* 4741 (1954).
Song of the Islands/Liebestraum *King* 4754 (1954).
Night and Day/Embraceable You *King* 4765 (1955).
Sweet Lorraine/Melody of Love *King* 4776 (1955).
Remember/Cherry Bean *King* 4799 (1955).
Beyond the Blue Horizon/For All We Know *King* 4829 (1955).
Poème/O Sole Mio *King* 4845 (1955).
Dream/East of the Sun *King* 4815 (1956).
Bugle Call Rag/I'll String Along with You *King* 4905 (1956).
Honeysuckle Rose/Back Beat *King* 5127 (c. 1957).
Over the Waves Rock/Twilight Time *King* 5136 (1958).

7" SINGLES (45 RPM)

845 Stomp/Earl's Rhumboogie *Gotham* G 7154 (1950).
The Man I Love/Apollo Theatre Jump *Gotham* G 7248 (1950).
Serenade to Beauty/Tiger Rag *Gotham* G 7255 (1950).
Seven Steps/Portrait of a Faded Love *King* 45-4387 (1951).
Sleep/September Song *King* 45-4444 (1951).
The Moon Is Low/Lover Come Back to Me *King* 45-4511 (1951).
Flamingo/I'm Getting Sentimental Over You *King* 45-4475 (1951).
Linger Awhile/Velvet Sunset *King* 45-4536 (1952).
Smoke Gets in Your Eyes/For You *King* 45-4570 (1952).
You Go to My Head/The Hour of Parting *King* 45-4586 (1953).
The Sheik of Araby/Steamwhistle Jump *King* 45-4603 (1953).
Cherokee/The Song Is Ended *King* 45-4623 (1953).
Melancholy Serenade/ What! No Pearls *King* 45-4644 (1953).
The Very Thought of You/Memories *King* 45-4653 (1953).
Deep Purple/Smoke Rings *King* 45-4674 (1953).
Cracked Ice/My Heart at Thy Sweet Voice *King* 45-4699 (1954).

Appendix C. Discography

Jungle Drums/Danube Waves *King* 45-4708 (1954).
Blue Skies/Mambolino *King* 45-4723 (1954).
These Foolish Things/Mambostic *King* 45-4730 (1954).
Oh Baby/There Is No Greater Love *King* 45-4739 (1954) (Sonny Carter with Earl Bostic Orch.).
Ubangi Stomp/Time on My Hands *King* 45-4741 (1954).
Song of the Islands/Liebestraum *King* 45-4754 (1954).
Embraceable You/Night and Day *King* 45-4765 (1955).
Melody of Love/Sweet Lorraine *King* 45-4776 (1955).
When Your Lover Has Gone/Cocktails for Two *King* 45-4790 (1955).
Remember/Cherry Bean *King* 45-4799 (1955).
Dream/East of the Sun *King* 45-4815 (1955).
For All We Know/Beyond the Blue Horizon *King* 45-4829 (1955).
O Sole Mio/ Poème *King* 45-4845 (1955).
'Cause You're My Lover/I Love You Truly *King* 45-4883 (1956).
Bugle Call Rag/I'll String Along with You *King* 45-4905 (1956).
Roses of Picardy/Where or When *King* 45-4943 (1956).
Pompton Turnpike/Lester Leaps In *King* 45-4954 (1956).
I Hear a Rhapsody/Harlem Nocturne *King* 45-4978 (1956).
Too Fine for Crying/Avalon *King* 45-5025 (1957).
Temptation/September Song *King* 45-5041 (1957).
Exercise/She's Funny That Way *King* 45-5056 (1957).
Vienna, City of My Dreams/Just Too Shy *King* 45-5071 (1957).
A Gay Day/Answer Me *King* 45-5081 (1957).
Josephine/Jeanine, I Dream of Lilac Time *King* 45-5092 (1957).
No Name Jive/Southern Fried *King* 45-5106 (1958).
Honeysuckle Rose/Back Beat *King* 45-5127 (1958).
Woodchopper's Ball/John's Idea *King* 45-5133 (1958).
Twilight Time/Over the Waves Rock *King* 45-5136 (1958).
Home Sweet Home Rock/Pinkie *King* 45-5144 (1958).
Goodnight Sweetheart/Indian Boogie Woogie *King* 45-5152 (1958).
Rockin' with Richard/Redskin Cha Cha *King* 45-5161 (1958).
My Reverie Cha Cha/Barcarolle *King* 45-5175 (1959).
Up There in Orbit/Sweet Pea *King* 45-5190 (1959).
Up There in Orbit Part 1/Part 2 *King* 45-S-5203 (1959) (Special Edition).
La Cucaracha Cha Cha/Dancing in the Dark *King* 45-5209 (1959).
Who Cares/Feeling Cool *King* 45-5229 (1959).
White Horse/Dark Eyes *King* 45-5252 (1959).
Gondola/Once in a While *King* 45-5263 (1959).
Tut-Strut/All the Things You Are *King* 45-4290 (1959).
Ebb Tide/Hildegarde *King* 45-5301 (1959).
Let's Move Out/Song of India *King* 45-5309 (1960).

Appendix C. Discography

Hello Sixty/Off Shore *King* 45-5314 (1960).
Out of Nowhere/Elegie *King* 45-5317 (1960).
Make Believe/A Gay Day *King* 45-5345 (1960).
Tuxedo Junction/Polanaise *King* 45-5362 (1960).
720 in the Books/Just in Time *King* 45-5402 (1960).
That Old Black Magic/Full Moon and Empty Arms *King* 45-5454 (1961).
Jersey Bounce/Because of You *King* 45-5477 (1961).
April in Portugal/The Thrill Is Gone *King* 45-5564 (1961).
Wrap It Up/How Deep Is the Ocean *King* 45-5600 (1962).
Dark Eyes/People Will Say We're in Love *King* 45-5636 (1962).
More Than You Know/Don't Blame Me *King* 45-5661 (1962).
Deep in My Heart/Ducky *King* 45-5683 (1962).
Autumn Leaves/Anitra's Dance *King* 45-5699 (1962).
El Choclo Bossa Nova/My Reverie Bossa Nova *King* 45-5711 (1962).
Cherry Pink and Apple Blossom White/Your Cheatin' Heart *King* 45-5742 (1963).
Love Letters in the Sand/Tammy *King* 45-5776 (1963).
Don't Do It Please/Apple Cake *King* 45-5819 (1963).
Telstar Drive/Fast Track *King* 45-5839 (1964).
Summertime/Let's Dance Little Girl *King* 45-5861 (1964).
Star Gazer/Make Believe *King* 45-5900 (1964).
Pink Panther/Lawrence of Arabia *King* 45-5925 (1964).
From Russia with Love/My Special Dream *King* 45-5944 (1964).
Dominique/Theme from The Unforgiven *King* 45-5955 (1964).
Walk on the Wild Side/Hello Dolly *King* 45-5961 (1964).

Long-Playing Records

10" LPs 33 RPM

Earl Bostic and His Alto Sax. A1 Flamingo A2 Wrap It Up A3 I Can't Give You Anything but Love B1 Always B2 Merry Widow B3 Filibuster *King* LP 295-64 (1951).

Earl Bostic and His Alto Sax. A1 Sleep A2 Earl Blows a Fuse A3 No Name Blues B1 Serenade B2 The Moon Is Low B3 Don't You Do It King LP 295-65 (1951).

Earl Bostic and His Alto Sax. A1 Lover Come Back to Me A2 Choppin' It Down A3 Earl's Imagination B1 Seven Steps B2 I'm Getting Sentimental Over You B3 Swing Low Sweet Boogie. *King* LP 295-66 (1951).

Earl Bostic and His Alto Sax. A1 Moonglow A2 Velvet Sunset A3 For You A4 Ain't Misbehavin' B1 You Go to My Head B2 Smoke Gets in Your Eyes B3 The Hour of Parting B4 Linger Awhile. *King* LP 295-72 (1953).

Earl Bostic His Alto Sax and His Orchestra. A1 Flamingo A2 Sleep A3 I'm Getting Sentimental Over You A4 Moonglow B1 Ain't Misbehavin' B2 Linger Awhile B3 Lover Come Back to Me B4 Seven Steps. *Vogue* Issued in France and England (1954) LD 110 in France LDE 100 in England.

12" LPs 33 RPM

The Best of Bostic. A1 Flamingo A2 Always A3 Deep Purple A4 Smoke Rings A5 What! No Pearls A6 Jungle Drums B1 Serenade B2 I Can't Give You Anything but Love B3 Seven Steps B4 I'm Getting Sentimental Over You B5 Don't You Do It B6 Steamwhistle Jump. *King* LP 395-500 (1956).

Earl Bostic for You. A1 Sleep A2 Moonglow A3 Velvet Sunset A4 For You A5 The Very Thought of You A6 Linger Awhile B1 Cherokee B2 Smoke Gets in Your Eyes B3 Memories B4 Embraceable You B5 Wrap Your Troubles in Dreams B6 Night and Day. *King* LP 395-503 (1956).

Altotude. A1 East of the Sun A2 When Your Lover Has Gone A3 Bugle Call Rag A5 Remember A6 Beyond the Blue Horizon B1 'Cause You're My Love B2 Melody of Love B3 Cocktails for Two B4 I'll String Along with You B5 I Love You Truly B6 Dream. *King* LP 395-515 (1956).

Dance Time. A1 Harlem Nocturne A2 Where or When A3 Sweet Lorraine A4 Poème A5 You Go to My Head A6 Off Shore B1 The Moon Is Low B2 Ain't Misbehavin' B3 The Sheikh of Araby B4 I Hear a Rhapsody B5 Roses of Picardy B6 Melancholy Serenade. *King* 525 (1957).

Let's Dance. A1 Lover Come Back to Me A2 The Merry Widow Waltz A3 Cracked Ice A4 Song of the Islands A5 Danube Waves A6 Wrap It Up B1 Blue Skies B2 Ubangi Stomp B3 Cherry Bean B4 Earl's Imagination B5 My Heart at Thy Sweet Voice B6 Liebestraum. *King* LP 529 (1957).

Invitation to Dance. A1 Temptation A2 Jeannine I Dream of Lilac Time A3 September Song A4 She's Funny That Way A5 Just Too Shy A6 Exercise B1 Josephine B2 Away B3 A Gay Day B4 Make Believe B5 Vienna, City of My Dreams B6 Answer Me. *King* LP 547 (1957).

C'mon Dance. A1 Avalon A2 The Bo-Do Rock A3 Laura A4 Mambostic A5 Mean to Me A6 Time on My Hands B1 For All We Know B2 Indiana B3 Too Fine for Crying B4 Mambolino B5 Bubbins Rock B6 How Deep Is the Ocean. *King* LP 558 (1958).

Bostic Rocks Hits of the Swing Age. A1 Southern Fried A2 Jersey Bounce A3 Jumpin' at the Woodside A4 Tuxedo Junction A5 720 in the Books A6 Airmail Special B1 Pompton Turnpike B2 Woodchopper's Ball B3 Night Train B4 Stompin' at the Savoy B5 Honeysuckle Rose B6 No Name Jive. *King* LP 571 (1958).

Showcase of Swinging Dance Hits. A1 Lester Leaps in A2 920 Special A3 Special Delivery Stomp A4 Anvil Chorus A5 Two O' Clock Jump A6

Back Beat B1 John's Idea B2 Royal Garden Blues B3 Indian Boogie Woogie B4 Fur Trapper's Ball B5 Lunceford Special B6 Back Bay Shuffle. *King* LP 583 (1958).

Alto Magic in Hi Fi. A1 Twilight Time A2 Stairway to the Stars A3 Rockin' with Richard A4 Be My Love A5 Pinkie A6 Goodnight, Sweetheart B1 Over the Wave Rock B2 Jer-On-Imo B3 C-Jam Blues B4 Wee-Gee Board B5 The Wrecking Rock B6 Sweet Home Rock. *King* LP 597 (1958).

Sweet Tunes of the Fantastic 50s. A1 Because of You A2 Unchained Melody A3 Stranger in Paradise A4 Ebb Tide A5 Lisbon Antigua A6 Love Is a Many-Splendored Thing B1 April in Portugal B2 Blue Tango B3 Three Coins in the Fountain B4 Canadian Sunset B5 Autumn Leaves B6 The Song from Moulin Rouge. *King* LP 602 (1959).

Dance Music from the Bostic Workshop. A1 Third Man Theme A2 The Key A3 Does Your Heart Beat for Me A4 El Choclo Cha Cha A5 Gondola A6 Sweet Pea B1 Ducky B2 Sentimental Journey B3 Barcarolle B4 Who Cares B5 Rose Marie B6 Up There in Orbit. *King* LP 613 (1959).

Sweet Tunes of the Roaring 20s. A1 Pagan Love Song A2 Manhattan A3 When Day Is Done A4 Softly as in a Morning Sunrise A5 Charmaine A6 Frasquita Serenade B1 Deep in My Heart B2 More Than You Know B3 Indian Love Call B4 Amour Toujours L'Amour B5 I Kiss Your Hand Madame B6 My Heart Stood Still. *King* LP 620 (1959).

Sweet Tunes of the Swinging 30s. A1 I Cover the Waterfront A2 In the Still of the Night A3 The Thrill Has Gone A4 The Night Is Young A5 My Reverie A6 Body and Soul B1 The Way You Look Tonight B2 Dancing in the Dark B3 The Breeze and I B4 Stars in My Eyes B5 There Is No Greater Love B6 All the Things You Are. *King* LP 632 (1959).

Sweet Tunes of the Sentimental 40s. A1 Moonlight in Vermont A2 Long Ago and Far Away A3 That Old Black Magic A4 It Might as Well Be Spring A5 I Think of You A6 Polonaise B1 Full Moon and Empty Arms B2 Mam'selle B3 Autumn Serenade B4 La Vie en Rose B5 While We're Young B6 I'll Walk Alone. *King* LP 640 (1959).

Musical Pearls. A1 Don't Blame Me A2 Dark Eyes A3 Feeling Cool A4 Once in a While A5 Anitra's Dance A6 Tut Strut B1 April Showers B2 Hildegarde B3 Song of India B4 Thinking of You B5 Let's Move Out B6 La Cucaracha. *King* LP 662 (1959).

Earl Bostic Memories. A1 Linger Awhile A2 The Very Thought of You A3 For You A4 Sleep A5 Embraceable You A6 Night and Day A7 Till the End of Time B1 Song of India B2 Don't Blame Me B3 Dark Eyes B4 Once in a While B5 April Showers B6 Long Ago and Far Away B7 It Might as Well Be Spring. *Polydor* LP 623 270 (Originally released 1959).

Plays the Hit Tunes of the Big Broadway Shows. A1 On the Street Where You Live A2 People Will Say We're in Love A3 Getting to Know

You A4 Some Enchanted Evening A5 Summertime A6 Bewitched B1 If I Loved You B2 Make Believe B3 How are Things in Glocca Morro? B4 Just in Time B5 So in Love. *King* LP 705 Issued in England as *Parlophone* PMC 1125 (1960).

By Popular Demand. A1 Temptation A2 Ebb Tide A3 Third Man Theme A4 Time on My Hands A5 The Key A6 More Than You Know B1 Avalon B2 Answer Me B3 Body and Soul B4 Anvil Chorus B5 That Old Black Magic B6 Velvet Sunset. *King* 786 (1961).

Plays Bossa Nova. A1 La Bossa A2 El Choclo Bossa Nova A3 Bossalino A4 My Reverie (Bossa Nova) A5 That Old Black Magic A6 La Cucaracha B1 Time on My Hands B2 Cha Bossa B3 Autumn Serenade B4 Softly as in A Morning Sunrise B5 Canadian Sunset B6 Be My Love. *King* 827 (1963).

Songs of the Fantastic 50s Vol. 2. A1 Cherry Pink and Apple Blossom White A2 Love Letters in the Sand A3 The High and the Mighty A4 Baubles, Bangles and Beads A5 Mr. Sandman A6 Too Young B1 Vaya Con Dios B2 It's No Sin B3 Your Cheatin' Heart B4 Tammy B5 O My Papa B6 I Can Dream Can't I. *King* 838 (1963).

Jazz as I Feel It. A1 Don't Do It Please A2 Ten Out A3 Telstar Drive A4 A Taste of Fresh Air B1 Hunt and Peck B2 Fast Track B3 Apple Cake. *King* 846 (1963).

A New Sound. A1 Blues for the Ivy Leagues A2 Touchstone A3 Que Jay A4 Wood Chuck A5 Chicken Little B1 Nita B2 Inquiry B3 Karen B4 Empathy B5 Wednesday's Child. *King* 900 (1964).

The Best of Earl Bostic Vol. 2. A1 Third Man Theme A2 Sentimental Journey A3 My Reverie A4 Be My Love A5 Twilight Time A6 Minkie Pinkie B1 Dark Eyes B2 Don't Blame Me B3 The Breeze and I B4 Softly as in a Morning Sunrise B5 More Than You Know B6 Indian Love Call. *King* LP 881 (1964).

Great Hits of 1964. A1 Pink Panther A2 Charade A3 Dominique A4 Walk on the Wild Side A5 Hello Dolly A6 More B1 From Russia with Love B2 Theme from The Unforgiven B3 Days of Wine and Roses B4 My Special Dream B5 Maria B6 Lawrence of Arabia. *King* LP 921 (1964).

7" EPs

Earl Bostic Vol. 3. A1 Memories A2 What! No Pearls B1 Melancholy Serenade B2 The Very Thought of You. *King* XP 123 (1953).

Vol 4. A1 Deep Purple A2 Velvet Sunset B1 Choppin' It Down B2 You Go to My Head. *King* XP 124 (1953).

Earl Bostic and His Alto Sax Vol. 1 A1 Flamingo A2 Swing Low Sweet Boogie B1 I Can't Give You Anything but Love B2 The Moon Is Low. *King* EP 200 (1953)

Earl Bostic Vol. 1. A1 Linger Awhile A2 Merry Widow B1 Always B2 Earl Blows a Fuse. *King* EP 202.

Earl Bostic Vol. 5. A1 Cherokee A2 No Name Blues B1 Seven Steps B2 Don't You Do It. *King* KEP 204 (1953).

Vol. 6. A1 Moonglow A2 For You B1 Blip Boogie B2 Wrap It Up. *King* GEP 205 (1953).

Vol 7. A1 Filibuster A2 Smoke Gets in Your Eyes B1 The Sheik of Araby B2 The Hour of Parting. *King* EP 206 (1953).

Vol. 9. A1 Melancholy Serenade A2 What! No Pearls B1 The Very Thought of You B2 Memories. *King* EP 245 (1953).

Vol. 10. A1 Jungle Drums A2 The Song Is Ended B1 Off Shore B2 Cracked Ice. *King* KEP 284 (1954).

Vol. 11. A1 Danube Waves A2 My Heart Sweet Voice B1 Poème B2 O Sole Mio. *King* KEP 285 (1954).

Mambo Stylings—Vol. 12. A1 Mambostic A2 Time on My Hands B1 Mambolino B2 Ven-a-Mi. *King* KEP 347 (1955).

The Artistry of Earl Bostic—Vol. 13. A1 Blue Skies A2 These Foolish Things B1 Song of the Islands B2 Ubangi Stomp. *King* KEP 350 (1955).

Earl Bostic and His Alto Sax—Vol. 14. A1 Cherry Bean A2 Liebestraum B1 Night and Day B2 Embraceable You. *King* KEP 355 (1955).

Earl Bostic and His Alto Sax—Vol 15. A1 Melody of Love A2 Cocktails for Two B1 Blue Moon B2 Remember. *King* KEP 363 (1956).

Earl Bostic with Strings—Vol 16. A1 Dream A2 Beyond the Blue Horizon B1 East of the Sun B2 For All We Know. *King* KEP 375 (1956).

Bostic Blows—Vol. 17. A1 Bugle Call Rag A2 I Love You Truly B1 'Cause You're My Lover B2 I'll String Along with You. *King* KEP 381 (1956).

Earl Bostic—All Time Hits, Vol. 18. A1 Harlem Nocturne A2 I Hear a Rhapsody B1 Roses of Picardy B2 Where or When. *King* KEP 398 (1956).

Earl Bostic—Bostic Rocks—Hits of the Swing Age Vol 1. A1 Southern Fried A2 Jersey Bounce B1 Jumpin' at the Woodside B2 Tuxedo Junction. *King* KEP 414 (1958).

Earl Bostic—Four Cha Cha Chas. A1 Softly as in a Morning Sunrise Cha Cha A2 My Reverie Cha Cha B1 El Choclo Cha Cha B2 Redskin Cha Cha. *King* EP 431 (1963).

Non-U.S. EP Releases

Earl Bostic and His Orchestra. A1 Flamingo A2 Sleep B1 Ain't Misbehavin' B2 Moonglow. *Vogue* EPV 1010 (1950) (England).

Earl Bostic and His Orchestra. A1 Flamingo A2 Swing Low Sweet Boogie B1 I Can't Give You Anything but Love B2 The Moon Is Low. *Angel* EP 1001 (1955) (Japan).

Appendix C. Discography

Earl Bostic. A1 Flamingo A2 Swing Low Sweet Boogie B1 I Can't Give You Anything but Love B2 The Moon Is Low. *Odeon* GEOW 31-1011 (1955) (Germany).

Earl's Imagination. A1 Earl's Imagination A2 Lover Come Back to Me B1 Sleep B2 I'm Gettin' Sentimental Over You. *Parlophone* GEP 8548 (c. 1955) (England). All the Parlophone releases were issued in Italy on the Parlophon American King Series with different cover designs, for instance, *Earl's Imagination* as KLP 25004.

Alto Sax and Mambo Strings. A1 Poème A2 O Sole Mio B1 Mambostic B2 Time on My Hands. *Parlophone* GEP 8565 (1956) (England).

Music à la Bostic No. 1. A1 The Sheik of Araby A2 The Hour of Parting B1 Serenade B2 Ain't Misbehavin' *Parlophone* GEP 8571 (1956) (England).

Music à la Bostic No. 2. A1 The Very Thought of You A2 Memories B1 Moonglow B2 Blip Boogie. *Parlophone* GEP 8574 (England).

Music à la Bostic No. 3. A1 Mambolino A2 Ven-a-mi B1 Off Shore B2 Cracked Ice. *Parlophone* GEP 8603 (England).

Bostic in Harlem. A1 East of the Sun A2 Sweet Lorraine B1 Harlem Nocturne B2 Avalon. *Parlophone* GEP 8637 (1957) (England).

Big Bostic Beat. A1 Love You Truly A2 'Cause You're My Lover B1 Josephine B2 Jeanine, I Dream of Lilac Time. *Parlophone* EP 8701 (1957) (England)

Rockin' With Bostic. A1 Rockin' With Richard A2 Home Sweet Home Rock B1 Pinkie B2 Goodnight Sweetheart *Parlophone* GEP 8741 (1957) (England).

Earl Bostic and His Orchestra. A1 Bugle Call Rag A2 I'll String Along with You B1 I Love You Truly B2 'Cause You are My Lover. *Odeon* 7 MOE 2064 (1957) (France).

Bostic Rocks. A1 Southern Fried A2 Tuxedo Junction B1 Air Mail Special B2 Jumpin' at the Woodside. *President* Hi Fi PRC 72 (1958) 7" EP (France).

Bostic Rocks 2. A1 Night Train A2 Pompton Turnpike B1 Woodchopper's Ball B2 No Name Blues. *President* Hi Fi PRC 76 (1958) 7" EP (France).

Earl Bostic—3. A1 Twilight Time A2 Over the Waves Rock B1 720 in the Books B2 Honeysuckle Rose. *President* Hi Fi PRC 88 (1958) 7" EP (France).

Bostic Plays Evergreens. A1 The Sheikh of Araby A2 Because of You B1 Sweet Lorraine B2 Autumn Leaves. *Odeon* O 41 273 (1960) 7" EP (Germany).

Earl Bostic. A1 La Cucaracha Cha Cha A2 Dancing in the Dark B1 Dark Eyes B2 Liebestraum. *Odeon* SOE 3559 (1960) 7" EP (France).

Earl Bostic. A1 Smoke Gets in Your Eyes A2 East of the Sun B1 I'm Getting Sentimental Over You B2 Smoke Rings. *Disques Vogue* EPL 8 084 (1963) 7" EP (France).

Recordings with Other Artists

Earl Bostic and Orchestra/Jimmie Lunceford. (Tracks by Bostic on Side A, Lunceford on Side B) A1 The Man I Love A2 All On A3 Hurricane Blues A4 The Man I Love. *Sparton* 4033 (1955).

Lionel Hampton All Star Groups. Bostic plays alto sax on track A6 The Heebie Jeebies Are Rockin' Town. *Jazztone* J 1246 (1956).

Earl Bostic and Bill Doggett. Mean to Me/The Bo-Do Rock *King* 4930 7" (1956).

Earl Bostic and Bill Doggett. Indiana/Bubbins Rock *King* 45-4954 7" (1956).

Earl Bostic and Bill Doggett—Bostic Meets Doggett. A1 Indiana (Bostic & Doggett) A2 Hammer Head (Doggett) A3 Answer Me (Bostic) A4 Shindig A5 Bubbins Rock (Both) B1 Mean to Me (Both) B2 A Gay Day (Bostic) B3 Ding Dong (Doggett) B4 Exercise (Bostic) B5 Bo-Do Rock (Both) 10" LP. *Parlophone* PMD 1054 (England) (1957).

Earl Bostic and Bill Doggett. Earl's Dog/ Special Delivery Stomp *King* 5427 7" single (1960).

Hot Lips Page—1944. A1 Big D Blues A2 Gee Baby Ain't I Good to You A3 The Lady in Red A4 It Ain't Like That A5 Florida Blues A6 Race Horse Mama Blues A7 The Lady in Debt B1 Corsicana B2 Willie Mae Willow Foot B3 Sunset Blues B4 They Raided the Joint B5 That's the Blues B6 I Want Every Bit of It B7 What's the Matter Now B8 4F Blues. *Black and Blue* BB 33008 (1967).

Cousin Joe—Cousin Joe from New Orleans in His Prime. A1 You Ain't Such a Much A2 Fly Hen Blues A3 Lonesome Man Blues A4 Little Eva B1 Baby You Don't Know It All B2 The Barefoot Baby. *Oldie Blues, Munich Records* OL 8008 LP (1984) (Netherlands).

Various Artists Compilations Featuring Tracks by Bostic

Earl Bostic, Tiny Bradshaw, Ernie Englund. Featuring Flamingo and Sleep by Bostic. *Vogue* 7" LP ELP 801.

Jam Session at Savoy. Includes "Swing Street" and "Jam Session" by Bostic. 10" LP *Savoy Records* MC 9030 (1954).

Posthumous Releases

Memorial to Earl Bostic. A1 Summertime A2 Polonaise A3 So in Love A4 Up There in Orbit A5 The Thrill Is Gone A6 Ducky A7 People Will Say We're In Love A8 Over the Waves Rock A9 The Way You Look Tonight A10 Minky Pinky A11 All the Things You Are A12 Barcarolle B1 Some Enchanted Evening B2 Song of India B3 On the Street Where You Live B4

Dark Eyes B5 In the Still of the Night B6 Anitra's Dance B7 Bewitched B8 Elegie B9 Third Man Theme B10 Hildegarde B11 If I Loved You B12 Let's Move Out. *King* LP K-947 (1965).

The Earl of Bostic. A1 Tiger Rag A2 Artistry by Bostic A3 Apollo Theater Jump A4 Serenade to Beauty A5 Earl's Rumboogie B1 Hot Sauce Boss B2 845 Stomp B3 Bostic Jump B4 My Special Dream B5 Away. *Grand Prix Series* K-404 (1966).

The Song Is NOT Ended. A1 Red Sails in the Sunset A2 Shangri La A3 On the Sunny Side of the Street A4 What's New A5 The Man I Love A6 My Funny Valentine B1 Misty B2 On Green Dolphin Street B3 Rose Room B4 People B5 The Song Is Ended. *Philips* PHS 600-262 (Stereo) PHS 200-262 (Mono) (1967).

Jazz History—Earl Bostic Vol. 20. Double gatefold 2 × LP. A1 Flamingo A2 What! No Pearls A3 Ubangi Stomp A4 Wrap It Up A5 Sweet Lorraine A6 Where or When B1 Steamwhistle Jump B2 Ain't Misbehavin' B3 Back Beat B4 John's Idea B5 Indian Boogie Woogie B6 Lunceford Special C1 All the Things You Are C2 Stars in My Eyes C3 The Way You Look Tonight C4 Dancing in the Dark C5 The Thrill Is Gone C6 Body and Soul D1 Dark Eyes D2 Exercise D3 Blue Skies D4 Does Your Heart Beat for Me D5 Let's Move Out D6 Tut Strut. *Polydor* 2679 024 S (Stereo) (1974).

Earl Bostic—14 Hits. A1 That's the Groovy Thing Pt. 1 & 2 A2 845 Stomp A3 Where or When (single version, previously unissued on LP) A4 Flamingo A5 Sleep A6 Blue Moon A7 Blue Skies B1 Harlem Nocturne B2 September Song B3 Stompin' at the Savoy B4 Twilight Time B5 Arrivederci Roma (previously unissued) B6 Cherry Pink and Apple Blossom White B7 Walk on the Wild Side. *King, Gusto* K-5010X. Originally released in Germany on Rare Bid & Bellaphon as BID 8010 (1977).

That's Earl, Brother. (Tracks recorded 1943–45) A1 All On A2 Lady Be Good (Lionel Hampton) A3 Choo Choo Baby (Hampton) A4 Dreamer's Blues (Rex Stewart) A5 The Man I Love A6 The Major and the Minor B1 The Major and the Minor (Hampton) B2 Nola (Hampton) B3 Pawnee (Stewart) B4 Hurricane Blues B5 Three-Horn Parley (Stewart) B6 Shady Side of the Street. *Spotlite Records* SPJ 152 (1985).

Earl Bostic Blows a Fuse. (Tracks recorded 1946–57) Compilation & sleeve notes by Danny Adler. A1 Night Train A2 8:45 Stomp A3 That's the Groovy Thing A4 Special Delivery Stomp A5 Moonglow A6 Mambostic A7 Earl Blows a Fuse A8 Harlem Nocturne B1 Who Snuck the Wine in the Gravy? B2 Don't You Do It B3 Disc Jockey's Nightmare B4 Flamingo B5 Steam Whistle Jump B6 What! No Pearls B7 Tuxedo Junction B8 Seven Steps. *Charly R & B Charly Records Ltd.* CRB 1091 (1985).

Cry Baby. Music from the Original Motion Picture includes Bostic's

Jungle Drums. *MCA Records* 2292-57183-1 LP (Europe), also released on cassette and CD (1990).

CD Compilations

Lionel Hampton and His Orchestra—The Chronological Lionel Hampton 1942-1944. CD Tracks featuring Bostic: Loose Wig/Chop Chop/ Flying Home No. 2/Hamp's Boogie Woogie / Flying Home Pt. 1/Flying Home Pt. 2/The Major and the Minor/I Wonder Boogie (Hamp's Boogie Woogie) (Recorded 1944). *Classics 803* (1994) France.

Rex Stewart—The Chronological Rex Stewart 1934-46. CD Bostic plays alto on four tracks: Pawnee/Three Horn Parlay/Dreamer's Blues/ Shady Side of the Street (Recorded July 30, 1945). *Classics 931* (1997) (France).

Hot Lips Page—The Chronological Hot Lips Page 1940-44. CD Bostic plays on tracks 14 to 21: I Got What It Takes/Good for Stompin'/Double-Trouble Blues/Blooey/Six, Seven, Eight or Nine/You Need Coachin'/These Foolish Things/Fish for Supper. *Classics 089* (1995) (France).

Hot Lips Page 1937-49: The Alternative Takes in Chronological Order. CD Bostic features on tracks 12 to 16: Good for Stompin'/Blooey/ Six, Seven, Eight of Nine/You Need Coachin' These Foolish Things. *Neatwork RP2064* (2003) (Europe). Limited edition of 500.

Earl Bostic—Member's Edition. Includes six-page booklet. (1) Rockin' with Richard (2) Up There in Orbit (3) C Jam Blues (4) Does your heart beat for me? (5) El Choclo Cha Cha (6) Gondola (7) Home Sweet Home Rock (8) Pinkie (9) Over the Waves Rock (10) Rose Marie (11) Sentimental Journey (12) Stairway to the Stars (13) Sweet Pea (14) The Key (15) The Wrecking Rock (16) Twilight Time (17) Wee Gee Board (18) Who Cares? (19) Be My Love (20) Barcarolle (21) Ducky (22) Goodnight Sweetheart. *TKO Records* (1997) (Holland).

Earl Bostic—The EP Collection. Twenty-six-track compilation of all the British Parlophone 7" EP releases. Includes photos and liner notes by Joop Vissar. (1) Flamingo (2) Sleep (3) Harlem Nocturne (4) The Moon Is Low (5) Linger Awhile (6) Smoke Gets in Your Eyes (7) Always (8) Steamwhistle Jump (9) Serenade (10) Smoke Rings (11) Wrap It Up (12) Velvet Sunset (13) East of the Sun (14) I'm Getting Sentimental Over You (15) Ain't Misbehavin' (16) Off Shore (17) Moonglow (18) For You (19) The Very Thought of You (20) Avalon (21) C Jam Blues (22) Sweet Lorraine (23) Cracked Ice (24) Mambostic (25) Mambolino (26) Stairway to the Stars. *See for Miles Records Ltd.* SEE CD 688 (1999) (UK).

Earl Bostic—The EP Collection Vol. 2. Twenty-six-track compilation of the original 7" King EP releases, with liner notes by Joop Vissar. (1) Blip

Boogie (2) Swing Low Sweet Boogie (3) Seven Steps (4) Don't You Do It (5) I Can't Give You Anything but Love (6) Lover Come Back to Me (7) You Go to My Head (8) The Hour of Parting (9) Cherokee (10) Memories (11) What! No Pearls (12) Deep Purple (13) O Sole Mio (14) Blue Skies (15) Time on My Hands (16) These Foolish Things (17) Song of the Islands (18) Liebestraum (19) Night and Day (20) Beyond the Blue Horizon (21) Bugle Call Rag (22) Indiana (23) Bubbins Rock (24) I Hear a Rhapsody (25) Two O'Clock Jump (26) Goodnight Sweetheart. *See for Miles Records Ltd.* SEE 720 (2000) (UK).

The Chronological Earl Bostic 1945-48. (1) The Man I Love (2) Hurricane Blues (3) The Major and the Minor (4) All On (5) Liza (6) That's the Groovy Thing—Part A (7) Tippin' In (8) Baby You Don't Know It All (9) Jumpin' Jack (10) That's the Groovy Thing—Part B (11) The Barefoot Boy (12) That's the Heat You Gotta Beat (13) Let's Ball Tonight—Part I (14) Let's Ball Tonight—Part II (15) Away (16) Where or When (17) Cuttin' Out (18) My Special Dream (19) I'm the Guy Who Loves You (20) Here Goes (21) Bostic's Jump (22) Earl's Rumboogie (23) Hot Sauce Boss (24) 845 Stomp. *Classics Records Blues and Rhythm Series* Classics 5005, France (2001).

The Chronological Earl Bostic 1948-49. (1) Disc Jockey's Nightmare (2) Slightly Groovy (3) Barfly Baby (4) Artistry by Bostic (5) Scotch Jam (6) Apollo Theater Jump (7) Serenade to Beauty (8) Tiger Rag (9) The Man I Love (10) Temptation (11) Bostic's Boogie Blues (12) Joy Dust (13) Wild Man (14) Watch Where You Walk, Boy (15) Blip Boogie (16) From Midnight to Dawn (17) Swing Low, Sweet Boogie (18) Earl's Imagination (19) Earl Blows a Fuse (20) Nay! Nay! Go Away! (21) Who Snuck the Wine in the Gravy (22) Earl's Blues. *Classics Records Blues and Rhythm Series* Classics 5022, France (2001).

The Chronological Earl Bostic 1949-1951. (1) Sugar Hill Blues (2) Choppin' It Down (3) Filibuster (4) No Name Blues (5) Serenade (6) Seven Steps (7) Portrait of a Faded Love (8) Wrap Your Troubles in Dreams (9) Way Down (10) Don't You Do It (11) Merry Widow Waltz (12) Wrap It Up (13) Rockin' and Reelin' (14) September Song (15) I Can't Give You Anything but Love (16) Flamingo (17) Sleep (18) How Could It Have Been You and I (19) Always (20) I'm Getting Sentimental Over You (21) The Moon Is Low (22) Lover Come Back to Me (23) Chains of Love (24) I Got Loaded. *Classics Records Blues and Rhythm Series*, Classics 5039, France (2002).

The Chronological Earl Bostic 1952-53. (1) Velvet Sunset (2) Moonglow (3) Linger Awhile (4) Ain't Misbehavin' (5) You Go to My Head (6) The Hour of Parting (7) Smoke Gets in Your Eyes (8) For You (9) The Sheik of Araby (10) Cherokee (11) Steam Whistle Jump (12) The Song Is Ended (13) Melancholy Serenade (14) The Very Thought of You (15) Memories (16) What! No Pearls (17) Smoke Rings (18) Deep Purple (19) Jungle Drums (20) Cracked Ice (21) Danube Waves (22) Poème (23) My Heart at Thy Sweet

Voice (24) O Sole Mio (25) Off Shore. *Classics Records Blues and Rhythm Series*, Classics 5093, France (2004).

The Chronological Earl Bostic 1954–55. (1) There Is No Greater Love (2) Oh Baby (3) Blue Skies (4) Mambostic (5) Ven-A-Mi (6) Time on My Hands (7) Mambolino (8) These Foolish Things (9) Ubangi Stomp (10) Song of the Islands (11) Cherry Bean (12) Liebestraum (13) Night and Day (14) Embraceable You (15) Sweet Lorraine (16) I Solemnly Swear (17) It's Strange but True (18) Cocktails for Two (19) Blue Moon (20) When Your Love Has Gone (21) Remember (22) Melody of Love. *Classics Records Blues and Rhythm Series*, Classics 5179, France (2007).

Let's Ball Tonight. (1) & (2) Let's Ball Tonight (3) Rockin' and Reelin' (4) Earl's Rhumboogie (5) Scotch Jam (6) Earl's Blues (7) 8:45 Stomp (8) Bar Fly Baby (9) Bostic's Jump (10) Earl Blows a Fuse (11) Who Snuck the Wine in the Gravy (12) Cuttin' Out (13) Don't You Do It (14) & (15) That's the Groovy Thing Parts A & B (16) Hot Sauce Boss (17) Bostic Boogie Blues (18) Watch Where You Walk Boy (19) Blip Boogie (20) That's the Heat You Gotta Beat (21) Swing Low Sweet Boogie (22) Sugar Hill Blues (23) Way Down (24) Choppin' It Down (25) Filibuster (26) Nay! Nay! Go Away (27) I Got Loaded (28) No Name Blues. *Rev-Ola* CR REV 163 (2006) (UK).

Magic Bostic 1944/52—Jazz Archives No. 209. (1) Flamingo (2) Sleep (3) Bostic's Jump (4) Artistry by Bostic (5) Temptation (6) Bostic's Boogie Blues (7) From Midnight to Dawn (8) Serenade (9) Lover Come Back to Me (10) Moonglow (11) Ain't Misbehavin' (12) You Go to My Head (13) The Hour of Parting (14) Cherokee (15) Steamwhistle Jump (16) All On (17) Shady Side of the Street (18) Fly Hen Blues (19) Ram Session (20) Double Trouble Blues (Lip's Blues) (21) Texas and Pacific (22) Birmingham Boogie. *EPM Musique* 160402 (2003) (France).

The Earl Bostic Story (Box Set)

Disc 1 The Major and the Minor

(1) The Man I Love (2) Hurricane Blues (3) The Major and the Minor (4) All On (5) Liza (6) That's the Groovy Thing—Part A (7) Tippin' In (8) Baby You Don't Know It All (9) Jumpin' Jack (10) That's the Groovy Thing—Part B (11) The Barefoot Boy (12) That's the Heat You Gotta Beat (13) Let's Ball Tonight—Part 1 (14) Let's Ball Tonight—Part 2 (15) Away (16) Where or When (17) Cuttin' Out (18) My Special Dream (19) I'm the Guy Who Loves You (20) Here Goes (21) Bostic's Jump (22) Earl's Rhumboogie (23) Hot Sauce Boss (24) 845 Stomp (25) Disc Jockey's Nightmare (26) Slightly Groovy (27) Barfly Baby.

Disc 2 Earl Blows a Fuse

(1) Artistry by Bostic (2) Scotch Jam (3) Apollo Theatre Jump (4) Serenade to Beauty (5) Tiger Rag (6) The Man I Love (7) Temptation (8) Bostic's

Boogie Blues (9) Joy Dust (10) Wild Man (11) Watch Where You Walk Boy (12) Blip Boogie (13) From Midnight Till Dawn (14) Swing Low Sweet Boogie (15) Earl's Imagination (16) Earl Blows a Fuse (17) Nay! Nay! Go Away! (18) Who Snuck the Wine in the Gravy (19) Earl's Blues (20) Sugar Hill Blues (21) Choppin' It Down (22) Filibuster (23) No Name Blues (24) Serenade (25) Seven Steps (26) Portrait of a Faded Love (27) Wrap Your Troubles in Dreams.

DISC 3 *FLAMINGO*

(1) Way Down (2) Don't You Do It (3) Merry Widow Waltz (4) Wrap It Up (5) Rockin' and Reelin' (6) September Song (7) I Can't Give You Anything but Love (8) Flamingo (9) Sleep (10) How Could It Have Been You and I (11) Always (12) I'm Getting Sentimental Over You (13) The Moon Is Low (14) Lover Come Back to Me (15) Chains of Love (16) I Got Loaded (17) Velvet Sunset (18) Moonglow (19) Linger Awhile (20) Ain't Misbehavin' (21) You Go to My Head (22) The Hour of Parting (23) Smoke Gets in Your Eyes (24) For You (25) Sheik of Araby (26) Cherokee (27) Steam Whistle Jump.

DISC 4 *CRACKED ICE*

(1) The Song Is Ended (2) Melancholy Serenade (3) The Very Thought of You (4) Memories (5) What! No Pearls (6) Smoke Rings (7) Deep Purple (8) Jungle Drums (9) Cracked Ice (10) Danube Waves (11) Poème (12) My Heart at Thy Sweet Voice (13) O Sole Mio (14) Offshore (15) Blue Skies (16) Mambostic (17) Time on My Hands (18) Mambolino (19) These Foolish Things (20) Song of the Islands (21) Liebestraume (22) Night and Day (23) Sweet Lorraine (24) Beyond the Blue Horizon (25) East of the Sun.

Four- CD Box Set including forty-four-page illustrated booklet with essay by Joop Vissar. *Proper Records* Properbox 112 (England) (2006). Reissued 2015.

John Peel & Sheila—The Pig's Big 78s—A Beginner's Guide. Includes Sleep. *Trikont* U.S.—0350 Germany (2006).

Earl Bostic Plays Jazz Standards. (1) Harlem Nocturne (2) When Your Lover Has Gone (3) Where or When (4) Blue Skies (5) Blue Moon (6) Twilight Time (7) Arrivederci Roma (8) Smoke Gets in Your Eyes (9) I'm Getting Sentimental Over You (10) Moonglow (11) Be My Love (12) Third Man Theme (13) Sentimental Journey (14) Who Cares (15) East of the Sun (16) The Very Thought of You (17) Stairway to the Stars (18) Always (19) Deep Purple (20) I Can't Give You Anything but Love (21) Lover Come Back to Me (22) You Go to My Head (23) O Sole Mio (24) Night and Day (25) These Foolish Things (26) I Hear a Rhapsody (27) Cherokee (28) Sweet Lorraine (29) Flamingo. *Definitive Records* DRCD 11295 (2006) Europe.

Complete Quintet Recordings. Viz. *Jazz as I Feel It* (1963) and *A New Sound* (1964). Phono 870 225 (2015) Europe.

Four Classic Albums. Viz. *Dance Time* (1956), *Let's Dance with Earl Bostic* (1957), *Alto Magic in Hi-Fi—A Dance Party with Bostic* (1958), and *Dance Music from the Bostic Workshop* (1959) (two CDs). *Avid Jazz* AMSC 1210 (2016) (UK).

The Earl Bostic Collection 1939-59. Two CDs, with booklet and liner notes. Disc 1, (1) Lionel Hampton & Orchestra "Haven't Named It Yet" (2) "All On" (3) Hot Lips Page "Double Trouble Blues" (4) Buck Ram's All Stars "Ram Session" (5) Hot Lips Page "You Need Coachin'" (6) Rex Stewart & His Orchestra "The Shady Side of the Street" (7) Earl Bostic Orchestra "The Man I Love" (8) "Hurricane Blues" (9) "The Major and the Minor" (10) "Liza" (11) "That's the Groovy Thing Pt. 1" (12) Hot Lips Page "Birmingham Boogie" (13) "Texas and Pacific" (14) Earl Bostic Orchestra "Let's Ball Tonight Pt. 1" (15) "Where or When" (16) "Cuttin' Out" (17) Earl Bostic Quartet "Hot Sauce Boss" (18) "845 Stomp" (19) Earl Bostic & His Orchestra "Artistry by Bostic" (20) "Apollo Theater Jump" (21) "Tiger Rag" (22) "Temptation" (23) "Watch Where You Walk Boy" (24) "From Midnight Till Dawn." Disc 2, (1) "Earl's Imagination" (2) "Choppin' It Down" (3) "Serenade" (4) "Don't You Do It" (5) "Flamingo" (6) "Sleep" (7) "Moonglow" (8) "Ain't Misbehavin'" (9) "You Got to My Head" (10) "Cherokee" (11) "Steam Whistle Jump" (12) "Bostic's Boogie Blues (Smoke Rings)" (13) "Cracked Ice" (14) "Blue Skies" (15) "Liebestraum" (16) "Blue Moon" (17) "Harlem Nocturne" (18) "Stompin' at the Savoy" (19) "Special Delivery Stomp" (20) "Goodnight Sweetheart" (21) "Wee-Gee Board" (22) "Up There in Orbit" (23) "Ducky" (24) "All the Things You Are" (25) "Jungle Drums" (26) "Where or When." *Acrobat Music* ADD CD 3131 (2015) (UK).

His Finest Albums. Viz. *Alto-Tude* (1956), *Dance Time* (1956), *Let's Dance with Earl Bostic* (1957), *Invitation to Dance with Bostic* (1957), *Bostic Rocks (Hits of the Swing Age)* (1958), *Bostic Showcase of Swinging Dance Hits* (1958), *Alto Magic in Hi-Fi* (1958), *Jazz as I Feel It* (1963). Four CDs. *Enlightenment* EN4 CD 9186 (2020).

Artists Who Recorded Bostic Songs and for Whom He Arranged

Cab Calloway & His Orchestra. Side B Trylon Swing (Mills–Bostic) *Vocalion* V5005 10" single (1939).

Larry Clinton's Bluebird Orchestra. Side A Let Me Off Uptown. *Bluebird* B-11240 10" Single (1941).

Lucky Millinder & His Orchestra Side B Let Me Off Uptown (Vocal by Trevor Bacon) *Decca* 4099 10" single (1941).

Alvino Rey & His Orchestra. Side B The Major and the Minor. 10" single *Bluebird* B-11573 (1942).

Appendix C. Discography

Louis Prima & His Orchestra. Side A Brooklyn Boogie. *Majestic* 1029 10" single (1946).

Gene Krupa—Columbia Presents Drummin' with Krupa. Side 8 Let Me Off Uptown. *Columbia* A-36 4 × 10" LP (1946).

Gotham's Four Notes Side A Away (Bostic-Smith) 10" single. *Gotham* G-164 (1948).

Gene Krupa, featuring Anita O'Day & Roy Eldridge– Drummer Man, Gene Krupa in HIghest-FI. Includes A1 Let Me Off Uptown. *Verve Records* MGV-2008 (1956).

Jimmy Cavello and His House Rockers—Rock, Rock, Rock. Track B1 That's the Groovy Thing. 7" EP *Coral* 94 077 EPC (Germany) (1956).

Joe Reisman & His Orchestra—Party Night at Joe's. B2 The Major and the Minor. *RCA Victor* LSP 1476 (1958).

Dakota Staton—Dynamic! B1 Let Me Off Uptown. *Capitol* T-1054 (1958).

The Five Keys—Rhythm and Blues Hits Past and Present. B5 Stop Your Crying. *King* 692 (1960), also on 7" Track A1 *King* 45-5496 (1961).

The Verlaires. Ubangi Stomp B-side of 7" single. *Jamie* 1211 (1962).

Bud Powell—A Portrait of Thelonious. A4 No Name Blues. *Columbia* CS 9092 (1965).

Mrs. Elva Miller—Will Success Spoil Mrs. Miller? B4 Sweet Pea. *Capitol Records* T-2759 (1966).

Patsy Cole. Disappointed Bride/Honeymoon Night (Bostic) 7" Single *Island* WI 271 (UK) (1966).

Jackie Davis—Tiger on the Hammond. B6 The Major and the Minor. *Capitol* ST-1419 (1970).

Sy Oliver and His Orchestra—Easy Walker. Track B1 I'm the Guy That Loves Ya. *Jazz Club* EP JC 6003 7" EP (c. 1970).

Eddie "Cleanhead" Vinson & Roomful of Blues. B1 That's the Groovy Thing. *Muse Records* MR 5282 LP (1982).

Barry Harris Live at "Dug." Track 3 No Name Blues. *Enja* CD (1995).

Edgar Hayes & His Orchestra 1937–1938 Swingfan Limited Edition LP 1003 (c. 1978) (Germany).

Don Redman—The Little Giant of Jazz 1938–1940 RCA LP Black & White Series Vol 68. RCA 741.061 (1972) (France).

Paul Whiteman & His Chesterfield Orchestra featuring Jack Teagarden. Two radio broadcasts, July 8 and August 17, 1938. *Mr. Music* MMCD 7008 (1999).

Paul Whiteman & His Orchestra a Great Combination. Chesterfield radio broadcasts from the early months of 1939. *Magic CDs* DAWE 45 (1991). (UK & France).

Gene Krupa—Let Me Off Uptown: Original Recordings 1939–1945.

Track 10 "Let Me Off Uptown" featuring Anita O'Day. *NAXOS Jazz Legends* CD 8.120749 (2004).

Artists Inspired by Bostic

Geoff Taylor Sextet—All of Me. A1 All of Me A2 Easy Going B1 Solitude B2 The One I Love (Belongs to Somebody Else). *Esquire* EP 55 (1954) 7" EP England.

Earl Cadillac—Paris Canaille. *Vogue* EPL 7110 (1955) 4-track 7" EP France.

Geoff Taylor All Stars—Sweet Suite. A) Sweet Sue B) Sweet Lorraine. *Esquire* EP 105 (1956) 7" EP England.

Geoff Taylor All Stars—Sweet Suite. A1 Sweet Sue A2 Sweet Lorraine B1 Sweet Eloise B2 Sweet Georgia Brown. *Esquire* 20–060 (1956) 10" LP England.

Earl Cadillac Son Saxophone Alto et Son Orchestre—*Le Nouveau Roi de la Danse* *Vogue* LD 221 (c. 1956) 10-track LP (France).

Earl Cadillac—King of Rock 'n' Roll. *Vogue* LD 313–30 (1956) 12-track LP France.

Earl Cadillac—Rock 'n' Roll Par Earl Cadillac. *Vogue* EPL 7220 (c. 1956) 4-track 7" EP (France).

Earl Cadillac Son Saxo Alto et Son Orchestre—Dansez Avec Earl Cadillac. *Vogue* LD 247 (c. 1956) 10-track 10" LP (France).

Earl Cadillac Son Saxo Alto et Son Orchestre—En Haute Fidelite. *Vogue* LD 284 (c. 1956) 10-track 10" LP (France).

Jay Orlando—Loves Earl Bostic. A1 Flamingo A2 Red Sails in the Sunset A3 Because of You A4 Where or When A5 Deep Purple B1 Sleep B2 Tenderly B3 Stardust B4 Dream. *Dobre Records* DR 1040 (1978) (U.S. & Canada).

Clous van Mechelin—A Tribute to Earl Bostic. A1 Flamingo A2 Deep Purple A3 Stranger in Paradise A4 Always A5 Moonglow A6 Cherokee B1 Liebestraum B2 Love Is a Many-Splendored Thing B3 Dream B4 Smoke Gets in Your Eyes B5 Autumn Leaves B6 King Bostic. *Polydor* 2441 093 (1979) (Netherlands).

Chaise Lounge—The Lock and Key. Track 5 "The Earl" dedicated to Bostic *Modern Songbook Records* MSR-008 CD (2017).

Appendix D

Radio, Film, and Television Credits

Radio

Xavier University Concert. WOW (Chicago) Broadcast performance by Xavier University Dance Band, bandleader Earl Bostic. Setlist included "The Model." October 1931.

Xavier Dance Band. WWL Loyola of the South (later affiliated with the CBS network) Broadcast performance by Xavier University Dance Band, bandleader, vocalist and arranger Earl Bostic. Playlist included "Dinah," "When Your Lover Has Gone," "Jig Time," "Double Check Stomp" and "The Model." November 21, 1931.

Chesterfield Time. CBS Paul Whiteman & His Orchestra. Earl Bostic was arranger for Paul Whiteman, December 31, 1938 to December 20, 1939.

Ralph Cooper's Jumpin' Jive. WINS (New York) With Earl Bostic Orchestra, Betty Sinclair. July 7, 1942.

Harlem Hospitality Club. Mutual Network. Weekly music variety show broadcast every Saturday presented by Willie Bryant. With music by Earl Bostic. October, November 1947.

Bostic Visits Home. KVOO Broadcast from Tulsa. June 30, 1949.

Bill Hawkins' Show. WDOK (Cleveland, Ohio) Earl Bostic (Guest). Circa 1952.

The Jim Hawthorne Show. KNX Los Angeles. Bostic plugs his record "The Sheik of Araby." Jim Hawthorne (Host) with guests Danny Welton, Richard Aurandt, George Kaufman, Earl Bostic. March 19, 1953.

Top Tune Time. KLAC Los Angeles. Bob McLaughlin host, with guests John Arcesi, Champ Butler, and Earl Bostic. April 1, 1953.

Monitor. WIBA Madison, Wisconsin. With Earl Bostic, Count Basie. December 17, 1955.

One Night Stand. Radio Luxembourg (208 meters). Featured artists: Perez Prado, Earl Bostic. September 25, 1956.

Appendix D. Radio, Film, and Television Credits 197

Jazz on Tap. Station WOLF (Syracuse). Charlie Shaw (host), featuring Eddie Condon, Chet Baker, Earl Bostic et al. January 12, 1957.

Earl Bostic Quintet. CBS October 11–16, 1958.

Phil Gordon. KGLA (Los Angeles) variety show. Phil Gordon, Bonnie Guitar, Earl Bostic. 1958.

Taylor at Large. KHIP-FM (Gonzales, CA. broadcasting to the Monterey–Salinas–Santa Cruz areas). Earl Bostic in concert live at the Blackhawk, San Francisco. December 4, 1960.

The Sentimental 40s. WDBN-FM (Ohio: Medina/Cleveland/Akron/Toledo). With Earl Bostic. August 1, 1961.

Candlelight Songs for a Summer Night. WDBN. Guest artists Les Baxter, Earl Bostic, Frankie Carle, Bobby Hackett. August 10, 1961.

Jazz. KRHM (Los Angeles). Featuring Paul Desmond, Earl Bostic, and Oscar Brown Jr. July 19, 1964.

Just Jazz. WJAS (Pittsburgh, PA). Earl Bostic with the greatest hits of 1964 and the George Roberts Sextette. November 12, 1964.

Stereo Showcase. WADV (Buffalo). Earl Bostic featured. August 24, 1969.

The Swingin' Years. Chuck Cecil interviews Bostic about his experiences working with Lionel Hampton and others. Interview recorded circa 1965, repeated several times on KGIL (California). September 7, 1979.

Profiles in Black History. WDAO (Dayton, Ohio). Celebrating the birth anniversary of Earl Bostic. April 25, 1973.

The History of Rock and Roll. WLRW-FM (Champaign, Illinois). Featuring Earl Bostic, Chuck Berry, Ray Charles, Bob Dylan, Elvis, Little Richard, The Beatles et al. Fifty-hour show, broadcast January 31–February 1, 1974. (Tapes donated to Lincoln Center.)

Films

Let Me Off Uptown. Cast: Anita O'Day, Gene Krupa & His Orchestra, Roy Eldridge, Jeanne Boyer. Dir.: Robert R. Snody (1942).

I Ain't Gonna Open That Door. Cast: Stepin Fetchit, Earl Bostic & His Orchestra: Danny Barker, George Jenkins, Huck King, Roger Jones, Ted Barnett, Joya Sherrell (vocalist). Astor Pictures (1947).

Television

Tonight, at Zardi's. KCOP Channel 13 (Los Angeles). Live show from Zardi's, Hollywood. Bill Balance (MC). April 1956.

Earl Bostic Orchestra. KTLA (Los Angeles). January 13, 1960.

Denny Sullivan & the Gang. WSYR-TV (Syracuse). Variety show hosted by Denny Sullivan, with Special Guest Earl Bostic, June 17, 1965. Recorded while Bostic was appearing at Florento's Club in Syracuse.

American Bandstand. Variety show. Dick Clark (Presenter). 11th Anniversary Specials, of Philadelphia's Bandstand Shows featuring Frankie Avalon, Earl Bostic, Jerry Lee Lewis, Bobby Rydell, Lovin' Spoonful. August 10, 1968 (Northern California).

Appendix E

Partial Itineraries of Tours, 1945–1965

1945

March, Backing Lena Horne at the Capitol Theater, New York.
May, Kelly's Stables, W. 52nd St., New York.
July, Revue (three shows nightly), Murrain's, New York.
Sept. 15 to Nov. 2, Onyx Club, with Roy Eldridge, Ben Webster, Sarah Vaughan.
Nov. 13, Guest with Gage Amber's Orch., The Paddock, 1550 Burnside Ave., E. Hartford, CT.
Nov. 29 to Dec. 6, Elks Rendezvous, Harlem, NY.

1946

Feb. 5 to March, Village Corners, 140 7th Av. S.
April, Murrain's, Harlem, NY.
April 22, Cavalcade of Jazz at the Academy of Music, New York, with Red Allen, Sidney Bechet, J.C. Higginbotham, Benny Moten et al.
May 9, Glen Island Casino, New Rochelle, NY.

1946–47

Dec. 1946 to Jan. 1947, Club Bengasi, Washington, D.C.
Feb. 7 to March 21, Club Baron, Harlem, with singers Gwen Tynes and Evelyn Freeman.
March 15, All Star *Pittsburgh Courier* Poll Winners Concert at Carnegie Hall, New York.
Late March, Horseshoe, New York.
March 17 onward, Club Bengasi, Washington, D.C.
June, Club 845, Bronx, NY.
Sep. 19 to Oct. 3, Club Bali, 14th Street, Washington, D.C.
Nov., Watt's Zanzibar Club, Philadelphia.
Dec., 845 Club, New York.

1948

March, Bengasi, Washington, D.C.
April 1, Audubon Ballroom, New York.
April 2, Memorial Hall, Trenton, NJ.
April 3, Carnegie Hall, New York (Sextet).
April 4, Memorial Auditorium, Buffalo, NY.

Appendix E. Partial Itineraries of Tours, 1945–1965

April 9 to 15, Club Astoria, Baltimore, MD.
April 19 to 24, Cotton Club, Dayton, OH.
April 25, Washington, D.C.
April 26, Richmond, VA.
April 27, Henderson, NC.
April 30, Grand Rapids, MI.
May 1, Cotton Club, Dayton, OH.
May 2–4, Club Sudan, Detroit.
May 5–8, Carnival, Detroit.
May 9, Cleveland.
May 10, Pittsburgh.
May 14, Watson's Smoke House, Salisbury, MD.
May 17, Greensboro, NC.
June 6, Sunset, Indianapolis.
June 11, Toledo.
June 12, Louisville, KY.
June 13, Chicago.
June 15, Akron, OH.
June 16, Youngstown, OH.
June 16–July 1, Atlantic City, NJ (Hi-Hat Club).
June, Emerson's Rainbow Room, Philadelphia.
June 18, Elate Ballroom, 711 S. Broad St., Philadelphia.
June 25–27, Tropical Gardens, Philadelphia.
July 2, Trenton, NJ.
July 3, Paterson, NJ.
July 4, Bridgeport, CT.
July, Renaissance Casino, New York City.
July 9, Millsboro, DE.
July 10, Wilmington, DE.
July 11, Washington, D.C.
July 12, Aliquippa, PA.
July 13, Washington, PA.
July 14, Greensboro, NC.
July 15, Knoxville, TN.
July 16, Phoenix City, AL.
July 18, New Orleans.
July 20, Galveston, TX.
July 23 to 25, Joe's Skyline Club, Oklahoma City, OK.
Aug. 1, Ft. Worth, TX.
Aug. 2, Dallas.
Aug. 3, Shreveport, LA.
Aug. 6, Champaign, IL.
Aug. 7, Gary, IN.
Aug. 8, Saginaw, MI.
Aug. 10, Cincinnati.
Aug. 11, Sunset Terrace, Indianapolis.
Aug. 12, Atomic Enterprise Club, Coliseum, Sandusky, OH.
Aug. 25, Apollo Theater, New York, Dr Neff's Madhouse of Mystery show.
Aug., Lorain, OH.
Sept. 1, City Armory, Danville, VA.
Sept. 2, City Armory, Lynchburg, VA.
Sept. 6, Labor Day Dance, Auditorium, Roanoke, VA.
Sept. 7 to 8, Emerson's, Philadelphia.
Sept. 19, Washington, D.C.
Sept. 20, Raleigh, NC.
Sept. 21, Greensboro, NC.
Sept. 22, Maxton, NC.
Sept. 23, Kingston, NC.
Oct. 9, Evansville, IN.
Oct. 10, Riviera, St. Louis, MO.
Oct. 12, Knoxville, TN.
Oct. 14, Ft. Wayne, IN.
Oct. 15, Civic Auditorium, Grand Rapids, MI.
Oct. 16, Ann Arbor, MI.
Oct. 17, Buffalo, NY.
Oct. 18, Pittsburgh.

Appendix E. *Partial Itineraries of Tours, 1945–1965*

Oct. 19, Aliquippa, PA.
Oct. 23, University of Michigan, Ann Arbor.
Oct. 26, Michigan Theater, Muskegon, MI.
Oct. 28, University of Illinois.
Oct. 29, W.K. Kellogg Auditorium, Battle Creek, MI.
Oct. 30, Sunset, Indianapolis.
Nov. 2, Election Day Dance, Chestnut St. Hall, Harrisburg, PA.
Nov. 19, Boston.
Nov. 20, Fall River, MA.
Nov. 24, Wilmington, DE.
Nov. 25, Philadelphia.
Nov. 26, Albany, NY.
Nov. 27, Newark, NJ.
Nov. 28, Bridgeport, CT.
Dec. 4, Sunset, Indianapolis.
Dec. 12, Ft. Wayne, IN.

1949

Jan. 5 to 6, Birmingham, AL, *with Roy Brown and Chubby Newsome.*
Jan. 7 to 10, Palace Theater, Memphis *with Roy Brown and Chubby Newsome.*
Jan. 15, Riviera, St. Louis, MO.
Jan. 16, Municipal Auditorium, Kansas City, MO, *Battle of Music with Cootie Williams.*
Jan. 17, Omaha, NE.
Jan. 20, Columbus, OH.
Jan. 21, Ann Arbor, MI.
Jan. 22, Louisville, KY.
Jan. 23, Cincinnati, OH.
Jan. 27, Philadelphia, PA.
Jan. or Feb., Turner's Club, Washington, D.C.

Feb. 4, Youth Center, Greensboro, NC.
Feb. 5, Huntington, WV.
Feb. 6, Bluefield, WV.
Feb. 7, Henderson, NC.
Feb. 8, Maxton, NC.
Feb. 9, Pre-Valentine Dance, New Bern (NC) Armory.
Feb. 11, Charleston, SC.
Feb. 12, Boynton Beach, FL.
Feb. 13, Miami, FL.
Feb. 14, Auditorium, Macon, GA.
Feb. 15, Belle Glade, FL.
Feb. 16, Orlando, FL.
Feb. 17, Sarasota, FL.
Feb. 18, St. Petersburg, FL.
Feb. 19, Tuskegee, AL.
Feb. 21, Jacksonville, FL.
Feb. 22, Albany, GA.
Feb. 23, Waycross, GA.
Feb. 24, Macon, GA.
Feb. 25, Augusta, GA.
Feb. 27, Savannah, GA.
Feb. 28, Lyans, GA.
March 1, Raleigh, NC.
March 2, Abingdon, VA.
March 3, Newport News, VA.
March 4 to 9, *Headlining with Roy Brown, Chubby Newsome* Howard Theater, Washington, D.C.
March 11 to 17, Royal Theater, Baltimore.
March 18 to 24, Apollo Theater, New York.
March 25, Chester, PA.
March 26 to April 8, Savoy Ballroom, New York.
April 9, Carnegie Hall, New York.
April 16, Trenton, NJ.
April 18, Newark, NJ.

Appendix E. Partial Itineraries of Tours, 1945-1965

April 20, Frances Movie Theater, Columbia, MO. Special Easter Show, Bostic at the piano.
April 21, Manoa, PA.
April 22, Camden, NJ.
April 23, Wilmington, DE.
April 28, Clairton, PA.
April 29, Columbus, OH.
May 1, Nashville.
May 2, Louisville.
May 4, Clarksville, TN.
May 9, Carnation Ballroom, Omaha, NE.
May 12, Wichita, KS.
May 13, Des Moines, IA.
May 14, St. Louis, MO.
May 15, Sunset Terrace, Indianapolis.
May 17, Davenport, IA.
May 20, Muskegon, MI.
May 21, Flint, MI.
May 22, Cleveland, OH.
May 29, Kimball, WV.
May 30, Westminster, MD.
June 3, Florence, AL.
June 5, New Orleans.
June 10, 11, Municipal Auditorium, Oklahoma City.
June 12, Indianola, MS.
June 13, Lake Charles, LA.
June 14, Opelousas, LA.
June 15, Monroe, LA.
June 16, Paris, TX.
June 17, Shreveport, LA.
June 18, Tyler, TX.
June 19, Ft. Worth, TX.
June 20, Dallas, TX.
June 21, San Antonio, TX.
June 24, Ft. Sill, OK.
June 25, Big Ten Ballroom, Tulsa, OK.
June 28, Oklahoma City, OK.
June 29, Crockett, TX.
June 30, Houston, TX.
July 1, Port Arthur, TX.
July 3-4, Birmingham, AL.
July 6, Logan, WV.
July 8, Albany, NY.
July 9, Atlantic City, NJ.
July 10, Carr's Beach, Annapolis, MD.
July 11-16, Show Boat Café, Philadelphia.
July 22, Asbury Park, NJ.
July 23, Millsboro, DE.
July 27, Cumberland, IN.
July 28, Charlestown, WV.
July 29, Sewickley, PA.
July 30, Youngstown, OH.
July 31, Cincinnati, OH.
Aug. 7, Regal, Washington, DC. *Headlining with Roy Brown & His Mighty Men, Herb Lance & Wini Brown.*
Aug. 12, Gary, IN.
Aug. 13, South Bend, IN.
Aug. 18, Clairton, PA.
Aug. 19, South Bend, IN.
Aug. 20, St. Louis, MO.
Aug. 21, Kansas City, MO.
Aug. 25, Atchinson, KS.
Aug. 26, Champaign, IL.
Aug. 27, Flint, MI.
Aug. 28, Cleveland, OH.
Aug. 29, Inkster, MI.
Sept. 1, Portsmouth, OH.
Sept. 2, Petersburg, VA.
Sept. 4, Charlestown, WV.
Sept. 5, Fairmount, WV.
Sept. 14, Auditorium, Macon, GA. Also appearing Mable Lee, dancer. *Battle of Music with Hal "Cornbread" Singer.*
Sept. 15, Atlanta, GA.

Sept. 16, Charleston, SC.
Sept. 17, Tuskegee, AL.
Sept. 22, Charlotte, NC.
Sept. 23, Greensboro, NC.
Sept. 26, Raleigh, NC.
Sept. 27, Danville, VA.
Sept. 28, Maxton, NC.
Sept. 29, Henderson, NC.
Sept. 30, Durham, NC.
Oct. 1, Charleston, WV.
Oct. 3, Fayetteville, NC.
Oct. 4, Opelousas, LA.
Oct. 5, Roanoke, VA.
Oct. 7, Norfolk, VA.
Oct. 8, Greensboro, NC.
Oct. 9, Washington, D.C.
Oct. 20, Brunswick, GA.
Oct. 21, St. Petersburg, FL.
Oct. 22, W. Palm Beach, FL.
Oct. 23, Miami, FL.
Oct. 24, Jacksonville, FL.
Oct. 25, Pahokee, FL.
Oct. 28, Sarasota, FL.
Oct. 29, Key West, FL.
Oct. 31, Tampa. FL, *supporting Dinah Washington.*
Nov. 1, Tallahassee, FL.
Nov. 2, Pensacola, FL.
Nov. 3, Meridian, MS.
Nov. 4, New Iberia, LA.
Nov. 6, New Orleans, LA.
Nov. 7, Biloxi, MS.
Nov. 8, Florence, AL.
Nov. 9, Augusta, GA.
Nov. 11, Wilmington, NC.
Dec. 2–22, Hi-Hat Club, Boston.
Dec. 26, 1949–Jan. 1, 1950, 421 Club, Philadelphia.

1950

Jan. 1, Ronceverte, VA.
Jan. 2, Rock Hill, SC.
Jan. 6, Paterson, NJ.
Jan. 7, Newark, NJ.
Jan. 13–19, Club Valley Ballroom, Detroit, MI.
Jan. 21–28, Club Riviera, 4460 Delmar, St. Louis, MO, Billie Holiday headliner.
Jan. 29, Sunset Terrace, Indianapolis, IN.
Feb. 17, Sarasota, FL.
Feb. 18, Key West, FL.
Feb. 19, Miami, FL.
Feb. 20, Ft. Lauderdale, FL.
Feb. 21, Waycross, GA.
Feb. 23, Waynesboro, GA.
Feb. 24, Wilmington, NC.
Feb. 25, Rock Hill, SC.
Feb. 26, Washington, D.C.
March 3, West Chester, PA.
March 4, Wilmington, DE.
March 11, Washington, D.C.
March 12, Buffalo, NY.
April 7, Camden, NJ.
April 9, Clairton, PA.
April 10, Lynchburg, VA.
Six-Date Vaudeville Tour of Virginia, with Helen Young, Red Foxx, and Slappy White (comedians), Lady Darlene (dancer), Jimmy Hawkins (tap dancer):
April 11, Gem Theater, Petersburg, VA.
April 12–14, Hippodrome, Richmond, VA.
April 15–17, Booker T., Norfolk, VA.
April 19, Jefferson, Newport News, VA.
April 20, Virginia, Roanoke, VA.
April 21, Harrison, Lynchburg, VA.

Appendix E. Partial Itineraries of Tours, 1945–1965

April 22, Washington, D.C.
April 23, Ronceverte, WV.
April 26, Atlanta, GA.
April 27, Rock Hill, SC.
April 28, Claflin University, Orangeburg, SC.
April 30, Nashville, TN.
May 27, Flint, MO.
June 2, 3, St. Louis, MO.
June 4, Kansas City, MO.
June 5, Junction City, KS.
June 6, Denver, CO.
June 7, Pueblo, CO.
June 8, Lubbock, TX.
June 9, Ft. Sill, OK.
June 10, 11, Oklahoma City, OK.
June 12, Sulphur Springs, TX.
June 13, Brennan, TX.
June 15, Houston, TX.
June 17, Big Ten Ballroom, Tulsa, OK.
June 22, San Antonio, TX.
June 23, Beaumont, TX.
June 25, New Orleans.
June 28, Little Rock, AR.
June 30, Laurel, MS.
July 5, Laurel, MS.
July 6, Opelika, AL.
July 7–10, W.C. Handy Theater, Memphis, TN, *with Harlem Revue.*
July 8, Kennedy Veterans' Hospital, Memphis, TN.
July 12, *Harlem Revue*, Lexington, KY.
July 13–15, *Harlem Revue*, Louisville, KY.
July 16–17, Columbus, OH.
July 19–20, Pittsburgh, PA.
July 21–22, Cincinnati, OH.
Aug. 18, Revere Beach, MA.
Aug. 20, Carr's Beach, MD.
Aug. 25, Salisbury, MD.
Aug. 27, Aliquippa, PA.
Aug. 28, Philadelphia, PA.
Sept. 1, Petersburg, VA.
Sept. 2, Huntington, VA.
Sept. 3, Charlestown, VA.
Sept. 4, Pittsburgh, PA.
Sept. 7, Mr. Carr's Beach, Annapolis, MD.
Sept. 14–30, Bop City, New York.
Oct. 1–11, Bop City, New York.
Nov. 12, Sunset Terrace, Indianapolis, IN.
Nov. 16, Farm Dell Night Club, Minneapolis, MN.
Nov. 24, Dreamland, Omaha, NE.
Nov. 25, C.I.O. Hall, Minneapolis, MN.
Dec. 1, 2, 3, New Harlem Night Club, Brooklyn, IL, *with Tab Smith.*
Dec. 2, Harlem Country Club, East St. Louis, IL.
Dec. 7 to 10, Holiday Inn, Newark, NJ.

1951

March 1 to 8, Apollo Theater, New York, *Supporting Dinah Washington.*
April 9, Labor Temple, Minneapolis, MN.
April 18, Municipal Auditorium, Atlanta, GA.
May 7, Rainbow Ballroom, Denver, CO.
May 12, Municipal Auditorium, San Bernardino, CA.
June 6, Rainbow Ballroom, Denver, CO.
June 29 to Aug., Surf Club, Wildwood, NJ.

Appendix E. *Partial Itineraries of Tours, 1945–1965* 205

Sept., William "Jap" Gleason's Musical Bar, Cleveland, OH.
Oct. 26 to Nov. 2, Apollo Theater, New York.

1952

May 18, St. Louis Memorial Auditorium.
May 24, 26, Shrine Auditorium, Los Angeles.
June 4, New Union Hall, Suffolk, VA.
June 9, Ebony Lounge, Cleveland, OH.
July 7, Rainbow Ballroom, Denver, CO.
July 13, Elks Hall, Los Angeles.
July 25, Primalon Ballroom, San Francisco.
July 27, Civic Auditorium, Richmond, VA.
July 29 to Aug. 10, Blackhawk Supper Club, San Francisco.
Aug. 23, Rendezvous Ballroom, Balboa, CA.
Aug. 24, Elks Hall, Los Angeles.
Sept. 20, Memorial Auditorium, St. Louis, MO.
Sept. 29, Municipal Auditorium, New Orleans.
Oct. 17 to Oct. 23, Howard Movie Theater, Washington, D.C., with Roy Milton, Camille Howard.
Oct. 31 to Nov. 6, Apollo Theater, New York, with Lloyd Price, Phyllis Branch.
Nov., Farm Dell Night Club, Dayton, OH.
Nov. 24, Trocaveria, Columbus, OH.

Dec. 20, Wilmington, NC.
Dec. 21, Charleston, SC.
Dec. 22, Wilson, NC.
Dec. 24, Orlando, FL.
Dec. 25, Miami, FL.
Dec. 26, Sanford, FL.
Dec. 27, Key West, FL.
Dec. 29, Lake City, FL.
Dec. 30, Florence Villa, FL.
Dec. 31, St. Petersburg, FL.

1953

Jan. 8, Douglas High School, Thomasville, GA.
Jan. 19 to 24, Pep's, Philadelphia.
Feb. 20 to 26, Regal Theater, Chicago.
March 3, Mountaineer Theater, Camp Carson, CO.
March 4, Rainbow Ballroom, Denver, CO.
March 15, Elks Hall, Los Angeles.
April 24 to 26, 5-4 Ballroom, Los Angeles.
May 10, Elks Hall, Los Angeles.
June 7, Wrigley Field, Los Angeles, The Ninth Cavalcade of Jazz, with Nat "King" Cole, Shorty Rogers, Louis Armstrong All Stars, Lloyd Price, et al.
July 10, Memorial Auditorium, Raleigh, NC.
Aug. 17, Graystone Ballroom, Detroit.
Sept. 5, Labor Temple, Minneapolis, MN.
Sept. 12, In person at Pooley's Music Shop, 12 Corners, Brighton, NY.
Nov. 30, Dec. 6, Quartier Latin, Montreal, Canada.

Appendix E. Partial Itineraries of Tours, 1945–1965

1954

Feb. 25, Elks' Masquerade Carnival Ball, Stevens Ball Room, Jackson, MS.
March 20, Dream Bowl, Napa, CA.
March 21, Oakland, CA.
March 26 to 28, 5-4 Ballroom, Los Angeles.
March 30 to April 11, Blackhawk Supper Club, San Francisco.
April 25, Gala Show, Elks Hall.
April 27, Chico State College, with Christine Kittrell.
April 28, Fort Ord Soldier's Club, with Christine Kittrell.
April, California State University.
May 2, Los Angeles, Elks Hall.
May, Vallejo Junior College.
May, Peninsula College.
May, Fresno State University.
June 4 to 6, Savoy new opening, Los Angeles.
June 11, Old Mill, Salt Lake City, UT.
June 12, Hotel Ben Lomond, Crystal Ballroom, Salt Lake City, UT.
June 15, Rainbow Ballroom, Denver, CO.
June 26, Kansas City, MO.
June 27, St. Louis, MO.
July 1, Rochester, NY.
July 2, Bradford Ballroom, Boston.
July 3, New London, CT.
July 4, Taunton, MA.
July 5, Bridgeport, CT.
July 9, York, PA.
July 10, Sarasota Springs, NY.
July 11, Annapolis, MD.
July 14, Cape Cod.
Aug. 8 to 14, Crystal Show Bar, Detroit.
Aug. 20, Vic's Cocktail Lounge, 507 Hennepin, Minneapolis, MN.
Sept. 5, Minneapolis Labor Temple.
Sept. 10, Boston.
Sept., Celebrity Club, Providence, RI.
Sept. 28, Basin Street East, New York, with Dave Brubeck, Carmen McRae.
Oct. 4 to 7, Pep's Musical Bar, 515 S. Broad Street, Philadelphia, PA.
Oct. 29 to Nov. 11, Crystal Show Bar, Detroit.
Dec. 6 to 12, Surf Club, Baltimore, MD.
Dec. 15 to 21, Markeez Club, Lowell, MI.
Dec., Basin Street East, New York.

1955

Jan. 28, E-J Recreation Center, Johnson City, TN.
Feb. 12, No Intermission Dance, Durham Armory, Durham, NC.
Feb. 16, Celtic Room, Nashville, TN.
Feb. 19, Columbus, GA.
Feb. 20, Pensacola, FL.
Feb. 24 to March 4, Palms Club, Hallandale Beach, FL.
March 5, Jacksonville, FL.
March 8 to 11, Battle of Music, Papa John Gordy, Celtic Room, Nashville, TN.
March 16, Municipal Auditorium, New Orleans.
March 26, Wichita, KS.
April 14, Carillo Auditorium, Santa Barbara, CA.

Appendix E. *Partial Itineraries of Tours, 1945–1965*

April 22, Shrine Auditorium, Los Angeles.
April 22 to 29, Club Oasis, Los Angeles.
April 29 to May 1, 5-4 Ballroom, Los Angeles.
May 18 to 28, Black Hawk Supper Club, San Francisco.
June, University of Oregon.
June, University of Portland.
June, University of Seattle.
June, Bay Meadows Club House, San Mateo, CA.
June, Carillo Auditorium, Santa Barbara, CA.
June 5, Knights of Honor Social Club, San Jose Civic Auditorium, San Jose, CA.
June 8 to 24, 1042 Club, Anchorage, AK.
July 6, Las Vegas.
July 15, Shrine Auditorium, Los Angeles.
July 22 to 25, 5-4 Ballroom, Los Angeles.
Aug. 13, Labor Temple, Minneapolis, MN.
Aug. 15, Stealer's Home of Jazz, Milwaukee, WI.
After Aug., Tony Di Martino's Terrace Lounge, St. Louis, MO.
Sept. 12, Hi-Hat Club, Boston.
Oct. 10 to 17, Flamingo Club, Lowell, MA.
Nov. 3, In Person at E.J. Record Store, Johnson City, TN.
Nov. 14 to 21, Pep's Musical Bar, 515 S. Broad Street, Philadelphia, PA
Nov. 28 to Dec. 5, Loew's Victoria, Baltimore, MD.
Dec., Blue Note, Chicago.

1956

March 17, Plantation, Dallas, TX.
April 3, Rainbow Ballroom, Denver, CO.
April 30, Shrine Auditorium, Los Angeles, *with Dave Brubeck.*
July 25, Savoy Ballroom, New York.

1957

Jan. 25, Civic Auditorium, Stockton, CA.
Jan. 26, Ballroom, 6th & E. Streets, Modesto, CA.
March 2, Elks Charity & Social Ball, Memorial Auditorium, Sacramento, CA.
March 9, Rainbow Gardens, Pomona, CA, *with Trini Menor.*
March 16, NAACP Benefit Dance, San Bernardino, CA.
April 13, Green Mill Ballroom, Ventura, CA.
May 3, McElroy's Ballroom, Portland, OR.
May 5, Evergreen Ballroom, Olympia, WA.
June 7, Fresno Auditorium, *with guest stars.*
June 9, Oakland, CA, *with Earl "Fatha" Hines.*
June 13, 14 Civic Auditorium, San Bernardino, CA.
June 22, NAACP Festival of Stars, Shrine Auditorium, Los Angeles, *with The Platters et al.*
June 28, Zenda Ballroom, Langston University, Langston, OK.

Appendix E. Partial Itineraries of Tours, 1945–1965

June 29, Civic Auditorium, Pasadena, CA, *with The Platters*.
July 16, Riverside Park Ballroom, Phoenix, AZ.
July 19 to Sept. 1, Brass Rail, New York.
Sept. 13, Rock 'n' Roll Festival, Civic Auditorium, Pasadena, *with Big J. McNeely, The Rockers, et al.*
Oct. 4 to 11, Apollo Theater, New York, *with the Del-Vikings, Slim Gaillard, et al.*
Oct. 12 to 19, Howard Theater, Washington, D.C.
Oct. 26, Elks Ballroom, Los Angeles.
Nov. 4 to 11, Frolic Show Bar, Detroit.
Nov. 17, "Battle of the Saxes," Ocean Beach Park, New London, CT, *with Arnett Cobb*.
Nov. 22 to 24, Jam Sessions, Flamingo Lounge, Lowell, MA.
Nov., Dates in Buffalo, Boston, and Chicago for Al Benson.
Nov. 26, Bandbox, Cleveland, OH.
Dec. 13, Rock 'n' Roll Festival, Civic Auditorium, San Bernardino, CA, *with Jesse Belvin, Six Teens, Richard Berry, Silhouettes, et al.*

1958 (Quintet)

March, Blue Note, Chicago.
March 25, Playdium, St. Louis, MO.
April, Brass Rail, Milwaukee, WI.
April (one week), Zanzibar, Buffalo, NY.
April, Surf Club, Baltimore, MD.
April 27, Ocean Beach Park, Nashua, NH.
April 28 to May 4, Flamingo Lounge, Lowell, MA.
May 13 to 20, Shuffle-Inn, Madison, WI.
May 30, Mambo Club, Kansas City, MO, *with Sonny Carter*
May 31, City Auditorium, Manhattan, KS,
July 18 to 24, Weekes Cocktail Lounge, 1760 Baltic Ave., Atlantic City, NJ.
July 27, Carr's Beach, Chesapeake Bay, *with Frankie Lymon & the Teenagers*.
Aug. 20, O'Clock Club, Cleveland, OH.
Aug. 22 to 24, Modern Jazz Room, E. 4th at Huron, Cleveland, OH.
Aug. 26 to Sept. 2, Playdium, St. Louis, MO.
Sept., Blue Note, Chicago.
Sept. 15 to 21, Shuffle Inn, Madison, WI.
Sept. 24, Jap-o-Land Ballroom, Benton Harbor, MI.
Oct. 1–12, Chicago Blue Note, *with Sig Millonzi Trio (Sunday Matinee)*.
Oct. 21, Minneapolis–St. Paul, MN, *with The Treniers*.
Oct. 22–31, The Key Club, Minneapolis, MN, with Ernestine Anderson. Personnel: Willliam Erskine drums, Fletcher Smith piano, Alan Seltzer guitar, Gene

Redd vibes, Herb Gordy bass.
Nov. 14, El Casino Ballroom, Tucson, AZ.
Nov. 22, Riverside Park, Phoenix, AZ.
Nov. 28, (Sextet) Blackhawk, San Francisco.

1959

Jan. 10, Auditorium, Arizona State College, Flagstaff, AZ.
Jan., Latin Quarter, El Paso, TX.
Jan. 21, Riverside Park, Phoenix, AZ.
Jan. 31, El Casino Ballroom, Tucson, AZ.
Feb. 4, Eastwood Country Club, San Antonio, TX.
Feb. 10, Miami.
Feb. 25, Battle of the Bands with Jack Teagarden, Fort Lauderdale, FL.
March 2, Porky's, Fort Lauderdale, FL.
March 14, Monarch Costume Ball, University of Florida, Gainesville.
March 19, Club 400, Evergreen, AL.
March 29, Copa Club, 333 Central Ave., Newport, NY.
March 30 to April 4, Brass Rail, Milwaukee, WI.
April 6, Clover Club, Peoria, IL.
April 12–26, Blue Note, Chicago.
April, Towne Club, Madison, WI.
May 3, Ocean Beach Park, New London, CT.
May 4 to 9, Pep's Bar, Philadelphia.
May 11 to 16, The Castle, Eggertsville, NY.
May 19 to 29, Playdium, St. Louis, MO.
July 20 to 26, The Ebb Tide, Norfolk, VA.
July 31, El Rancho, Wilmington, DE.
Aug. 8, Chicago Stadium Playboy Jazz Festival.
Aug. 9, Edgewater Park, Celina, OH.
Aug. 14, Sept. 21 to 26, The Castle, Eggertsville, NY.
Oct. 10, 12, Pep's, 516 South Broad St., Philadelphia, PA.
Oct. 14, Ebb Tide, East Ocean Ave., Norfolk, VA.
Oct. 20 to 25, Club Miami, State Route 4, Richmond, IN.
Oct. 30, Calderon Ballroom, 1610 E. Henshaw Road, Phoenix, AZ.

1960

Sextet

Jan. 11, Beverly Hilton Ballroom, Los Angeles (fundraiser for the Rinky Dinkers).
Jan. 28, Bob's Place Ballroom, St. Mary's Road, Tucson, AZ.
Jan. 29, Calderon Ballroom, Phoenix, AZ.
Feb. 8 to 15, Porky's, 3900 N. Federal Highway, Fort Lauderdale, FL.
April 18 to May, The Castle Rest Lounge, 2066 Eggert Road, Eggertsville, NY.
May 30, The Embers Supper Club, St. Louis, MO.
July 19 to 22, Minor Key, 11541 Dexter, Detroit, MI.

Aug. 19 to 21, Ebb Tide, 2106 E. Ocean View Ave., Norfolk, VA.
Aug. 23 to 28, Durgan's, Route 86, north of Saranac Lake, New York State.
Sep. 15, Baltimore Towers, Philadelphia.
Sep. 16 to 25, Lammanias, Merchantville, NJ.
Sep. 26 to Oct. 1, Coronet Club, Lancaster, PA.
Oct. 4 to 9, New Surf Club, Baltimore, MD.
Oct. 11 to 16, The Castle Rest Lounge, 2066 Eggert Road, Eggertsville, NY.
Nov. 25, Dallas Arts Festival, Dallas, TX.

1961

Jan. 1, Hollywood Palladium, Los Angeles, Ray Charles headliner.
Jan. 13, Hotel, 331 S. Duke St., York, PA.
Jan. 14, Shrine Auditorium.
Jan. 28 to 31, Mardi Gras Room, Kansas City, MO.
Feb. 10, Benefit Show, Henson Hall Gym, Dillard University, New Orleans.
Feb. 17, 18, Clemson College Midwinter Dance, Columbia, SC.
Feb. 24, Township Auditorium, University of South Carolina, Columbia, SC.
March 4, 10, Esquire Show Bar, Montreal, Canada.
March 24, La Maina's Musical Bar, Camden, NJ.
April (1 week), New Gene's Inn, Glen Park, Watertown, NY.
April, Memorial Hall, Dayton, OH, Louis Armstrong headliner.
April 11 to 15, Coronet, 155 N. Queen St, Lancaster, PA.
April 21, Armory, Dayton, OH.
April 28, 7th Annual Dance, Jersey City Park Police, Jersey City, NJ.
May 19 to 25, King Arthur's Lounge, Philadelphia.
May 29 to June 4, Ebb Tide, East Ocean Drive, Norfolk, VA.
Aug. 5, In person, Stockton, CA.
Aug., Opening of Flying Fox, Santa Barbara, CA.
Aug., Starlight Lounge, Kansas City, MO.
Oct. 2, The Cove, Hazelton.
Oct. 9 to 14, The Castle Rest Lounge, 2066 Eggert Road, Eggertsville, NY.
Oct. 20 to 22, El Rancho, Wilmington, DE.
Nov. 10, The Key Club, 1325 Washington St., Minneapolis, MN.
Nov. 21 to 25, Surf Club, Cincinnati, OH.
Nov. 27 to Dec. 4, Esquire Club, Montreal, Canada.
Dec. 31, New Year's Eve Dance, Club Laurel, Chicago.

1962

Jan. 5, King Arthur's Lounge, 1115 E. Armour, Kansas City, MO.
Jan. 19, Bryant Center Auditorium, 2701 N.E. 21st St., Oklahoma City, OK.

Appendix E. *Partial Itineraries of Tours, 1945-1965*

Jan. 19, Club Checkmate, Norman, OK.
Feb. 4, Evergreen Ballroom, Tacoma, WA.
Feb. 12, Annual Community Auxiliary Dinner Dance, Fraternal Hall, Hanford, CA.
March 9 to 11, El Condado, Bristol, PA.
March 15 to 24, Red Hipp's Vogue Room, Chambersburg, PA.
April 6 to 15, Casablanca Club, 258 East West Street, New York.
June 30, Wichita, KS.
July 6, Mardi Gras Room, 19th & Vine, Kansas City, MO.
July 13, Blue Dahlia, 4255 West Port St., Detroit.

1963

Quintet

Jan. 17, Feb. 14, Ivanhoe, Arcadia, CA.
Feb. 8 to 10, Town Market, Del Mar, CA.
March 10, Crossbow Inn, North Hollywood, CA.
March 13, Civic Auditorium, San Bernardino, CA.
April 1, April Fool Dance Panorama, Hollywood Palladium, with René Touzet and The Rivingtons.
May 27, Why Not Club, Canoga Park, CA.
June 8, Jam Session, Precious Moment Club, Sherman Square Bowl, Sherman Way, Reseda, CA.
June 14 to 16, jaMan Trio, featuring James Manuel, Earl Bostic, Frank and Teresa's Anchor Bay Restaurant, Buffalo, NY.
July to Aug. 3, Azusa Lanes, 645 E. Foothills, Azusa, CA.
Aug. 9, Why Not Club, Canoga Park, CA.
Aug. 15, Crescendo, Sunset Strip, Ink Spots, Dick Gregory (comedian).
Aug. 30 to Sept. 27, Club Sahara, Ontario, CA.
Oct. 3 to 28, Crescendo, Sunset Strip, with Louis Nye, Nancy Wilson.

1964

Quintet

Jan. 27, Why Not? Club, Canoga Park, Van Nuys, CA.
Jan., Crescendo, Sunset Strip, CA.
Feb. 2, also June 12, 13, The Crossbow Inn, 7625 Van Nuys Bld., Pan City, North Hollywood, CA.
Feb. 6 to 13, Apollo Room, Caesar's Supper Room, Palos Verdes, CA.
May 8 to July, Royal Tahitian, Pomona, CA.
July, Henri's Whip, Long Beach, CA.

Trio

Nov., White Horse, Redondo Beach, CA.

1965

Jan. 10, Lazy X, Lankershim & Vanowen, North Hollywood, CA.

Appendix E. Partial Itineraries of Tours, 1945–1965

Jan., White Horse, Redondo Beach, CA.

TRIO

Feb. 8 to 13, The Castle, Eggertsville, NY.
Mar. 22 to 27, Crawford Grill, 2142 Wylie Avenue, Pittsburgh, PA (Trio).
April 20 to 22, Paul's Steak House, Albany, NY.
April 23 to 26, The Castle Rest Lounge, 2066 Eggert Road, Eggertsville, NY.
April, Lennie's, Turnpike, West Peabody, Boston.
May 11, 12, Chassey's, 11th Street, Philadelphia.
May 12, Bar X, Frankford Av. & Levick Street, Philadelphia.
May 24 to June 13, (Trio) Pillow Talk Bar & Lounge, 307 Central Avenue, New York.
June 15 to 21, Florento's Supper Club, Brewerton Road, Syracuse
June 28 to July 4, Lennie's, W. Peabody, Boston, MA.
July 26 to 31, Pushnik's, Waterfall Room, Theatre-Restaurant, Cumberland Street, Lebanon, PA.
Aug., Top of the Plaza, Midland Tower Hotel, Rochester, NY.
Aug. 24 to Sept. 6, Florento's Supper Club, Brewerton Road, Syracuse, NY.
Sept. 6 to 11, Pushnik's, Waterfall Room, Theatre-Restaurant, Cumberland Street, Lebanon, PA.
Sept. 13, Aku Aku Clubm Town House Motel, 1111 West Bancroft, Toledo, OH.
Sept. 15 to 19, The Castle, Eggertsville, NY.
Oct. 11 to 24, Baker's Keyboard Lounge, 20510 Livernois Avenue, Detroit, MI.
Oct. 25, Top of the Plaza, Midland Tower Hotel, Rochester, NY.

Appendix F

Sessions

Key to Abbreviations

Alto sax (as); Soprano Sax (ss); Baritone sax (bs); Tenor sax (ts); Drums (d); Bass (b); Guitar (g); Vocal (vcl); Trumpet (tp); Trombone (tb); Piano (p); Clarinet (cl); Vibes (vib); Percussion (perc); Organ (org)

Majestic

NOVEMBER TO DECEMBER 1945

Earl Bostic (as, vcl), Roger Jones, Dick Vance, Benny Harris (tp) Claude Jones, Benny Morton (tb) Eddie Barefield (cl) Don Byas, Walter "Foots" Thomas (ts) Ed Finkel (p) Tiny Grimes (g) Al Hall (b) Cozy Cole (d).

Gotham

NEW YORK

FEBRUARY 1946

Cousin Joe with the Earl Bostic Sextet: Cousin Joe (vcl) Eart Bostic (as) John Hardee (ts) Tony Scott (cl) Ernie Washington (p) Jimmy Shirley (g) "Pops" Foster (bs) J.C. Heard (dr).

MARCH AND JULY 1946

Earl Bostic (as, vcl) Lemon Boler (tp) Tony Scott (cl) John Hardee (ts) George Parker (p) Jimmy Shirley (g) Jimmy Jones (b) Eddie Nicholson (d).

AUGUST 1946

Earl Bostic's Orchestra with Cousin Joe: Cousin Joe (vcl) Earl Bostic (as) John Hardee (ts) Tyree Glenn (tr) Tony Scott (cl) Hank Jones (p) Jimmy Shirley (g) "Pops" Foster (bs) Eddie Nicholson (dr).

July 1947

Earl Bostic (as) Roger Jones (tp) Rudy Powell (as, cl) Ted Barnett (ts) George Parker (p) Jimmy Shirley (g) Vernon King (b) Chick Cruickson (d).

Late 1947

Earl Bostic (as) George Parker (p) Vernon King (b) Shep Shepherd (d); probably late 1947: Roger Jones (tp, vcl) Earl Bostic (as) Ted Barnett (ts) George Parker (p) Vernon King (b) Shep Shepherd (d).

King

January 12 and 13, 1949

Earl Bostic (as, vocal) Roger Jones (tp,vcl) Lowell "Count" Hastings (ts) Jaki Byard (p) Vernon King (b) Shep Shepherd (d).

May 28 and August 1949

As above, but Rufus Webster (p) Keter Betts (b) replace Jaki Byard, Vernon King.

March 23, 1950

Earl Bostic (as, vcl) Lowell "Count" Hastings (ts) Gene Redd (vib) Cliff Smalls (p) Al Casey (g) Keter Betts (b) Joe Marshall (d) Helen Young (vcl).

October 13, 1950

As above but Edward Barefield (g) replaces Al Casey.

January 10 and 23, 1951

Earl Bostic (as) Gene Redd (tp,vib) Earl Bostic (as) Lowell "Count" Hastings (ts) Cliff Smalls (p) René Hall (g) Keter Betts (b) Jimmy Cobb (d) Clyde Terrell (vcl).

October 4, 1951

Earl Bostic (as) Buddy Miles (as,bar) Wilbur Campbell (ts) Gene Redd (vib) Cliff Smalls (p) Ike Isaacs (b) Jimmy Cobb (d) unknown (vcl).

April 7, 1952

Earl Bostic (as) Blue Mitchell (tp) Pinky Williams (as,bar) John Coltrane (ts) Gene Redd (vib) Joe Knight (p) Jimmy Shirley (g) Ike Isaacs (b) Specs Wright (d).

August 15, 1952

As above, but Harold Grant (g) replaces Jimmy Shirley.

December 17, 1952
Earl Bostic (as) Blue Mitchell (tp) Ray Felder (ts) Gene Redd (vib) Joe Knight (p) Mickey Baker (g) Ike Isaacs (b) George Brown (d) Bill Williams (vcl).

June 6, 1953
Earl Bostic (as) Blue Mitchell, Tommy Turrentine (tp) Earl Bostic (as) Stanley Turrentine (ts) Luis Rivera (p) Herman Mitchell (g) Mario Delagarde (b) Albert Bartee (d).

August 24, 1953
Earl Bostic (as) Blue Mitchell, Tommy Turrentine (tp) Stanley Turrentine (ts) Edward Richley (vib) Alexander Sample (p) Charles Grayson (g) Bob Breston (b) Granville T. Hogan (d).

October 4, 1953
Earl Bostic (as) Blue Mitchell, Tommy Turrentine (tp) Stanley Turrentine (ts) Stash O'Laughlin (p) Clarence Kenner (g) George Tucker (b) Granville T. Hogan (d).

May 27, 1954
Earl Bostic (as) Blue Mitchell, Eldridge Morris (tp) Stanley Turrentine (ts) Stash O'Laughlin, Celia Lopez (p) Mitchell Webb (g) George Tucker (b) Granville T. Hogan (d) Bob Bustamente, Bill Gallardo, Jose Mendoza (perc) Sonny Carter (vcl).

October 8 and 9, 1954
Earl Bostic (as) Blue Mitchell, Eldridge Morris (tp) Benny Golson (ts) Teddy Charles (vib) Stash O'Laughlin (p) Jimmy Shirley (g) George Tucker (b) Granville T. Hogan (d) Sonny Carter (vcl) Oct. 9.

January 27, 1955
Earl Bostic (as) Elmon Wright, Johnny Coles (tp) Benny Golson (ts) Teddy Charles (vib) Stash O'Laughlin (p) Jimmy Shirley (g) George Tucker (b) Granville T. Hogan (d) Sonny Carter (vcl).

May 4, 1955
Earl Bostic (as) Elmon Wright, Johnny Coles (tp) Benny Carter (as) Benny Golson (ts) Frank Flynn (vib) Stash O'Laughlin (p) Ulysses Livingston (g) George Tucker (b) Granville T. Hogan (d).

January 11, 1956
Earl Bostic (as) Elmon Wright, Johnny Coles (tp) Phil Olivella (cl)

Hymie Schertzer (as) Benny Golson (ts) Stash O'Laughlin (p) George Barnes (g) George Tucker (b) Granville T. Hogan (d) Kenneth Tyler (perc) and strings.

LOS ANGELES

APRIL 19, 1956

Earl Bostic (as) Bill Doggett (org) Billy Butler (g) George Tucker (b) Shep Shepherd (d).

APRIL 23, 1956

Elmon Wright, Johnny Coles (tp) Earl Bostic (as) Benny Golson (ts) Larry Bunker (vib) Stash O'Laughlin (p) Barney Kessel (g) George Tucker (b) Ralph Jones (d) Kenneth Tyler (perc).

FEBRUARY 2, 1957

Earl Bostic (as) John Anderson, Ronnie Lewis (tp) Jewell Grant (as) Bill Green (as,bar) Teddy Edwards (ts) Larry Bunker (vib) Charlie Lawrence (p) Adolphus Alsbrook (b) Roy Porter (d) Billy Jones (vcl).

FEBRUARY 28, 1957

As above, but Irving Ashby (g) added, Lou Singer (vib) replaces Larry Bunker, with addition of unnamed vocal group.

Billy Jones accompanied by Earl Bostic and his Orchestra:

MAY 1, 1957

Similar personnel (Billy Jones accompanied by Earl Bostic and his Orchestra).

JULY 24 AND 25, 1957

Earl Bostic (as) Joseph Dolny, Art DePew (tp) Jewell Grant (ts) Tom Suthers, Bill Green (ts,bar) Elmer Schmidt (vib) Charlie Lawrence (p) René Hall (g) Adolphus Alsbrook (b) Earl Palmer (d).

DECEMBER 18 AND 19, 1957

Earl Bostic (as) Wallace Snow (vib) Ernest Crawford (p) Tony Rizzi (g) H.J. Timbrell (b) Earl Palmer (d).

JANUARY 30, 1958

Earl Bostic (as) Elmer Schmidt (vib) Charlie Lawrence (p) Tony Rizzi (g) H.J. Timbrell (b) Earl Palmer (d).

FEBRUARY 26, 1958

Earl Bostic (as) Elmer Schmidt (vib) Fletcher Smith (p) Allan Seltzer (g) Margo Gibson (b) Earl Palmer (d).

MAY 8, 1958
   Earl Bostic (as) Gene Redd (vib) Fletcher Smith (p) Allan Seltzer (g) Margo Gibson (b) Charles Walton (d).

CINCINNATI

JULY 14 AND 15, 1958
   Earl Bostic (as) Gene Redd (vib) Fletcher Smith (p, org) Allan Seltzer (g) Edwyn Conley (b) William Erskine (d).

OCTOBER 7, 1958
   Earl Bostic (as) Claude Jones (p, org) Johnny Gray (g) Johnny Pate (b) Alrock Ducan (d) Frank Rullo (perc).

OCTOBER 10, 1958
   As above but Isaac "Red" Holt (d) replaces Alrock Ducan, Allan Seltzer (g) also added.

OCTOBER 20, 1958
   As on October 7 but Herb Gordy (b), Walter Perkins (d) replace Johnny Pate, "Red" Holt.

LOS ANGELES

DECEMBER 1 TO 3, 1958
   Earl Bostic (as) Elmer Schmidt (vib) Hal Hidey (p) René Hall (g) Herb Gordy (b) Earl Palmer (d).

DECEMBER 4, 1958
   Earl Bostic (as) Gerald Wilson, Oliver Mitchell, Joseph Dolny, Anthony Terran (tp) Ernie Freeman (p) René Hall, Allan Seltzer (g) Herb Gordy (b) Earl Palmer (d).

JANUARY 26, 1959
   Earl Bostic, Benny Carter, Jewell Grant (as) Bill Green, Plas Johnson (ts) Buddy Collette (as,ts,bar) Elmer Schmidt (vib) Sir Charles Thompson (p) René Hall (g) Herb Gordy (b) Earl Palmer (d).

JANUARY 27 AND 28, 1959
   Earl Bostic (as) Elmer Schmidt (vib) Sir Charles Thompson (p) René Hall, Allan Seltzer (g) Herb Gordy (b) Earl Palmer (d).

JANUARY 29, 1959

As above, with addition of George Roberts (tb) Lloyd Ulyate (tb) Bob Pring (tb) Hoyt Bohannon (tb) Joe Howard (tb).

CINCINNATI

MARCH 25 TO 28, 1959

Earl Bostic (as) Roland Johnson (vib) Jon Thomas (p) Allan Seltzer (g) Herb Gordy (b) William Erskine (d), same lineup until March 28.

APRIL 6 TO JUNE 15, 1959

Earl Bostic (as) Roland Johnson (vib) Claude Jones (p) Warren Stephens, Allan Seltzer (g) Herb Gordy (b) William Erskine (d).

LOS ANGELES

FEBRUARY 14, 1963

Earl Bostic (cl, sop, as) Elmer Schmidt (vib) Evelyn Roberts (p, org) Ernest McLean (g) René Hall (el-b) Sharkey Hall (d).

AUGUST 13, 1963

Earl Bostic (as) Richard "Groove" Holmes (org) Joe Pass (g) Jimmy Bond (b) Charles Blackwell (d).

AUGUST 14, 1963

Earl Bostic (as) Richard "Groove" Holmes (org) Joe Pass (g) Herb Gordy (b) Shelly Manne (d).

JANUARY 22, 23, AND 27, 1964

Earl Bostic (as) Richard "Groove" Holmes (org) Joe Pass (g) Jimmy Bond, Al McKibbon (b) Earl Palmer (d),

Chapter Notes

Introduction

1. Jeff Pike, *The Death of Rock 'n' Roll* (Boston: Faber & Faber, 1993), 62.
2. Matthew Wright, "Obituary: Victor Schonfield," *Jazz Journal*, May 20, 2022.
3. See Owen Callahan, "Up There in Orbit," Honors thesis, Wesleyan University, 2012, https://digitalcollections.wesleyan.edu/object/ir-1194.

Chapter 1

1. Earl Bostic in interview with Karl Zanco. Karl Zanco, "Teenager, Earl Bostic Talk Music at Ocean Side Center as Swingsters Rock 'n' Roll," *Blade Tribune*, April 25, 1956, 16.
2. Ike Bostic and Druzilla Gipson, marriage license entry, August 10, 1912, Missionary Baptist Chapel, Tulsa, OK.
3. Earl E. Bostic, birth certificate, Tulsa, Oklahoma, April 25, 1913.
4. Ike Bostic draft card, June 1917; Charlie and Maria Bostic and family in 1900 Census Van Buren City, Van Buren Township, Second Ward, Crawford County, Arkansas, June 26, 1900, Image 438. There is no Charles Bostic listed in Van Buren in 1870 and 1880, but all the evidence indicates that they appear instead as Charles and Maria Foster. Qv. Charles and Maria (Foster) Van Buren, 1880 Census, Image 110; Charles and Maria (Foster) Van Buren 1870 Census, Image 208. Unfortunately, the 1890 Federal Census for Van Buren does not survive.
5. Ike Boston [sic], 1910 Census, 504 Kenosha Avenue, Tulsa City, Oklahoma.
6. Bostic apparently inherited the title after the death of Viscount Eligio Arroyo. "Earl Bostic Inherits a New Title," *The California Eagle*, July 14, 1949, 15.
7. 1910 Census (Coweta, Waggoner County, Tulsa, Oklahoma), Charles Gibson and family. See also 1900 Census (Freestone, Texas).
8. 20 North Detroit Street, Ike Bostic draft card, June 1917; "Mr and Mrs Ike Bostic," *The Tulsa Star*, September 7, 1918, 4. See also 1920 Census. Although Ernie Fields once described Ike as a junk peddler, there is no other evidence which supports this, and all records, official and otherwise since 1900, describe him as a cook.
9. "Our Totterie," *The Tulsa Star*, October 19, 1918, 2.
10. See the lengthy and detailed report about the riot: Various authors, *Tulsa Race Riot: A Report by the Oklahoma Commission to Study the Tulsa Race Riot of 1921*, February 28, 2001, https://www.okhistory.org/research/forms/freport.pdf.
11. See Miss Mary E. Jones Parrish, *Events of the Tulsa Disaster* (Tulsa: Privately printed, 1922), 42. The remarkable Rev. Charles Lanier Netherland died in his 92nd year in 1958 after a lifetime of service to the church. See obituary: "Rev. C. L. Netherland, Tulsa's Oldest Cleric, Dies," *The Oklahoma Eagle*, January 23, 1958, 1.
12. "Chattel Mortgages," *Tulsa Daily Legal News*, August 12, 1913, 2.
13. "People Places: Greenwood Tour," *The Oklahoma Eagle*, July 19, 1951, 4; "Theatricals," *The Pittsburgh Courier*, February 8, 1947, 8.

Chapter 2

1. Marc Crawford, "Bostic's Discs Help Him Click," *The Pittsburgh Courier*, February 25, 1956, Sec. 2, p. 5.
2. "Bandmaster" (with photo), *The Oklahoma Eagle*, February 14, 1942, 11.
3. Carmen Fields, *Going Back to T-Town* (Norman: University of Oklahoma Press, 2023), 48.
4. "Tonkawa Man Given Rene Morento Medal," *The Cushing Daily Citizen*, January 7, 1928, 6. (Includes photograph.)
5. "Tulsa Clerk Finds Hobby Working Among Negroes," *Tulsa World*, November 12, 1933, 22.
6. "Troop No. 41 St. Monica's Church," *The Oklahoma Courier*, September 17, 1927, 3.
7. "Troop No. 41 St. Monica's," *The Oklahoma Courier*, March 30, 1929, 4.
8. "Give Minstrel Show" *The Oklahoma Courier* June 28, 1930, 7.
9. "Earl Bostic Here June 25th," *The Oklahoma Eagle*, June 16, 1949, 7.
10. "Tulsa Clerk Finds Hobby Working Among Negroes," *Tulsa World*, November 12, 1933, 22.
11. "Troop No. 41," *The Oklahoma Courier*, September 13, 1930, 2.
12. "Patron Saint Passes," *The Oklahoma Eagle*, March 30, 1972, 1, 10A.

Chapter 3

1. Bill Lewis quoted by Buddy Tate in Nathan W. Pearson Jr., *Goin' to Kansas City* (Urbana: University of Illinois Press, 1987), 58.
2. See Ross Russell, *Jazz Style in Kansas City and the South West* (Berkeley: University of California Press, 1971).
3. Buddy Tate interview in Nathan W. Pearson, Jr., *Goin' to Kansas City* (Chicago: University of Illinois Press, 1987), 58.
4. Helen McNamara, "Buddy Tate: Still Keeping Up," *Downbeat*, April, 29, 1971.
5. "Earl Bostic," *IAJRC Journal* Vols. 24–25 (International Association of Jazz Record Collectors, 1991), 49.
6. Albert J. McCarthy, *Big Band Jazz* (New York: Exeter Books, 1983), 101–2.

Chapter 4

1. L. Masco Young, "Earl Bostic, Noted Sax Man, Blazing New Trails in Music," *The Indianapolis Recorder*, November 26, 1955, 13.
2. "Band Elects New Officers for 1930–31," *The Creightonian*, October 23, 1930, 1.
3. "Arts College to Hold Fun Fest Tonight," *The Creightonian*, November 20, 1930, 1.
4. "Negro Students," *The Creighton Alumnus*, Vol. 5, No. 5, February 1931, 12.
5. "Xavier Dance Orchestra Appears—Music Greatly Applauded," *The Xavier Herald*, Vol. 7, No. 1, November 1931, 1.
6. "Instrumental Music," *The Xavier Herald*, Vol. 7, No. 1, November 1931, 2.
7. "Music Review," *The Xavier Herald*, Vol 7, No. 3, January 1932, 2.
8. "Earl Bostic Draws Reprimand for Barfly Baby Blues," *The Ohio State News*, July 24 1948, 26. There is some doubt whether Bostic attended Langston University, as this article, which appeared in several other newspapers, including *The Chicago Defender*, is one of the few mentioning that he did. None of the available yearbooks at Langston list either Bostic or Professor Lester Hines. An enquiry to the university authorities did not produce a response.
9. See Richard Payne's recollections of his time at Xavier University in Charles Suhor, *Jazz in New Orleans: The Postwar Years Through 1970* (Lanham. MD: Scarecrow Press, 2001), 278.
10. "How He Proposed by Mrs Earl Bostic," *Tan*, Vol. 31, Issue 1, November 1952, 15.
11. "Earl Bostic Here June 25th," *The Oklahoma Eagle*, June 23, 1949, 12.
12. Stanley Dance, *The World of Count Basie* (New York: Scribners, 1980), 144.
13. "Meet Joe Newman, Another New Orleans Gift to Jazz," *Down Beat*, October 20, 1954, 21.

Chapter 5

1. Zutty Singleton, quoted in Kathy J. Ogren, *The Jazz Revolution: Twenties America and the Meaning of Jazz* (New York: Oxford University Press, 1992), 48.
2. Albert J. McCarthy, *Big Band Jazz* (New York: Exeter Books. 1983), 136.
3. Father Al Lewis. Transcript of interview with Father Al Lewis recorded February 1972, 6.

4. Eddy Determeyer, *Big Easy Big Bands* (Groningen, Netherlands: RhythmBusiness Publishing, 2012), 165; "Joe Robichaux: After the Sun Goes Down," *The Jazz Archivist*, Vol. IV, No. 1, May 1989.
  5. "Re: Joe Robichaux," *Coda: The Canadian Jazz Magazine*, Vol. 4, 1961, 32.
  6. Bostic spent a year in St. Louis, MO, 1934–1935, according to Alice Pardoe West, "Earl Bostic Tries 3 Years, Finally Makes Trip to Utah," *Ogden Standard-Examiner*, June 13, 1954, 8.
  7. Leonard Feather, "Riverboat Jazz Sets Sail Again," *Los Angeles Times*, June 9, 1969, 91.
  8. Pops Foster, *The Autobiography of Pops Foster, New Orleans Jazzman* (Berkeley: University of California Press, 1971), 106.
  9. John Chilton, *Ride, Red, Ride* (Cassell, 1999), 30.
  10. William Howland Kenney, *Jazz on the River* (Chicago: University of Chicago Press, 2005), 171.
  11. "Earl Bostic Member of Clarence Olden's Band," *The Call*, November 29, 1935, 21.
  12. See David Meyers, Howard Arnett, James Loeffler, James, and Candice Watkins, *Images of America: Columbus: The Musical Crossroads* (Charleston, SC: Arcadia Publishing, 2008).
  13. "Cedar Gardens Goes 'Non-Union', But It's Because They Have To," *The Pittsburgh Courier*, March 20 1937, 18.
  14. Joe Mosbrook, *Cleveland Jazz History* (Northeast Ohio Jazz Society, 2003), 120–22.

Chapter 6

  1. Harry Kramer, "Notes to You," *The New York Age*, August 24, 1940, 4.
  2. "Five Years Ago," *Down Beat*, April 1, 1943, 3.
  3. "Ed Smalls Dies at 92; Owned Famous Harlem Spot," *Jet*, November 7, 1974, 30.
  4. Arnold Shaw, *The Jazz Ages Pop Music in the 1920s* (New York: Oxford University Press, 1987), 62.
  5. "Earl Bostic," *Billboard*, May 16, 1942, 8.
  6. Gilbert Gaster, "Miss Rhapsody," *Storyville*, No. 43, Oct–Dec, 1972.
  7. E. E. Bostic Draft Card dated October 17, 1940. Census 1940, Earl Bostic lodging in Manhattan, New York, listed as Band Leader Orchestra.
  8. "Blitz Show," *Pittsburgh Courier*, December 20, 1941, 23; "Musical Patriots Who are Keeping America Singing in the Midst of a War-Torn World," *Pittsburgh Courier*, with photo, May 2, 1942, 21.
  9. Irving (Jimmy) Hines, "Club World," *The New York Age*, June 29, 1940, 12.
  10. Hugues Panassié, "Earl Bostic," *Jazz Journal*, Vol. 10, Issue 7, July 1957, 11.
  11. "Earl Bostic," *The Phoenix Index*, October 4, 1941, 3.
  12. Herbert H. Nichols, "The Jazz Life," *The New York Age*, September 6, 1941, 10.
  13. "Bostic Bands on Showboat," *New York New Amsterdam Star-News*, August 16, 1941, 21.
  14. Alfred A. Duckett, "Seeing the Show," *The New York Age*, April 29, 1939, 1.
  15. "Earl Bostic Celebrates," *New Pittsburgh Courier*, July 10, 1948, 23.
  16. "Bostic, The Man Who Came Back," *The Afro American*, April 9, 1949, 6.

Chapter 7

  1. Undated magazine clipping, circa 1951.
  2. 1940 Census, 1809 West Easton Place, Tulsa: Lloyd Owen and family.
  3. "Greenwood Tour: Places, People," *The Oklahoma Eagle*, July 19, 1951, 4.
  4. "Card of Thanks," *The Oklahoma Eagle*, November 3, 1941, 2.
  5. 1930 Census 1833 Burdette Street, New Orleans: Fred White and family.
  6. Undated magazine clipping, circa 1951.
  7. Ibid.
  8. "How He Proposed by Mrs Earl Bostic," *Tan*, Vol. 31, Issue 1, November, 1952, 25.
  9. In an interview, Hildegarde said that she and Earl married in February 1942. However, her divorce petition of 1965 listed the marriage date as November 30, 1942.

Chapter 8

  1. Buddy Tate interview in Nathan W. Pearson, Jr., *Goin' to Kansas City* (Chicago: University of Illinois Press, 1987), 58.
  2. "Swing: Alvino Rey," *Down Beat*, September 1, 1942, 8.

3. Tim Gayle, "Alvino Rey," *The Baton*, 1941, 10.
4. "Anita O'Day: Revisiting A Classic Voice," *Fresh Air* (Radio Broadcast), July 24, 2009.
5. "Entertainment," *The Jackson Sun*, November 25, 1941, 8.
6. See Carmen Fields, *Going Back to T-Town*, 145.
7. "Leslie Johnakins—Always a Big Band Musician: His Life Story as Told to David Griffiths," *Storyville*, No. 70, April–May 1977, 146.
8. Gene Allen, interviewed in 2000. See Jack Gordon, *Fifties Jazz Talk: An Oral Retrospective* (Lanham, MD: Scarecrow Press, 2004), 2.
9. Johnny Simmen, "Some Piano Compositions of Willie 'the Lion' Smith Played by Other Musicians Concluded," *Storyville*, No. 45 (London: Storyville Publications Co., Feb–Mar 1973), 98.

Chapter 9

1. "Lionel Hampton Given Works By 'Billboard,'" *The Pittsburgh Courier*, July 31, 1943, 20.
2. "Earl Bostic Has New Rig," *The Afro American*, January 23, 1943, 9.
3. "Earl Bostic to Play with Hamp," *Down Beat*, July 1, 1943.
4. Lucius Jones, "'I Refuse to Put My Bandmen in a Musical Straight-jacket; I Let 'Em Play'—Hamp," *The Pittsburgh Courier*, August 21, 1943, 12.
5. Joe Williams, "Frankly Speaking," interview with *Jazz Professional*, January, 1962, 11.
6. Lucius Jones, *The Pittsburgh Courier*, August 21. 1943, 12.
7. "Original Band Member Still with Hampton," *The Pittsburgh Courier*, January 1, 1944, 13.
8. "Lionel Hampton in Boston Concert," *The Pittsburgh Courier*, April 1, 1944, 13.
9. For an excellent appraisal of Lionel Hampton, see the chapter "Lionel Hampton Major Contributions" in Martin Williams, *Jazz in Its Time* (New York: Oxford University Press, 1991), 70–78.
10. Hal Singer, quoted in Ira Gitler, *Swing to Bop* (New York: Oxford University Press, 1987), 76.

Chapter 10

1. James Moody, quoted in *The Earl Bostic Story* sleeve notes, Proper Box Set, 2006.
2. Gordon Gullickson, *The Record Changer*, Vol. 3, 1944, 53.
3. "Miss Weston, Singer," *The Portsmouth Star*, February 2, 1945, 14.
4. Herman Rosenberg, "Manhattan Melange," *The Record Changer*, Vol. 4, March 1945–Feb. 1946, 70.
5. Alvin Moses, "Night Life in New York," *The Daily Bulletin*, July 14, 1945, 3.
6. "Here and There," *Hartford Courant* November 14 1945, 7.
7. "Cousin" Joe, with Harriet Ottenheimer, *Blues from New Orleans* (Chicago: University of Chicago Press, 1987), 116.
8. "Earl Bostic," *Down Beat*, August 26, 1946, 20.
9. "Jazz Cavalcade Has Some Kicks," *Down Beat*, April 18, 1946, 2.
10. "Jazz Concert At Academy Aids Elks' Charity," *Brooklyn Eagle*, April 23, 1946, 18.

Chapter 11

1. "Bostic's 'Temptation' Looms as Hot Wax Hit," *The Pittsburgh Courier*, April 3, 1948, 17.
2. George F. Brown, "Courier's Carnegie Music Hall Concert Smash Hit," *New Pittsburgh Courier*, March 22, 1947, 16.
3. "Ace Jazz Artists in Solo Battles to Swing NM Up!," *New Masses*, Vol. LXIII, Number Four, April 22, 1947, 32; "Duels in Jazz Concert," *Daily Worker*, April 16, 1947, 11.
4. "Pitching Platters," *The Guilfordian*, February 19, 1949, 2. See also "Bostic Says Bop and Swing to Blend," *California Eagle*, March 10, 1949, 16.
5. "Bostic Cracks Philly Record," *The Pittsburgh Courier*, June 29, 1948, 20.
6. "Earl Bostic at N. Y. Club," *The Pittsburgh Courier* June 21, 1947, 17.
7. "Earl Bostic Waxes Four Gotham Sides," *New Pittsburgh Courier*, August 2, 1947, 16.
8. "Earl Bostic's Ork Hits DC Club Bali, Sept. 19," *The Pittsburgh Courier*, September 20, 1947, 17.
9. "Earl Bostic's Ork and Revue Comes

to Apollo Stage," *The New York Age*, December 20, 1947, 63.
10. "Universal Attractions Signs E Bostic's Ork," *New Pittsburgh Courier*, November 8, 1947, 17; "Boone Joins Shaw Agency," *Jackson Advocate*, April 13, 1957, 2.
11. Morris Ball in J. Jerome Zolten, *Great God A'mighty! The Dixie Hummingbirds* (New York: Oxford University Press, 2003), 171.
12. "Ball Parks Bounce to Bostic Bash," *New Pittsburgh Courier*, June 12, 1948, 17.
13. Les Mernon, "Records of the Month," *Radio Best*, March, 1948, 40.
14. "Earl Bostic Repeats Philadelphia Story," *The Afro American*, September 11, 1948, 6.
15. "Transportation 'Fleet' for Earl Bostic," *The New York Age*, July 31, 1948, 4.
16. "Earl Bostic Celebrates," *New Pittsburgh Courier*, July 10, 1948, 23.
17. "Apollo, N. Y. Dr Neff's Madhouse of Mystery," *Variety*, August 25, 1948, 48.
18. Victor Schonfield, "The Forgotten Ones: Earl Bostic," *Jazz Journal International*, November, 1984, 14.
19. "Torrid Tempo Exponent Bostic Turns to Blues," *The Ohio State News*, January 29, 1949, 21.

Chapter 12

1. Duke Orsino in Shakespeare, *Twelfth Night*, Act 1, Scene 1.
2. E.B. Rae, "Encores and Echoes," *Afro-American*, October 16, 1948, B6.
3. *Addisleigh Park Historic District Designation Report*, NYC Landmarks Preservation Commission, 2011, 323.
4. "Bostic Takes Time Off to Fix Home," *Washington African American*, November 13, 1948, 20.
5. Jacobs Richard Gilbert, "Horn of Plenty in Queens," *The Times*, October 23, 1999. See also Lee Cotten, *The Golden Age of American Rock 'n Roll* (Ann Arbor, MI: Pierian Press, 1989).
6. 1950 Census Addisleigh Park, New York; 1950 Census, Tulsa. See also "Mrs. A. Z. Reed Dies at Chicago; Rites Sunday," *The Oklahoma Eagle*, February 13, 1958, 4.
7. "Wives Wear Aprons as well as Minks," *Jet*, April 12, 1952, 27; "New York Beat," *Jet*, January 8, 1953, 63.
8. "Earl Bostic Urges Theatricals to Join Fight to Aid Civil Rights Program," *The New York Age*, August 7, 1948.
9. "Ruth MacArthur," *Chicago World*, September 18, 1948, 1.
10. "Earl Bostic, Village Corners," *Daily News*, March 14, 1946, 19.
11. "Musicians Ask Meany's Help on Union Bias," *The California Eagle*, March 20, 1958, 3.
12. Frances Theater, Columbia, Missouri: Renamed the Tiger in 1951, the theater closed in 1955, but later reopened under different management. For a detailed history of the Frances/Tiger Theater see the chapter "Tiger Theater" in Dianna Borsi O'Brien, *Historic Movie Theaters in Columbia, Missouri* (Charleston, SC: The History Press/Arcadia Publishing, 2021), 109–13; "Special Easter Attraction: Earl Bostic at the Piano," *Columbia Missourian*, April 16, 1949, 2.
13. "Earl Sees Brighter Days Ahead for Musicians in Dixie Change," *Washington African-American*, September 6, 1949, 5.
14. "Turntable Tintypes: No. 17 of a series: Hunter Hancock," *Radio Life*, December 19, 1952, 39.
15. "Bostic to be First Beige Band in Spot," *The Pittsburgh Courier*, July 20, 1950, 20.
16. "Toy Firecracker Nearly Wrecks Birmingham Holiday Dance," *Jackson Advocate*, July 9, 1949, 5.
17. "Earl Bostic Sets Precedent Playing Southern Nightery," *The Call*, March 11, 1955, 7; Eddie Jones, "$5000 (Confederate) Riding on Coming Battle of Jazz," *Nashville Banner*, February 11, 1955, 10.
18. L. Maceo Young, "The Lowdown," *Minneapolis Spokesman*, 13 April, 1956, 6.
19. *Jet*, Issue 26, Vol. 9, May 3, 1956, 16.
20. "Bostic Suggests Music as Means to Temper Juvenile Delinquency," *The Afro American*, May 29, 1948, 6.
21. "Earl Bostic One Step Ahead of Diplomats," *The Black Dispatch*, September 18, 1948, 3.

Chapter 13

1. Earl Snider, "Turrentine: He's Got Stories to Tell," *Tampa Bay Times*, March 28, 1986, 60.
2. "Earl Bostic, Roy Brown Package Tops on Tour," *New Pittsburgh Courier*, January 22, 1949, 22.

3. "Music Critic Group Awards Earl Bostic," *The Detroit Tribune*, June 4, 1949, 11.
4. "Earl Bostic Plans Symphony Orchestra," *The California Eagle*, 11 August, 1949, 15.
5. "Sax King Puts Final Touches on Musical Score," *New England Bulletin*, June 4, 1949, 5.
6. "Bostic in Market for a New Thrush," *Baltimore Afro American*, August 2, 1949, 7.
7. "Earl Bostic Searches for Trombonist," *The Detroit Tribune*, May 14, 1949, 13.
8. "Headliners to Top KC Music Festival," *The New York Age*, August 20, 1949, 19.
9. "Earl Bostic Praises New Vaude Wheel," *The Call*, July 14, 1950, 10.
10. "Bostic Leads Bop Conga at NY Savoy," *New Pittsburgh Courier*, April 2, 1949, 19.
11. Dan Burley, "Ovation for Billie at Jazz Concert," *The New York Age*, April 16, 1949, 3.
12. "Earl Bostic Has Traveled One Million Miles," *The Indianapolis Recorder*, November 12, 1949, 8.
13. "Earl Bostic Keeps Date With Help of Snowplow and Cops," *The Oklahoma Eagle*, December 7, 1950, 8.
14. Gerald Horne, *Jazz and Justice: Racism and the Political Economy of the Music* (New York: Monthly Review Press, 2019), 189.
15. Peter Vacher, *Swingin' on Central Avenue* (Lanham, MD: Rowman & Littlefield, 2015), 164.
16. "Song-Writing Bus Driver Ace Adams from New York," *Ebony*, Vol. 12, Issue 9, July 1957, 39.
17. Stanley Turrentine, interviewed by Pete Hammill, "On Jazz," *Daily News*, August 14, 1977, 212.

Chapter 14

1. "Earl Bostic's Six-Piece Combo Looms as Band of Tomorrow," *The Afro American*, March, 20 1948, 6.
2. "Earl Bostic to Serenade Dinah Washington," *The Northwest Enterprise*, August 24, 1950, 7.
3. "Paging Mr Ripley Musician Turns Down Pay for Play," *The Afro American*, September 9, 1950, 8.

4. "St. Louis Song Writer Ballad is Recorded," *St. Louis Globe-Democrat*, August 24, 1950, 19.
5. "Bostic Adds Three to Ork," *Pittsburgh Courier*, April 1, 1950, 21.
6. "It's Viscount of Bostic Now," *The Pittsburgh Courier*, July 16, 1949, 18.
7. "Earl Bostic Sees Modern Music Lagging," *The Detroit Tribune*, April 23, 1949, 15.
8. "Bostic Eyes Little Towns," *The Detroit Tribune*, July 1, 1950, 2.
9. "Earl Bostic to go Caribbean," *Washington Afro-American*, July 11, 1950, 19.
10. "Earl Bostic Scores in Sax Battle in New York," *Indianapolis Recorder*, August 12, 1950, 13.
11. "Jazz Train Chugs into City of Bop," *The Pittsburgh Courier*, September 22, 1950, 14.
12. Al Salerno, "Brooklyn and Broadway Night Life," *The Brooklyn Eagle*, September 22, 1950, 8.
13. "Off the Record with Disker," *Liverpool Echo*, April 6, 1963, 6.

Chapter 15

1. Jack Hutton, "Family Favourites: Earl Bostic—The Man the Jazz World Forgot," *Melody Maker*, September 4, 1954, 13.
2. Nigel Hunter, "Vogue in the U. K.," *Billboard*, October 7, 1967, 44.
3. John Peel, radio show transcript, January 7, 1996, British Forces Broadcasting Service (BFBS).
4. "Best Selling Retail Rhythm & Blues Records," *Billboard*, April 28, 1951, 37.

Chapter 16

1. J.C. Thomas, *Chasin' the Trane* (New York: Da Capo, 1975), 60.
2. "Earl Bostic, Top Musician, Injured in Car Collision," *Tampa Bay Times*, December 10, 1951, 19.
3. "Earl Bostic Removed to New York," *The Indianapolis Recorder*, December 22, 1951, 13; "Earl Bostic Injured in Head-On Crash," *The Pittsburgh Courier*, December 15, 1951.
4. "New Yorker Arrested," *The News-Messenger*, Fremont, Ohio, April 13, 1951, 13.

5. "Speeder Fined $10," *Press of Atlantic City*, July 12, 1951, 11.
6. "Jazz Musician Who Hit Boy Denies Dangerous Driving," *The Republican*, November 7, 1955, 20.
7. "Earl Bostic Appeals Fine on Auto Count," *The Republican*, December 28, 1955, 22. "Bostic Faces $50,000 Suit for Accident," *The Republican*, January 26, 1956, 20.
8. "Suit Against Bandmaster is Settled," *The Republican*, May 17, 1957, 27.
9. Cliff Smalls, interview with Sue Terry, *The Jazz Artist*, Vol. III, No. 1, July 1999.
10. Cliff Smalls, interviewed in Stanley Dance, *The World of Earl Hines* (New York: Scribners, 1977), 270.
11. "New York Beat," *Jet*, November 7, 1957, 63.
12. "Peacock Scores as Pinch-Hitter," *The Call*, December 21, 1951, 8.
13. Photo with caption "Bandleader Earl Bostic," *The St. Louis American*, February 28, 1952, 6.

Chapter 17

1. Art Blakey, quoted in J.C. Thomas, *Chasin' the Trane: The Music and Mystique of John Coltrane* (New York: Doubleday, 1975), 58.
2. "Bostic to Chicago's Blue Note," *Pittsburgh Courier*, March 1, 1958, 23.
3. Dan Morgenstern, "Ready, Willing and Able: Jackie Byard," *Down Beat*, October 21, 1965, 17.
4. See Ingrid Monson, *Saying Something: Jazz Improvisation and Interaction* (Chicago: University of Chicago Press, 1987), 184. Monson states that Byard was with Bostic between 1947 and 1949; however, the *Grove Dictionary* states that he stayed three years. Author Richard Vacca maintains that Byard was fired. See Richard Vacca, *The Boston Jazz Chronicles: Faces, Places and Night Life 1937–62* (Belmont, MS: Troy Street Publishing, 2012), 172.
5. "These Artists Gather Stardust on Nation's Marquees," *The Pittsburgh Courier*, December 4, 1954, 14.
6. Lou Donaldson, sleeve notes from *Flamingo: The Very Best of Earl Bostic*.
7. "Bobby Booker's Life Story as told to David Griffiths and Frank Diggs," *Storyville*, No. 101, June–July 1982, 183.

8. "E B Scores in Sax Battle in N. Y.," *The Indianapolis Recorder*, August 12, 1950, 13.
9. Herb Wong, "Alto Saxophone," *Jazz on My Mind* (Jefferson, NC: McFarland & Company, 2016), 77.
10. Benny Golson, quoted by Paul Watts in liner notes of *The Earl Bostic Collection 1939–59*, Acrobat Music ADD CD 3131 (2015).
11. John Porter, *John Coltrane: His Life and Music* (Ann Arbor: University of Michigan Press, 1998), 90.
12. Roy Haynes, audio interview, quoted in sleeve notes of *The Ultimate Blue Train*. (Blue Note CD 1997).
13. Lewis Porter et al., *The John Coltrane Reference* (New York: Routledge, 2007), 75.
14. John Coltrane to August Blume, in *The Jazz Review*, quoted in *The John Coltrane Companion Five Decades of Commentary* (London: Omnibus Press, 1998), 25.
15. Earl Snider, "Turrentine: He's Got Stories to Tell," *Tampa Bay Times*. March 28, 1986, 60.
16. Al Hunter, Jr., "Turrentine Finds Sanctuary for Jazz," *Philadelphia Daily News*, May 17, 1996, 58.
17. Lewis Porter, *Coltrane, His Life & Music* (Ann Arbor: University of Michigan Press, 1999), 90. See also Marc Myers, interview with Benny Golson, on *Jazz Wax*, September 9, 2008.
18. Art Blakey, quoted in J.C. Thomas, *Chasin' the Trane: The Music and Mystique of John Coltrane* (New York: Doubleday, 1975), 58.
19. Thomas Putnam, "Pianist Afraid He'll Get Stale," *Buffalo Courier-Express*, July 18, 1967, 43.
20. Bill Kirchner, interview with George Goldsmith, *Down Beat*, June 21, 1979, 81.
21. Joe Knight, quoted in J.C. Thomas, *Chasin' the Trane: The Music and Mystique of John Coltrane* (New York: Doubleday, 1975), 58.
22. "Pitching Platters," *The Guilfordian*, February 19, 1949, 2.

Chapter 18

1. Karl Zanco, "Teenager, Earl Bostic Talk Music at Ocean Side Center as

Swingsters Rock 'n' Roll," *Blade Tribune*, April 25, 1956, 16.

2. "Rhythm and Blues Record Reviews," *Billboard*, July 4, 1953, 46.

3. "Songwriters' Test Going Fine—Bostic," *Washington Afro American*, November 18, 1952, 4.

4. Hugues Panassié, "Earl Bostic," *Jazz Journal*, Vol. 10, Issue 7, July 1957, 11.

5. John Hardin, "Melody Time," *The Springfield News-Leader*, November 21, 1954, 26.

6. Barbara L. Wilson, "Bostic, Eldridge and Hawkins on Earle Stage," *The Philadelphia Inquirer*, February 7, 1953, 10.

7. Harry Levette, "Movie Lots Gossip," *The Call*, June 19, 1953, 8.

8. "Earl Bostic" by Steve Hoffman in Edward M. Komara, *Encyclopaedia of the Blues Vol. 1* (London: Psychology Press, 2006), 140.

9. "Dance Fans Will Hear One of Nation's Top Bands On July 3 When Bostic Plays," *The Carolinian*, July 4, 1953, 4.

10. "Brubeck & Bostic At Basin St, New York," *The Cash Box*, October 16, 1954, 22.

11. "Big Bands on Rise—E. Bostic," *The Pittsburgh Courier*, April 19, 1950, 21.

12. Bret Primack, interview with Stanley Turrentine, "We're in the Market Place Now," *Down Beat*, October 19, 1978, 13.

13. Bill Soberanes, "So They Tell Me," *Press Democrat*, August 1, 1952, 18.

14. Robert P. Laurence, "Rock 'n Roll Celebrates its 25th Birthday," *Beaver County Times*, February 7, 1979, 64.

15. Pete Hamill, "The City That Changed My Life," *San Bernardino Sun*, July 21, 1985, 102.

Chapter 19

1. Alice Pardoe West, "Earl Bostic Tries 3 Years, Finally Makes Trip to Utah," *Ogden Standard-Examiner*, June 13, 1954, 8.

2. "Bostic Blows for Forgotten G. I. Eagles," *New Pittsburgh Courier*, February 19, 1949, 19; "Earl Bostic Drafted for Fort Sill," *New Pittsburgh Courier*, June 17, 1950, 11.

3. "Patients to See Revue," *The Commercial Appeal*, July 8, 1950, 10.

4. "Earl Bostic Campus Dates Stir-Up Booking Agencies," *The Detroit Tribune*, April 15, 1950, 7.

5. "Alpha Phi Alpha to Hold Regional Meet at Colleges," *The Times & Democrat*, October 5, 1951, 22

6. "Earl Bostic Helps RC," *The Detroit Tribune*, February 4, 1950, 7.

7. "College, Army Camp Deal for Bostic Package May Open New Coast Route," *Variety*, April 14, 1954, 109.

8. Phil Guthrie, "Bostic's Band Scores Hit in Jazz Concert," *Enterprise-Record*, April 28, 1954, 2.

9. "Fullbackers to Present Earl Bostic, Band Feb. 10," *The Louisiana Weekly*, January 28, 1961, 14.

10. "On the Upbeat," *Variety*, May 25, 1955, 59.

11. "Top Jazz Man Earl Bostic to Play Here," *Arizona Daily Sun*, January 9, 1959, 6.

12. Grace Hinson, "Greeks Leave Local Campus Scenery to Celebrate Fraternity Weekends," *The Florida Alligator*, March 13, 1959, 2.

13. "Greek Week Activities Begin Monday: Dave Brubeck Quartet, Bostic Provide Music," *The Gamecock*, February 24, 1961, 1; "Jazz in Concert in Person" (advertisement), *The Kentucky Kernel*, May 13, 1960, 2.

14. "Valentines, Parties, Jazz, Bostic," *Taps* (Clemson University), 1961, 16.

15. *T. C. Ram* (Winston-Salem Teachers College, 1962), 29.

Chapter 20

1. Edith McCormick, president of International Fan Club of America, "International Fan Club Salutes Earl Bostic," *The Call*, December 27, 1957, 8.

2. "Earl Bostic Sets Precedent Playing Southern Nightery," *The Call*, March 11, 1955, 2; "Drama Notes," *New York Post*, January 14, 1955, 23.

3. Lee F. Hewitt, "Musical Celebrity Collects Coins," *Numismatic Scrapbook*, 1954, 1433.

4. "Earl Bostic, Saxman, Coin Collector, Seeks 1913 Liberty-Head," *Washington Afro-American*, January 17, 1956, 16.

5. "Tulsa Man Offers $6000 for Missing Coin," *The Oklahoma Eagle*, January 26, 1956, 9.

6. "Earl Bostic," *Jet*, Vol. 7, Issue 25, April 24, 1955, 13.

7. "They're Talking About," *New Pittsburgh Courier*, May 17, 1958, 23.

8. Marion Brown, *Recollections, Essays, Drawings, Miscellanea* (Frankfurt am Main, Germany: J.A. Schmitt, 1984), 120.
9. "Citrus Curves Dangerous for Bostic," *Pittsburgh Courier*, February 6, 1949, 12.
10. "Have You Hurd?," *The Enterprise*, July 6, 1951, 3.
11. "Earl Bostic Urges Teenagers To Drive Safely Launches Public Appeal to Curb Teenicide," *The Indianapolis Recorder*, August 13, 1955, 13.
12. "Rhythm & Blues: Dance Time," *Billboard*, February 23, 1957, 64.
13. "Doll League Spring Dance" *California Eagle*, April 5, 1956, 8.
14. "Bostic, Jazz Ace, Stricken on Bandstand," *Oakland Tribune*, June 15, 1956, 17.
15. *Jet*, Vol. 11, Issue 2, November 15, 1956, 23.

Chapter 21

1. Lou Donaldson, sleeve notes from *Flamingo: The Very Best of Earl Bostic*.
2. Plas Johnson, quoted in Michael Segell, *The Devil's Horn: The Story of the Saxophone, from Noisy Novelty to King of Cool* (New York: Farrar, Straus & Giroux, 2005), 146.
3. "Record Ramblin,'" *Springfield Post*, May 17, 1956, 6.
4. Sleeve notes, Geoff Taylor All Stars, *Sweet Suite*, Esquire LP 20-060 1955; Jack Florin, "Jazz Roundabout," *Manchester Evening News*, June 28, 1954, 23.
5. See Matthew Barton, "So Rare: The Last Days of Jimmy Dorsey," *ARSC Journal*, Vol. 51, Issue 2 (Association for Recorded Sound Collections, 2020).
6. Allan MacMillan, *Indianapolis Recorder*, December 7, 1957.
7. "Earl Bostic Ponders International Tour," *The St. Louis Argus*, January 10, 1958, 19.
8. Hugues Panassié, "Earl Bostic," *Jazz Journal*, Vol. 10, Issue 7, July 1957, 11.
9. Gerald Lascelles, "Records: Can Jazz-Players Hit the Jackpot?" *The Tatler*, February 18, 1959, 313.
10. Gerald Lascelles, "Records: A Clarinettist in Rampart Street," *The Tatler*, May 4, 1960, 8.
11. Rudolph Nureyev, quoted by Elizabeth Kaye, "Nureyev: Dancing in His Own Shadow," *Esquire*, Vol. 115 (March 1991), 128.
12. "Wooed to the Wail of Bostic," *Daily Mirror*, September 2, 1964, 16. Letters: Mrs D. Lenanton of Seaward Road, Woolston, Southampton.
13. *About Larkin*, Issue 6, The Philip Larkin Society, 1999, 6.

Chapter 22

1. "Dave Brubeck Quartet, Bostic Provide Music," *The Gamecock*, February 24, 1961, 1.
2. "NAACP Plans Benefit Dance," *The San Bernardino County Sun*, March 15, 1957, 15.
3. "Brotherhood Slates Gala Anniversary," *California Eagle*, October 14, 1957, 8.
4. "Joe Glaser Signs Earl Bostic to Long Term Contract," *The Louisiana Weekly*, February 15, 1958, 14.
5. "Chicago Jazz Fans Praise Earl Bostic," *Philadelphia Tribune*, March 25, 1958, 12.
6. "Bostic in Cutting Marathon for King Records," in Galen Gart (Editor & Compiler), *First Pressings: The History of Rhythm & Blues Vol. 9 1959* (Winter Haven, FL: Big Nickel Music Publications, 2002), 59.
7. Chris Perlee, "Greatest Array of Artists," *San Bernardino Sun*, May 1, 1960, 52.
8. Dom Cerulli, "The Playboy Festival," *International Music*, September 1959, 9.
9. George Harris, "Platter Chatter: Album of the Week," *The Daily Notes*, March 30, 1959, 2.
10. Stanley Turrentine, interviewed in Gene Lees, *Friends Along the Way: A Journey Through Jazz* (New Haven, CT: Yale University Press, 2003), 64.

Chapter 23

1. Albert Anderson, for ANP, "This Week in Records: Contrast in Jazz," *The Call*, May 30, 1958, 9.
2. "Popular," *Billboard*, May 11, 1959, 33.
3. "Says Bostic Like Old Man River," *The Call*, May 2, 1958, 9.
4. Earl Wilson, "Marilyn Monroe—Revolt of the Love Goddess Her Ambition:

'To Grow and Develop!'" *Sunday Herald*, June 6. 1955, M-3.

Chapter 24

1. Karl Zanco, "Teenager, Earl Bostic Talk Music at Ocean Side Center as Swingsters Rock 'n' Roll," *Blade Tribune*, April 25, 1956.
2. Jackie Wolffer, "Teen Talk," *Lake Elsinore Valley Sun-Tribune*, January 14, 1960, 14.
3. "Bostic Has Heart Attack Scare," *Pittsburgh Courier*, July 25, 1960, 12.
4. Chester L. Lane, quoted in Peter Vacher, *Swingin' on Central Avenue* (Lanham, MD: Rowman & Littlefield, 2015), 164.
5. *Tampa Bay Times*, January 10, 1960, 80.
6. "'Pops' Blows into Town and Wows Audience," *The Journal Herald*, April 20, 1961, 3.
7. "The Lighthouse," *Downbeat Yearbook*, 1962, 23.

Chapter 25

1. Earl Bostic, quoted by Hal Neely in sleeve notes of *Jazz as I Feel It* (1963).
2. Ibid.
3. Ibid.
4. Barry McRae, sleeve notes *Jazz Time*, Charly Records Le Jazz CD 52 (1996).
5. Albert Anderson, "The Week in Records," *The Carolinian* (Raleigh, NC), March 7, 1964, 14.
6. Mark Gardner, "Jazz Notes," *Whitstable & Herne Bay Herald*, January 11, 1974, 30.
7. "Earl Bostic, Jazz As I Feel It (King 1963)," *Flophouse Magazine*, November 22, 2022.
8. Ibid.
9. Jamboree Jazz Events: January 2016." Translated from the Spanish original. See also https://jamboreejazz.com/en/events/benjamin-herman-abel-boquera-dave-mitchell-anton-jarl-2.
10. Don A. Yoder, "Just Jazz," *The Denver Blade*, January 24, 1963, 6.
11. "Opening Set for Young Adults Club," *The Van Nuys News & Valley Green Sheet*, May 24, 1963, 47.
12. David Allen, "Former Royal Tahitian Now at Tiki Teardown," *Daily Bulletin*, September 4, 2010.

Chapter 26

1. Ken Barnard, "That New Detroiter, Mr. Earl Bostic," *Detroit Free Press*, October 17, 1965, 27.
2. "Hildegarde Quits Earl Bostic: Earthquake Named as Cause," *Jet*, October 28, 1965; "Earl Bostic Misses 'Earthquake,'" *Jet*, November 11, 1965.
3. Ken Barnard, "That New Detroiter, Mr. Earl Bostic," *Detroit Free Press*, October 17, 1965, 27.
4. Letter from Mrs. Kenneth J. Shipman, "Midtown Plaza Gave Good Entertainment," *Democrat & Chronicle*, Rochester, NY, September 13, 1965, 10A.
5. Ken Barnard, "That New Detroiter, Mr. Earl Bostic," *Detroit Free Press*, October 17, 1965, 27.
6. "Wife Sues Orchestra Man Bostic," *Los Angeles Evening Citizen News*, October 14, 1965, 3.
7. "Bostic, Noted Sax Player, Stricken Here," *Rochester Democrat & Chronicle*, October 27, 1965, 6C.
8. "Heart Attack Proves Fatal to Earl Bostic," *North Tonawanda Evening News*, October 28, 1965, 15.
9. Maxie Maxwell, "Jazz Great Dies," *The Buffalo Challenger*, November 4, 1965, 6.
10. Leonard Feather, *Encyclopaedia of Jazz* (New York: Random House, 1988), 432.
11. Gerry Niewood, *Democrat & Chronicle*, September 23, 1977, 21.
12. "Earl Bostic Buried, Widow Tells Why She Didn't Cry," *Jet*, November 18, 1965.
13. Ibid.
14. United States Social Security Death Index, Hildegarde Theresa Bostic, née White, died October 10, 2002.
15. Los Angeles Cemetery Records Druzella Bostic, Evergreen Cemetery, Los Angeles. Died March 23, 1985. Informant Martin D. Hamilton, Nephew.

Epilogue

1. "Earl Bostic Ork," *Los Angeles Sentinel*, August 21, 1952, B2.

2. Kal Rudman, "Money Music," *Record World*, September 3, 1966, 33.

3. Michael Bone, interview with Dr. John, "Dr. John's Temple of Big Band," *Down Beat*, July 1995, 18–19.

4. Ivor Lee (Coventry), "Smoke Rings True," Letters, *Jazz UK*, December 1982, 37.

5. John Peel, transcript of radio show, British Forces Broadcasting Service (BFBS), September 1999.

6. David Bowie, interview, *The San Diego Union-Tribune*, April 18, 1993, 63; George Varga, "David Bowie in His Own Words," *The San Diego Union-Tribune*, January 11, 2018.

7. Pharoah Sanders, "In my own playing I was more or less into rhythm and blues. I liked Earl Bostic a lot." Quoted in the chapter "Pharoah's Tale" in Martin Williams, *Jazz Changes* (New York: Oxford University Press, 1993), 121.

8. Albert Ayler, quoted by Frank Kofsky in sleeve notes for Albert Ayler LP *Love Cry*, Impulse! Records (1968).

9. Victor Schonfield, "The Forgotten Ones: Earl Bostic," *Jazz Journal International*, November 1984, 15.

Bibliography

Amis, Kingsley. "Rhythm and Blues. J.R. Discusses the Career of Earl Bostic et al." *The Observer,* October 21, 1956, 13.

Barton, Matthew. "So Rare: The Last Days of Jimmy Dorsey." *ARSC (Association for Recorded Sound Collections) Journal,* Vol. 51, Issue 2, 2020.

Berish, Andrew S. *Lonesome Roads and Streets of Dreams.* Chicago: University of Chicago Press, 2012.

Birnbaum, Larry. *Before Elvis: The Prehistory of Rock 'n' Roll.* Lanham, MD: Scarecrow, 2013.

Bjorn, Lars, with Jim Gallert. *Before Motown: A History of Jazz in Detroit 1920–1960.* Ann Arbor: University of Michigan Press, 2001.

Broven, John. *Walking to New Orleans: The Story of New Orleans Rhythm & Blues.* Bexhill-on-Sea: Blues Unlimited, 1974.

Brown, Marion. *Recollections: Essays, Drawings, Miscellanea.* Frankfurt am Main: J.A. Schmidt, 1984.

Callahan, Owen. *Up There in Orbit.* Middletown, CT: Wesleyan University, 2012.

Catalog of Copyright Entries Third Series (Music) Published & Unpublished Music. Washington, D.C.: Library of Congress, 1938–1977.

Chilton, John. *Let the Good Times Roll: The Story of Louis Jordan and His Music.* London: Quartet Books, 1992.

Chilton, John. *Ride, Red, Ride: The Life of Henry 'Red' Allen.* London: Cassell, 2000.

Chilton, John. *Who's Who of Jazz: Storyville to Swing Street.* London: Macmillan, 1972.

Clark, Peter W. *Delta Shadows: A Pageant of Negro Progress in New Orleans.* New Orleans: Graphic Arts Studios, 1942.

Cohodas, Nadine. *Queen: The Life and Music of Dinah Washington.* New York: Knopf Doubleday Publishing Group, 2007.

Cotten, Lee. *The Golden Age of American Rock 'n' Roll 1952–1955.* Ann Arbor, MI: Pierian Press, 1989.

Dance, Stanley. *The World of Count Basie.* New York: Charles Scribner's Sons, 1980.

Dance, Stanley. *The World of Earl Hines.* New York: Charles Scribner's Sons, 1977.

Deffaa, Chip. *Voices of the Jazz Age: Profiles of Eight Vintage Jazzmen.* Champaign: University of Illinois Press, 1992.

Driggs, Frank, and Harris Lewine. *Black Beauty, White Heat.* Boston: Da Capo Press, 1996.

The Earl Bostic Collection of United States Coins. Public Auction Sale, Wednesday December 19, 1956, at the Carl Fischer Concert Hall. New York: Stacks, 1956. 49 pp.

"Earl of Music." *Rhythm and Blues,* Vol. 1, No. 1 (Derby, CT: Onyx Publishing Co.), August 1952, 10.

Feather, Leonard, and Ira Gitler. *The Biographical Encyclopedia of Jazz.* New York: Oxford University Press, 1999.

Fields, Carmen. *Going Back to T-Town: The Ernie Fields Territory Big Band.* Norman: University of Oklahoma Press, 2023.

Foster, Pops. *The Autobiography of Pops Foster, New Orleans Jazzman as told to Tom Stoddard.* Berkeley: University of California Press, 1971.

Fox, John Hartley. *King of the Queen City: The Story of King Records.* Champaign: University of Illinois Press, 2010.

Bibliography

Fox, Ted. *Showtime at the Apollo.* New York: Da Capo Press, 1993.

Gerber, Cheryl. *Cherchez La Femme: New Orleans Women.* Jackson: University Press of Mississippi, 2020.

Gitler, Ira. *Swing to Bop: An Oral History of the Transition in Jazz in the 1940s.* New York: Oxford University Press, 1985.

Goosman, Stuart L. *Group Harmony: The Black Urban Roots of Rhythm and Blues.* Philadelphia: University of Pennsylvania Press, 2005.

Gordon, Jack. *Fifties Jazz Talk: An Oral Retrospective.* Langham, MD: Scarecrow, 2004.

Gregory, Hugh. *The Real Rhythm and Blues.* London: Cassell/Blandford, 1998.

Hampton, Lionel, with James Haskins. *Hamp: An Autobiography.* New York: Warner Books, 1989.

Hutton, Jack. "Family Favourites: Earl Bostic—The Man the Jazz World Forgot." *Melody Maker,* September 4, 1954, 13.

Kennedy, Rick, and Randy McNutt. *Little Labels—Big Sound: Small Record Companies and the Rise of American Music.* Bloomington: University of Indiana Press, 1999.

Kenney, William Howland. *Jazz on the River.* Chicago: University of Chicago Press, 2005.

Mather, Dan. *Charlie Barnet: An Illustrated Biography & Discography of the Swing Era Band Leader.* Jefferson, NC: McFarland & Company, 2008.

McCarthy, Albert. *Big Band Jazz.* New York: G.P. Putnam's Sons, 1974.

McClellan, Lawrence. *The Later Swing Era, 1942–55.* Westport, CT: Greenwood Press, 2004.

McNutt, Randy. *King Records of Cincinnati.* Charleston, SC: Arcadia Publishing, 2009.

Miller, Paul Edward (Ed.). *Esquire's 1946 Jazz Book.* New York: A.S. Barnes, 1946.

"Musical Celebrity Collects Coins." In *Numismatic Scrapbook,* Vol. 20. New York: Lee F. Hewitt, 1954, 1424, 1433.

Owsley, Dennis. *City of Gabriels: The History of Jazz in St. Louis 1895–1973.* St. Louis: Reedy Press, 2006.

Owsley, Dennis. *St. Louis Jazz: A History.* Charleston, SC: The History Press, 2019.

Panchyk, Richard. *Hidden History of Queens.* Charleston, SC: Arcadia Publishing, The History Press, 2018.

Pearson, Nathan. *Goin' to Kansas City.* Champaign: University of Illinois Press, 1987.

Porter, Lewis. *John Coltrane: His Life & Music.* Ann Arbor: University of Michigan, 1999.

Porter, Lewis [Ed.], Chris Devito, David Wild, DeVito, Yasuhiro Fujioka, and Schmaler Wolf. *The John Coltrane Reference.* New York: Routledge, 2008.

Reisner, Robert George. *Bird: The Legend of Charlie Parker.* London: The Jazz Book Club, 1962.

Richards, Tad. *Small Group Swing 1940–1960.* New York: State University of New York, 2024.

Russell, Ross. *Jazz Style in Kansas City and the Southwest.* Berkeley: University of California Press, 1971.

Savage, William W. *Singing Cowboys and All That Jazz: A Short History of Popular Music in Oklahoma.* Norman: University of Oklahoma Press, 1983.

Scherman, Tony. *Backbeat: Earl Palmer's Story.* Washington, D.C.: Smithsonian Books, 1999.

Schonfield, Victor. "The Forgotten Ones: Earl Bostic." *Jazz Journal International,* Vol. 17, No. 11, November 1984.

Schroeder, Peter. *From the Minds of Jazz Musicians: Conversations with the Creative and the Inspired.* New York: Taylor & Francis, 2024.

Segell, Michael. *The Devil's Horn: The Story of the Saxophone, from Noisy Novelty to King of Cool.* New York: Farrar, Straus & Giroux, 2005.

Shaw, Arnold. *Honkers and Shouters: The Golden Years of Rhythm and Blues.* London: Macmillan, 1986.

Shaw, Arnold. *The Rockin' '50s: The Decade That Transformed the Pop Music Scene.* New York: Hawthorn Books, 1974.

Simmons, Rick. *Carolina Beach Music Encyclopedia.* Jefferson, NC: McFarland & Company, 2018.

Smith, Jay D., and Len Guttridge. *Jack Teagarden: The Story of a Jazz Maverick.* London: The Jazz Book Club, 1962.

Southern, Eileen. *Biographical Dictionary of Afro-American & African Musicians.* Westport, CT: Greenwood Press, 1982. Profile of Bostic, 42.

Stewart, Rex. *Boy Meets Horn.* London: A. & C. Black, 1995.

Suhor, Charles. *Jazz in New Orleans: The*

Post-War Years Through 1970. Lanham, MD: Scarecrow, 2001.

Tracy, Steven C. *Going to Cincinnati: A History of the Blues in the Queen City*. Champaign: University of Illinois Press, 1993.

Vacher, Peter. *Swingin' on Central Avenue: African American Jazz in Los Angeles*. Lanham, MD: Rowman & Littlefield, 2015.

Weekes, Todd Bryant. *Luck's in My Corner: The Life and Music of Hot Lips Page*. New York: Routledge, 2014.

Wintz, Cary D., and Paul Finkelman. *Encyclopedia of the Harlem Renaissance, 2 Vols*. New York: Routledge, 2012.

Wood, Ean. *Born to Swing: The Story of the Big Bands*. London: Sanctuary, 1996.

Index

Academy of Music, New York 62
Adams, Stanley "Ace" 83
Adderley, Cannonball 72, 130, 155
"Adios" 131
Adler, Danny 173
AEF Radio 48
"Air Mail Special" 144
"All On" 60
"All the Things You Are" 148
Allen, Gene 48
Allen, Henry "Red" 30, 32, 45, 62, 64, 89
Allen, Lee 129, 167
Allen, Marshall 130
Allen, Woody 156
"Always" 93
American Federation of Musicians 67
Amis, Kingsley 134
"Andalusia" 131
Anderson, Albert 145, 155
Anderson, John 108
Anderson, Leroy 142
Angel Records 173
"Angelina" 48
Apollo Theater 37, 38, 47
"Apple Cake" 154
"April in Portugal" 142
Armstrong, Louis 2, 23, 30, 50, 53, 59, 74, 86, 113, 137, 145, 169
"Arrivederci Roma" 142
Assoc. Booking Co. (ABC) 137
"At Twilight" 111
"Auld Lang's Syne" 34
Austin, Sil 129
"Avalon" 118
"Away" 65
Ayler, Albert 166, 168

"Baby Rockin' Daddy" 80
"Bach Is in the Groove" 55
"Back Beat Boogie" 141
Bailey, Buster 64
Bailey, Mildred 94

Baker, Chet 154, 163
Baker, Josephine 94
Baker, Lavern 3
Baker, "Shorty" 34–35
Ballin, Ivin 60, 66
Bankhead, Tallullah 35
Barefield, Eddie 19, 27
"Barfly Baby" 24, 61
Barnard, Ken 161
Barnet, Charlie 47, 144
Barnett, Ted 61, 65
Bart, Ben 66
Bartholemew, Dave 108
Basie, Catherine 72
Basie, Count 25, 27, 28, 61, 72, 141
Bass, Ralph 93
Bassman, George 93
The Baton 47
Baxter, Les 142
Bazzle, Germaine 24
"Because of You" 132, 142
Bechet, Sidney 26–27, 62, 64
"Beggin' Woman" 60
Belvin, Jesse 137
Bennett, Tony 132
Benton, Walter 106
Bernstein, Artie 45
Berton, Vic 61
Betts, Keter 89, 91, 106, 107
"Bewitched" 148
Billboard 50, 78, 109, 110, 125, 132, 144
"Birmingham Boogie" 51
Black & White Records 133
Black Hawk, San Francisco 121, 136, 150
Black Outs 137
Blackwell, Charlie 151
Blakey, Art 100, 106
"Blip Boogie" 79
"The Blizzard" 48
The Blue Devils 27, 50
Blue Note, Chicago 121, 136, 137
Blue Note Records 1, 104, 105, 107, 153

233

Index

"Blue Tango" 142
Blue Train 104
"Blues for the Ivy Leagues" 154
Blythe, Arthur 129
"Bo Do Rock" 130
"Body and Soul" 38
Bond, Graham 166
Bond, Jimmy 151
"Bones, Bones, Bones" 60
Booker, Bobby 102
Boone, Dick 66
Boquera, Abel 155
Borders, the Rev. William 137
Bostic, Charles (Grandfather) 7
Bostic, Dorothy 87–88
Bostic, Druzella (née Gibson, mother) 5–7, 8, 10–11, 13, 40, 72, 132, 160, 164
Bostic, Hildegarde (née White, wife) 22, 24–25, 40–42, 71, 72–73, 88, 96, 98, 127, 132, 136, 147, 148, 149, 150–51, 162–64, 221ch7n9
Bostic, Ike (father) 5–7, 10–11, 13; death 40
Bostic, Joe 87–88
Bostic, Maria (grandmother) 7
Bostic Meets Doggett **129**, 130
Bowen, James 15
Bowen, Ruth 73
Bowie, David 167
Bradshaw, Tiny 79, 129
Breston, Bob 110
"Brooklyn Boogie" 48
Brown, George F. 64
Brown, James 66, 86, 93, 136, 139
Brown, Marion 123
Brown, Nacio Herb 67, 94
Brown, Olive 36
Brown, Roy 78, 80
Brown, Wini 80
Brubeck, Dave 113, 119, 141
Bryant, "Rusty" 167
Bryant, Willie 66
Buckner, Milt 54, 86
Burtnett, Earl 93
Bushell, Garvin 166
Buck Ram All Stars 55
Byard, Jaki 78–79, 100
Byas, Don 50, 55, 56

Callahan, Owen 2
Calloway, Cab 43, 45, 61
Campos, Rafael 149
Cannon, "Ace" 167
Carline, Ray 108
Carnegie Hall 63
Carrington, Jeff 18
Carter, Benny 27, 143

Carter, Sonny 113
Casa Loma Orch. 110
Casey, Al 86
Catlett, Sid 45
Cavalcade of Jazz 62, 112–13
Cedar Gardens Club, Cleveland, OH. 32–33
Celestin, Papa 29
Cerulli, Dom 141
Chaise Lounge 167
Charles, Ray 127, 149
Charly Records 164, 173
"Cherokee" 48, 56, 118, 172
Chess Records 93
The Chicago Defender 21, 53
Chilton, John 49
"Chinatown, My Chinatown" 48
"El Choclo" 148
"Choppin' It Down" 79
Christian, Charlie 45
Christy, June 141
Clarke, Kenny 34
Clemmons, Clarence 166
Clinton, Larry 47
"Close Your Eyes" 80
Cobb, Arnett 54, 55, 98
Cobb, Jimmy 82, 91, 106–07
Cole, Cozy 55
Cole, Freddy 107
Cole, Maria 73
Cole, Nat "King" 2, 64, 73, 74, 77, 107, 108, 111, 113
Coleman, Ornette 155
Coltrane, John 2, 96, 100, **101**, 102–04, 105, 134, 155, 166, 168
Condon, Eddie 74
Corley, George 18
Cotton Club 33, 35
The Cotton Club 98
"Cracked Ice" 110, 141
Crawford, Hank 166
Creath, Charlie 29, 30
Creighton University, Omaha 15, 18, 20–22, **21**, 23
Crosby, Bing 67
Crouch, William F. 65
Cry-Baby 110, 167
"Cuttin' Out" 65, 68

Dameron, Tadd 33
Dance Time 1, 125, **126**
"Danube Waves" 110
Darin, Bobby 141
"Dark Eyes" 148
Davidson, Wild Bill 62, 130
Davis, Bill 16
Davis, "Don" John 24

Index

Davis, Eddie "Lockjaw" 69
Davis, Miles 33, 107, 141
Dearing, Ulysses "Sweets" 32–33
"Deep in My Heart" 143
"Deep Purple" 110
Del-Vikings 137
Dell, Alan 1
Delta Rhythm Boys 47
Dennis, Kenny 108
Depp, Johnny 110
Desmond, Paul 155
Dexter, Dave 114
Diamond, Leo 111
Di Fabio, Frank 47
Dillard, Bill 18
"Dinah" 23
Dr. John 166
Dodds, Baby 30
Doggett, Bill 65, 119, **129**, 130, 132
Dolphy, Eric 166
"Dominique" 157
Domino, Fats 2, 107, 113
Donaldson, Lou 101–02, 105, 120, 128
"Don't Blame Me" 148
"Don't You Do It" 89
Dorsey, George 55
Dorsey, Jimmy 93, 118, 131–32
Dorsey, Tommy 35, 75, 81, 93, 111, 118, 119, 132
"Double Check Stomp" 23, 24
"Double Trouble Blues" 50
Down Beat 46, 60, 62, 150
Drexel, Mother Katherine 22, 23
Drexel, Thomas 22
Duckett, Alfred 38
Duffle Bag 48
Duncan, Hank 62
Dupree, Bill 145
Dupree, Champion Jack 69

"The Earl" 166
"Earl Blows a Fuse" 79
Earl Cadillac (Rostaing, Hubert) 130, 131
The Earls 23
"Earl's Blues" 79
"Earl's Imagination" 79
Edwards, Teddy 163, 167
"845 Stomp" 65, 68
Eldridge, Roy 47, 112, 197, 199
Elizabeth II 134
Ellington, Duke 24, 27, 47, 59, 73, 74, 81, 91, 108, 144, 145, 156
Ellington, Mercer 72
Esquire 62, 63, 67, 86
Evans, Redd 47, 54
Everly Brothers 67
Ewing, John 108

Farmer, Art 55
"Fast Track" 154
Feather, Leonard 17, 29, 136, 140–41, 163
"Feeling Cool" 148
Fetchit, Stepin 65, **66**
Fields, Ernie 13, 15, 28
"Filibuster" 79
Fitzgerald, Ella 63, 72, 81, 141
"The Five O'clock Whistle" 45
"Flamingo" 27, 85, 89, 91–93, **92**, 118, 128, 134, 141, 167, 170
Fletcher, Leroy 52
Fletcher, Sam 163
Flophouse Magazine 155
"Flying Home No. 2" 54
Forrest, Jimmy 144
Foster, George "Pops" 30, 108
Fowlkes, Charles 54
Francis, Connie 83
"Frankie and Johnny" 30
Franklin, John Hope 13
"Frasquita Serenade" 143
Freed, Arthur 67, 94
Freeman, Evelyn 63
Freymuth, Leo W. 12, 13–14, 15, 21
Fulsom, Lowell 104

Gage, Amber 59
Gaillard, Slim 137
"Gambler's Blues" 80
Gardner, Mark 155
Garner, Erroll 100–01, 108
Geibel, Alan 93
Gershwin, George 43, 60, 62
Gibeling, Howard 131
Gibson, Charles (Grandfather) 7–8
Gibson, Charles (Uncle) 10
Gibson, Sarah (née Hart, grandmother) 7–8
Gifford, Gene 110
Gillespie, Dizzy 63, 141
Glaser, Joe 50, 100, 137, 146
Gleason, Jackie 109
Glenn, Lloyd 18
Going Hollywood 67
The Golden Gate Quintet 60
Goldsmith, George 106
Golson, Benny 83, 102, 105–06
Gomez, Phil 39
"Good for Stompin'" 51
"Good Rockin' Tonight" 78
Goodman, Benny 47, 53, 144
Goodwin, Herbie 52
Goody, Sam 60, 66
Gordon, Dexter 54, 108
Gordy, Herb 143, 151, 154
Gordy, Papa John 76

Gotham Records 60–61, 65, 66, 69, 171
Gotham's Four Notes 65
Grayson, Charles 110
Greer, Sonny 35
Gregg, Gary 167
Gregory, Dick 156
Gros, Leon 48
Grouya, Ted 91
Guthrie, Phil 118

Haley, Bill 128
Hall, Edmond 57
Hall, Rene 91
Hamm, Herrington 14
Hammill, Pete 114
Hammond, Butch 51
"Hamp's Boogie Woogie" 54
Hampton, Gladys 55
Hampton, Lionel 34, 45, 48, 50, 52–55, **53**, 57, 64, 80, 83, 133, 173
Hancock, Hunter 75
Handy, Capt. John 26, 30
Hardin, John 111
"Harlem Nocturne" 125, 172
"Harlem Serenade" 36, 47
Harlematinee 75
Harris, Charlie 63–64
Harris, George 142
Harris, Wynonie 72
Hart, Clyde 45
Hastings, Lowell "Count" 78–79, 86, 89, 91
"Haven't Named It Yet" 45
Hawkins, Coleman 108, 112, 141
Hawkins, Erskine 81
Hawkins, Louis 80
Hawkins, Screaming Jay 67
Hayes, Edgar 34, 163
Hecht, Joseph 32–33
"The Heebie Jeebies Are Rockin' the Town" 45
Hefflin, Leon, Jr. 113
Hefti, Neal 131
"Hello Sixty" 147
Henderson, Fletcher 29, 34, 88–89
Henderson, Horace 57, 108
Henderson, Ray 144
Henry, Buddy 161, 162
"Here Goes" 65
Herman, Benjamin 155
Herman, Florian 148
Herman, Woody 162
Hibbler, Al 60
Higginbotham, J.C. 45, 62, 64
"High Sweep" 122
"Hildegarde" 148
Hines, Earl 86, 98
Hines, Jimmy 37

Hines, Prof. Lester 24
Hite, Les 53
Hodges, Johnny 27, 47, 63, 67, 133
Hoffman, Steve 113
Hogan, Granville T. 110
Holder, Torrence 16, 17, 19, 27
Holiday, Billie 81, 85
Holmes, Harold 29
Holmes, Richard "Groove" 151, 152–54, 165
"Honky Tonk" 65, 132
Hooker, John Lee 93
Hopkins, Lightnin' 154
Horne, Lena 57, 72, 199
Hospitality Club 66
"Hot Sauce Boss" 65
Hunter, Ivory Joe 69
"Hurricane Blues" 60
Hutton, Ina Ray 45–46
Hutton, Jack 134

I Ain't Gonna Open That Door 65, **66**
"I Can't Give You Anything But Love" 91, 172
"I Cover the Waterfront" 144
"I Kiss Your Hand, Madame" 45, 144
"I Love You Truly" 48
"I Will Be Home Again" 60
"If I Loved You" 148
"I'm Getting Sentimental Over You" 93
"I'm on My Way from You" 45
"I'm the Guy Who Loves You" 65
"In the Mood" 28, 34
Ink Spots 130, 156
International Music 141
Isaacs, Ike 108, 163
Ivanovici, Josef 110

Jackson, "Bull Moose" 98, 114
Jackson, Jimmy 149
Jackson, Joyce 80
Jackson, Milt 54
Jacquet, Barbara 72
Jacquet, Illinois 55, 61, 64, 72
Jamal, Ahmad 141
James, Harry 27, 61
Jarl, Anton 155
Jarmusch, Jim 167
"Jazz for the Playboy" 141
Jazz Monthly 133
The Jazz Train 89
Jefferies, Herb 91
Jett, William M. 12–13
"Jig Time" 23, 24
Joe, Cousin 59–60, 61
Johnakins, John 48
Johnson, James P. 114

Johnson, Plas 130, 163
Johnson, Roland 143, 148, 157
Jones, Quincy 55
Jones, Roger 52, 60, 61, 65, 78
Jordan, Louis 2, 3, 59, 61, 64, 79, 130, 149, 165
Jourard, Marty 2
"Joy Dust" 65
"Jumpin' Jack" 61
"Jungle Drums" 110, 167, 172

Kahn, Gustave 109
"Kansas City Jive" 51
Katscher, Robert 144
Kearns, David 97
Kearns, George 98
Keenan, Norman 36
Kelly, Wynton 107
Kenton, Stan 141
Kern, Jerome 144
Kershaw, E.A. 117
"The Key" 148
King, Charles 111
King, Junior 166
King, Vernon 32, 61, 65, 78, 108
King Curtis 86, 130, 166
King Records 63, 68–69, 78, 86, 89, 93, 94, 136, 147, 154, 172
Kirk, Andy 16, 18
Kittrell, Catherine 118
Knight, Joe 106
"Knock Me a Kiss" 45
Kool and the Gang 86
Krupa, Gene 29, 35, 40, 41, **46**, 47

Lacy, Sam 122
Lady Darlene 80
Laetitia, Sister Mary 24–25, 157, 160
Laffler, William 165
Lance, Herb 80
Lane, Chester L. 83, 147
Larkin, Philip 134–35
Lascelles, Gerald 134
Lecuana, Ernest 110
Lehar, Franz 89, 143
Leo XIII 21
"Let Me Off Uptown" 29, 41, 46, 56
"Let's Ball Tonight" 113, 118
"Let's Move Out" 148
Lewis, "Father" Al 28
Lewis, Jerry Lee 114
Lewis, "Little" Joe 18
Lewis, Robert 13
"Liebestraum" 111
Liszt, Franz 111
Little Richard 2, 78, 89, 140, 167
"Liza" 55, 60

London, Johhny 128
"Lonely Blues" 80
"Long Tall Sally" 140
Louis, Joe 35, 41, 72
Louis, William 32
"Louisiana Bobo" 18
"Love Is a Many Spendid" 142
"Love Letters in the Sand" 148
"Lover Come Back to Me" 94
Lucy, Autherine 76
Lunceford, Jimmie 27, 36
Lymon, Frankie & the Teenagers 130, 137
Lynch, Lillian 154
Lyttelton, Humphrey 133

MacArthur, Ruth 73
"Make Me Know It" 46
Majestic Records 60
"The Major and the Minor" 46, 54. 60
"Make Believe" 148
Malcolm X 38
"Mambolino" 111, 120
"Mambostic" 111, 120
"The Man I Love" 60
Mann, Herbie 154
Manne, Shelley 151, 152, 153–54
Manuel, Jimmy 156, 157
Marabel, Fate 28, 29–32, *31*, 64, 100, 123
"Margie" 34
Marrett, Maurine 161
Marshall, Eddie 167
Marshall, Kaiser 32
Martin, George 93
Maxwell, Maxie 162
Maxwell, Robert 165
May, Billie 43
Mayer, Dr. Leo 96
Mays, Willie 121
McCormack, Edith 120, 137
McDuff, Brother Jack 153
McGhee, Howard 108
McGriff, Jimmy 153
McKay, Andy 167
McKibbon, Al 154
McLean, Ernest 108
McPhatter, Clyde & Drifters 113, 119
McRae, Carmen 108, 113, 163
McVea, Jack 133
"Mean to Me" 130
"Melancholy Serenade" 109
Melody Maker 131, 134
"Memories of You" 53
Mercers, Wallace 18
Mercury Records 129
"Merry Widow Waltz" 89
The Meters 148
Middleton, Edward 15

Index

Middleton, Edwin 15
Miller, Glenn 28, 35, 41, 45, 69, 109, 131
Miller, Harry 34
Miller, Helen 41
Millinder, "Lucky" 2, 47, 61, 98
Mingus, Charles 55, 104
"Mingus Fingers" 55
Mitchell, David 155
Mitchell, Richard "Blue" 103, 107, 110, 118
"The Model" 23
The Modern Jazz Quartet 54
The Modernaires 44
Mole, Miff 64
Molina, Carlos 110
Monk, Thelonious 108
Monroe, Marilyn 145
Monteiro, Arthur 64
Moody, James 57, 129
"The Moon Is Low" 94
Moore, Ardenne 72
Moore, Phil 48–49
"More" 157
Morgan, Sam 29
"A Morning Mist" 56
Morris, Joe 54
Morrison, Eldridge 107–08
Morton, Benny 57
Most, Sam 154
Moten, Bennie 19, 27–28, 62
Mullican, Moon 114, 139
Mullins, Ed "Moon" 36
Murphy, Dr. Fred E. 96
"My Heart at Thy Sweet Voice" 110
"My Special Dream" 61, 65

NAACP 136–37
Nathan, Syd 69, 138
Neely, Hal 153
Nel-lo, Dani 155
Nelson, Leslie 18
Nelson, Mervyn 89
Netherland, the Rev. C.L. 5, 9, 219n11
New Masses 64
The New Moon 94
New Musical Express (NME) 133
New York Age 37
Newman, Joe 25, 54
Newsome, Velma "Chubby" 78, 80
Nichols, Herbert 38
"Night Train" 144
"No Name Blues" 156
"No Name Jive" 121
"No Restricted Signs (in Heaven)" 60
Noble, Ray 109
Norman, Gene 156
Norvo, Red 55
Nureyev, Rudolph 134

"Obobereba" 62
The Observer 134
O'Day, Anita 46, 47
Odeon Records 173
"Off Shore" 111
"Oh, How I Miss You Tonight" 133
Okeh Records 30
Olden, Clarence 32
Oliver, King 18
"Open the Door, Richard" 65, 133
Osby, Greg 166
Owen, Lloyd 40

Page, Oran "Hot Lips" 27, 48, 50–52, **51**, 56, 57, 61, 125, 173
Page, Walter 50
Palmer, Earl 108, 122
Palmieri, Reno 55
Panassie, Hugues 38, 94, 110, 133
"Paradise Shuffle" 47
Paris, Art 58
"Paris Canaille" 131
Parker, Charlie 27, 56, 167
Parker, Clarence 14
Parker, George 65
Parlophone 1, 129, 145, 173
Pass, Joe 151, 152, 153–54, 163
Pastor, Tony 47
Pate, Johnny 154
Payne, Percival "Sonny" 61
Payne, Richard 24
Peacock, Burnie 96, 98
Peel, John 1, 93, 166
Pepper, Art 154
Permanent Vacation 167
Peterson, Oscar 153
Petrillo, James 67
Phillips, Sam 128
"Pink Panther" 130
The Pittsburgh Courier 33, 54, 63, 64, 67, 81
Pius XI 14
The Platters 137
Playboy Jazz Festival 1959 136, 140–41
Playboy Jazz Poll 136, 146, 155
"Poeme" 111
"Poet and Peasant Overture" 16
"Polonaise" 144
Pompilli, Rudy 128
"Pompton Turnpike" 48, 144
Porter, Cole 144
"Portrait of a Faded Love" 86
Powell, Bud 100, 157
President Records 173
Presley, Elvis 60, 85, 108, 113
"Pretend" 132
Price, Lloyd 113

Price, Sam 60
Prima, Louis 3, 48, 163
Procul Harum 153
Prysock, Arthur 72
Prysock, Wilbert "Red" 129
Puma, Joe 154

Quebec, Ike 50

Race, Steve 131
Raft, George 35
Rainey, Ma 50
"Ram Session" 56
Randolph, "Mouse" 32
The Record Changer 57
"Red Sails in the Sunset" 165
Redd, Gene 86, 89, 113
Redman, Don 34–35
Reed, Aslean (aunt) 72
Reed, Augustus (cousin) 10, 160
Reed, Augustus, Jr. 160
Reed, Curtis 160
Reed, Juanita (cousin) 10
Rey, Alvino 46
Rich, Buddy 161
Richley, Edward 110
Riddle, Nelson 43
The Ring (1952) 112
"Rippling Waters" 49
Rivera, Louis 109
Riverside Records 107
The Rivingtons 156
Roach, Max 105
Robichaux, Joe 28–29
Robinson, Bill "Bojangles" 58
Robinson, Jackie 72
Robinson, Smokey 98
"Rockin' and Reelin'" 91
Rockin' in Rhythm 79
Rodrigues, Amalia 142
Rollins, Sonny 103, 130, 141
Romano, Joe 162
Romberg, Sigmund 143
"Roses of Picardy" 125
Roxy Music 167
Rudman, Kal 165
"Rudy's Rock" 128
Rushing, Jimmy 27
Rutherford, Rudy 52

Sahl, Mort 141
St. John, Dell 38
Saint-Saens, Camille 110–11
Salerno, Al 89
Sample, Alexander 110
Samson & Delilah 111
Sanders, Pharoah 168

Sands, Tommy 156
Saulter, Dotty 89
Savage, Archie 125
Savoy Records 55, 93, 171
Sax, Adolphe 90
"Say, Hey" 121
Schonfield, Victor 2, 69, 169
Schubert, Franz 86
Scott, Cecil 59
Scott, Hazel 38, 104
Scott, Leslie 89
Scott, Tony 61
Sears, Al 32, 38, 68, 88, 102
Sears, Marion 32, 33
"Serenade" 86, 88
"Serenade to Beauty" 65
"Seven Steps" 87
"720 in the Books" 144
"Shangri La" 165
Shaw, Artie 48, 65
Shearing, George 156
Sheffield, Leslie 18
"The Sheik of Araby" 51, 125
Shepherd, Shep 65, 78
"She's Got It" 167
The Shirelles 107
Silver, Horace 107
Simmen, Johnny 49
Simmons, John 13
Simone, Nina 141
Sinatra, Frank 43, 61, 75, 108
Singer, Hal 13, 56, 102, 166
Singing Nun 157
Singleton, Zutty 26, 32
The Skatalites 166
"Skyliner" 48
"Sleep" 92, 93, 172
Smalls, Clifton 86, 89, 91, 93, 95, 96, 97–98
Smalls, Edwin 35
Smalls' Paradise 34, 35–39, *37*, 42, 47, 48, 50, 55, 56, 57
"Smalls' Special" 36, 47
Smith, Bessie 36
Smith, Jimmy 153
Smith, "Professor" Buster 27
Smith, Sonny 37
Smith, Tab 26, 132
Smith, Willie 27
Smith, Willie "The Lion" 49
Smith Sisters 58
"Smoke Gets in Your Eyes" 112
"Smoke Rings" 110
Snow, Wallace 144
"So Rare" 131–32
Soberanes, Bill 114
"Softly as in a Morning Sunrise" 143
"The Song Is Ended" 165

"Song of the Islands" 111
Spanier, Muggsy 62
"Special Delivery Stomp" 48
Spencer, Francis 80
Staton, Dakota 47
Stewart, Chester 52
Stewart, Rex 58–59, 156, 163, 173
Stewart, Slam 55
Stitt, Sonny 155
"Stompin' at the Savoy" 144
Stone, Jesse 17
Storey, Nat 32
Streckfus, Joseph, Sr. 29
Streeter, Bob 62
Streisand, Barbra 137
"String of Pearls" 109
"Il Sufit d'une Melodie" 131
Sun Ra 130
Sun Records 128
"Sweet Lorraine" 111, 172
"Swing Low Sweet Boogie" 79
"Swing Street" 56

Tate, Buddy 17–18, 25, 43
Tatum, Art 59
Taylor, Geoff 130–31
Taylor, Sam "The Man" 129
Tazelaar, Gideon 167
Teagarden, Jack 44, 48–49, 141, 148
The Teenagers 118
"Telstar Drive" 152
"Temptation" 63, 65, 67, 69
"Ten Out" 152
Terrell, Clyde 91
"Texas and Pacific" 51
"That's the Groovy Thing" 61, 129
"There Is No Greater Love" 113
"They Raided the Joint" 50
Thomas, J.C. 96
Thomas, Maude 80
Thomas, Walter "Foots" 45, 61
Thompson, Sir Charles 108
The Three Keys 24
"The Thrill Is Gone" 144
Till, Emmett 76
Timbrell, Tiny 144, 148
"Tippin' In" 61
Tonkins, Van 118
Trumbauer, Frank 17
"Trylon Swing" 45
Turpin, Clyde 33
Turrentine, Rosetta 105
Turrentine, Stanley 78, 84, 104, **105**, 110, 114, 118, 141, 157, 166
Turrentine, Thomas, Sr. 105
Turrentine, Tommy 104–05
"Tut Strut" 118, 148

Twelve Clouds of Joy 16–18
"Twilight in Tehran" 56
Tynes, Gladys 63

Unchained 142
"Unchained Melody" 142
"United Nations Stomp" 77
United Records 133
Universal Attractions 66, 99, 137
"Up There in Orbit" 167

v-disc 54, 57
Van Alstyne, Egbert 109
Variety 68
Vaughan, Sarah 161
"Velvet Sunset" 110
"The Very Thought of You" 109
"La Vie en Rose" 144
Vinson, Eddie "Cleanhead" 2, 61, 102, 165
The Viscounts 166
Vissar, Joop 173
Vito, Victor 122
Vogue 1, 92, 173

Wall, Alvin "Fats" 18
Waller, Fats 2, 72, 86, 94, 107
Ward, Booty 54
Waring, Fred 93
Washington (riverboat) 28, **30**, 32
Washington, Dinah 54, 55, 66, 85–86, 94, 98, 107, 149
Washington, Ned 110
Washington, Oscar 15, 20, 86
"Washington and Lee Swing" 25
Watanabe, Sadao 132
"Watch Where You Walk Boy" 79
Waters, Ethel 35
Waters, John 110, 167
Watts, Charlie 167
Watts, Paul 173
"Way Down" 86
Webb, Chick 144
Webster, Ben 50, 59, 108, 199
Webster, Freddie 33
Weinberg, Ralph 75
Wells, Viola 36
West, Luther Spurgeon 28
Weston, Ruth 57
"What! No Pearls" 109
"When Day Is Done" 144
"When I've Done the Best I Can" 163
"When Your Mother's Gone" 60
"Where or When" 79, 125, 172
White, Blanche (mother-in-law) 41
White, Fred (brother-in-law) 41
White, Fred (father-in-law) 41, 132
White, Slappy 163

Whiteman, Paul 43–45, *44*
"Why Do Fools Fall in Love?" 129
Wickliff, Vernon 14, 20, 21
Wilder, Joe 54
Williams, Al 163
Williams, the Rev. C.B. 163
Williams, Claude "Fiddler" 18
Williams, Cootie 66, 86, 102
Williams, Floyd "Horsecollar" 51
Williams, Irene 89
Williams, Joe 54, 141
Williams, Pinkie 103
Williams, Skippy 108
Williams, Tony 173
Wilson, Barbara 112
Wilson, Charles 21
Wilson, Dwayne "Fatman" 107
Wilson, Gerry 163
Wilson, Jackie 78
Wilson, Mabel (cousin) 160
Wilson, Marie (cousin) 160
Wilson, Nancy 125, 156
Wilson, Teddy 111

Wong, Herb 102
Woods, Ellis W. 12, 13
Wright, Jimmy 130
Wright, Lamar, Jr. 54
Wright, Specs 103

Xavier Herald 23
Xavier University, New Orleans 21–25, *22*, 40, 41, 118, 160

"You Belong to Me" 132
"You Go to My Head" 141
"You Need Coachin'" 51
Young, Helen 86
Young, L. Masco 20
Young, Lester 27, 108

Zanco, Karl 109
Zappa, Frank 137
Zdenek, Fibich 111
The Zombies 153
"Zon, Zon, Zon" 131

www.ingramcontent.com/pod-product-compliance
Lightning Source LLC
Chambersburg PA
CBHW032037300426
44117CB00009B/1097